The Idea of Japan

Ian Littlewood

THE IDEA OF JAPAN

Western Images, Western Myths

Ivan R. Dee
Chicago 1996

THE IDEA OF JAPAN. Copyright ©1996 by Ian Littlewood. All rights reserved, including the right to reproduce this book or portions thereof in any form. For information, address: Ivan R. Dee, Inc., 1332 North Halsted Street, Chicago 60622. Manufactured in the United States of America and printed on acid-free paper.

Published in Great Britain by Martin Secker & Warburg Limited, an imprint of Reed Books International Limited. The author has asserted his moral rights.

The author and publisher have taken all possible care to determine the copyright owners of materials used in this book, and to make acknowledgment of their use. Omissions that may have occurred will be corrected in subsequent editions provided notification is made to the publisher.

Library of Congress Cataloging-in-Publication Data:
Littlewood, Ian.
 The idea of Japan : western images, western myths / Ian Littlewood.
  p.   cm.
 Includes bibliographical references and index.
 ISBN 1-56663-117-3
 1. Japan—Civilization. I. Title.
DS821.L58   1996
952—dc20   96-24432

For Ayumi and Hanako

Contents

List of Illustrations

Between pages 128 and 129

Preface

In December 1941 the Canadian troops defending Hong Kong were assured that at least one thing was in their favour: no Japanese were going to risk a night-attack by sea. As a race, they were prone to seasickness and their slant eyes were bad for night vision. The attack, of course, came by night from the sea. Fifty years after the end of the war, this sounds like a story from another age. We know more about the Japanese now; we eat their food, drive their cars, rub shoulders with them in the street. But how much have our ideas really changed?

This is not a question that can be answered by turning to standard academic texts. Popular impressions of Japan owe little to historians or social scientists; they are more likely to have been scrambled together from a cultural miscellany of television programmes, bestselling novels, gadgets around the house and fading echoes of the Second World War. The great names of modern Japanese studies have no place here, unless, like Ruth Benedict, they have worked their way into general currency. In this hall of mirrors, where the object of enquiry is the image rather than the reality, the ten-second advertisement can be more revealing than the expert's monograph, the casual reference more significant than the detailed survey. It is one area where a book's cover sometimes tells us more than its contents.

Take the *Cambridge Encyclopedia of Japan* (1993). The picture on the front is of Mount Fuji seen across Kawaguchi Lake against a cloudless sky. On the back are four more images: a class of *kendo* students, their faces indistinguishable behind the masks;

an elegant woman in kimono leading her two small daughters, also in traditional dress, down the steps of a shrine; the moon rising beside a temple in Kyoto; finally, the interior of a McDonald's, a scene that might have been photographed any-where in the world, except that the westerner's eye is drawn straight to the incongruous band of Japanese writing across the top of the service counter. What do these snapshots add up to? Against the primary image of essential, unchanging Japan, they set out for us the four most familiar faces of Japanese culture: the Japan of warriors in masks, of women in kimono, of temples in a poetic landscape, and of ordinary Japanese – a people whose daily lives show them to be like us and yet not like us, marked always by an ineradicable difference. By accident or design, these pictures highlight the main categories that have domi-nated western perceptions of Japan. In this book I have called them Aliens, Aesthetes, Butterflies and Samurai.

To give them a rough context, we can divide the history of our relations with Japan into four stages: the initial contacts, which began in the 1540s and ended a century later when Japan shut itself off from the outside world; the period after its reopening in the mid-nineteenth century, during which, under the gener-ally patronising gaze of the west, it developed into a powerful modern state; the Second World War and the ensuing years of regeneration; and the last three decades, which have seen Japan's rise to the status of economic superpower. This is the broad framework within which western images have been formed.

Two points should be made at the outset. First, to talk of 'the west' as a single entity is to lump together a vast range of dis-parate and conflicting responses. I have not tried to do justice to their complexity. My aim has been to select from them those images of Japan which recur most often and which have left the deepest imprint on popular attitudes.

Second, it is not my intention to suggest that stereotypes are necessarily foolish or valueless. As a rule, in spite of aberrations, they have gained acceptance because there is a basis of truth to them. If the sadistic Japanese soldier retains his hold on our imagination, it is in part because the atrocities of Nanking and the POW camps were a well-documented reality. If Japan is still associated with images of aesthetic refinement, we need only step inside a traditional Japanese inn to understand why.

Western visitors to the country are often struck by how reliably it confirms their expectations. Amid polite, bowing people, they find themselves in just the world they were told about, where the trains are a miracle of punctuality, the Ginza is a dazzling stretch of neon, and cherry trees line the paths to ancient shrines. One by one, the time-honoured images turn out to be true. But in doing so, they obscure all the other things that are true – which is why they are dangerous. They teach us what to look for, and that is what we find; everything else becomes a background blur. We are left with a reality selected for us by our stereotypes.

The process is not peculiar to the west. The concepts of racial difference which underpin these stereotypes have been embraced no less eagerly by the Japanese, with results no less pernicious. But old habits of thought can be revised, and there is at least a possibility that this is starting to happen. For as long as we have known about Japan, it has been our natural opposite. East to our west, it has helped to maintain the crucial axis along which the world is divided. Today we cannot be so sure. As we begin to talk less of the cultural divide between east and west and more of the economic divide between north and south, there are signs that our imaginative map of the world may be changing. If this weakens the grip of established attitudes, it can only be to our advantage. The chapters that follow present a Japan which we have turned into a place of myth, an image either of our fears or of our fantasies. It belongs to the past. The Japan we must live with at the end of the twentieth century has grown too important to be left to the mercy of clichés.

Acknowledgements

I'm very grateful to the many friends and colleagues who gave me advice and suggestions while I was writing this book, among them the unfailingly helpful staff of the Sussex University library. In particular, I would like to thank Andrew Gibson and Patrick Conner, who read parts of the typescript and saved me from numerous errors.

The author gratefully acknowledges permission to reproduce the following quotations:

From *The Chrysanthemum and the Sword* by Ruth Benedict (1946), granted by Routledge.

From *The Naked Island* by Russell Braddon, granted by Curtis Brown Ltd, on behalf of Russell Braddon. Copyright © 1951 by Russell Braddon.

From *Shogun* by James Clavell, granted by Hodder & Stoughton Ltd. Copyright © 1975 by James Clavell.

From *Japan-Think, Ameri-Think* by Robert J. Collins, granted by Penguin Books USA Inc.

From *They Came to Japan: An Anthology of European Reports on Japan, 1543–1640*, Michael Cooper, editor (1965), granted by Thames & Hudson. Copyright © 1965 by the Regents of the University of California.

From *War Without Mercy* by John W. Dower, *Rising Sun* by Michael Crichton, (copyright © 1992 by Michael Crichton), *The Good War* by Studs Terkel (copyright © 1984 by Studs Terkel) and *Fodors 93 Japan*, granted by Alfred A. Knopf Inc.

From 'Manga Mania' by Catherine Eade, granted by *The Big Issue*.

From *You Only Live Twice* by Ian Fleming, granted by Glidrose Publications Ltd. First published by Jonathan Cape Ltd. Copyright © 1964 by Glidrose Productions Ltd. U.S. copyright renewed 1992.

From *Into the Valley* by John Hersey, granted by Laurence Pollinger Ltd.

From *The Secret Sun* by Fred Hiatt, granted by Simon & Schuster Ltd. Copyright © 1992 by Fred Hiatt.

From *A Circle Round the Sun* by Peregrine Hodson, William Heinemann Ltd, and *Sayonara* by James Michener, Secker & Warburg Ltd., granted by Reed Books.

From *The Lady and the Monk* by Pico Iyer, granted by Bodley Head.

From *Travels in China and Japan* by Nikos Kazantzakis, granted by Patroclos Stavrou.

From *The Japanese* by Joe Joseph (copyright © 1993 by Joe Joseph) and *Japanese Frenzy* by Simon Harcourt-Smith (copyright © 1942 by Simon Harcourt-Smith), granted by Penguin Books Ltd.

From the letters of Rudyard Kipling, granted by A.P. Watt on behalf of The National Trust for Places of Historic Interest or Natural Beauty.

From *The Lotus and the Robot* by Arthur Koestler, granted by Peters, Fraser & Dunlop Group Ltd.

From *The Ninja, The Miko* and *White Ninja* by Eric Van Lustbader, granted by Grafton, an imprint of HarperCollins Publishers Ltd.

From the Mass Observation Archive, granted by Curtis Brown Group Ltd, London. Copyright © Trustees of the Mass Observation Archive at the University of Sussex.

As always, my greatest debt is to my wife, Ayumi, without whom the book would not have been written.

PART I

Aliens

1. A Question of Category

B y the middle of the sixteenth century western travellers were used to encountering remote people who seemed absurdly different from themselves. With the confidence that comes from superior weaponry and a monopoly on religious truth they cheerfully defined these anomalous creatures as subhuman. But from the start Japan was untypical. There was no military confrontation, no element of conquest. The traders and missionaries who made their way there were dependent on the favour of hosts who had a clear and unflattering perspective of their own. To the Japanese, these large and malodorous southerners were the barbarians; the usual European distinction between savage natives and civilised westerners became difficult to apply.

In other respects, too, things were less than simple. Japan displayed many of the features of a savage land – it was remote, it was unchristian, its people had an odd appearance and some even odder habits – but the Japanese were polite, brave and much preoccupied with questions of honour and etiquette. They were, from a western point of view, something of a paradox, and the language of paradox has dominated descriptions of Japan ever since.

'On the one hand,' wrote the Italian Jesuit Alessandro Valignano in 1580, 'they are the most affable people and a race more given to outward marks of affection than any yet known. [...] On the other hand, they are the most false and treacherous people of any known in the world.'[1] A few years later Valignano returned to the theme in his *Historia del Principio*. After listing a range of Japanese peculiarities ('everything is so different and opposite that they are like us in practically nothing'), he continues:

> Now all this would not be surprising if they were like so many barbarians, but what astonishes me is that they behave as very prudent and cultured people in all these matters. To see how everything is the reverse of Europe, despite the fact that their customs and ceremonies are so cultured and founded on reason, causes no little surprise to anyone who understands such things.[2]

If the Japanese had merely been different from Europeans, there would have been no problem; the same was true of all the savages Europe had been coming across for the past century, from Greenland to Brazil. What troubles Valignano is that a society can apparently be both the opposite of Europe and at the same time cultured and rational. It produces a note of mild discomfiture which for another fifty years sounds through the reports that went back to Europe.

And then the door slammed shut.

When the first westerners set foot in Japan in 1543, the country was a warring collection of semi-independent provinces under the control of feudal lords, or *daimyo*. The first sixty years of European contact coincided with the turbulent period of unification that created modern Japan. This achievement was the work of the three great warlords who ruled in succession from the 1570s onwards – Oda Nobunaga, Toyotomi Hideyoshi and Tokugawa Ieyasu.

Until the end of the century, the European presence, largely Portuguese, was dominated by the Jesuits. With brilliant suppleness they brought off the delicate task of keeping on friendly terms with each of the three rulers as well as with other leading *daimyo*. Trouble came with the arrival of Spanish friars from Manila in the 1590s. These were a coarser breed, fiery in their zeal and impatient of the niceties of Jesuit strategy. They wanted souls and, if that meant bruising heathen sensibilities, they were willing to pay the price. When the British and Dutch appeared on the scene a few years later with their Protestant heresies and lust for trade, the embarrassment was even greater. Buddhist priests had long been warning against the motives of the Jesuits, and now there were plenty of other Europeans with sound religious and financial reasons for reinforcing these suspicions. The tide began to turn. By the time Ieyasu died in 1616, Christianity had become a dangerous commitment.

For the Japanese it was impossible to separate Christianity from the Europeans who had introduced it. In 1637 an unsuccessful rebellion against two *daimyo* in Kyushu brought the whole issue to a crisis. Many of the rebels were Christian and there was evidence that the Portuguese had lent them support. The Tokugawa government decided to act. From this time, with the exception of a small Dutch trading post on the artificial island of Dejima in Nagasaki harbour, Japan was sealed off from the outside world. No Japanese was allowed to leave the country, on pain of death, and no foreigner was allowed to enter it – this, too, on pain of death. When the Portuguese sent a deputation of prominent citizens from Macau in 1640 to beg for a resumption of trade, they were executed to a man, along with all but thirteen of the crew. These thirteen, witnesses to the executions, were sent back with a message for the Macanese, 'Let the people of Macao think no more of us; as if we were no longer in the world.'[3]

For the next two hundred years Japan might just as well have been no longer in the world as far as most westerners were concerned. Cut off from all but the trickle of Dutchmen who had dealings in the carefully supervised enclave at Dejima, it was as remote as the moon. And when the country was reopened in the mid-nineteenth century, accounts sent back to the west had something of the excitement of bulletins from another planet. Since the voyages of discovery in the fifteenth and sixteenth centuries there had been nothing like it.

But again there is an element of perplexity. It's not just that these people are strange; they are strange in ways which elude the normal classifications. When Rudyard Kipling sees Chinese men in the streets of Kobe, he can place them without difficulty, but the Japanese are more of a problem, as he explains to his friend, the professor: '"The Chinaman's a native, 'Fessor," I said. "That's the look on a native's face, but the Japanese isn't a native, and he isn't a *sahib* either."'[4]

It's a question of category. The Japanese defied not only the crucial distinction between native and sahib but the no less crucial distinction between western and oriental. Part of the problem was that Japan never quite fitted the images of oriental decadence which seemed to serve so well for the rest of Asia. In sexual matters it was everything that might be expected: prostitution was rife, the common people bathed naked together without a blush, and earlier visitors had reported buggery among the priesthood. On the other hand, it was well known that orientals were effeminate, and this could hardly be said of the Japanese samurai. Their way of life was spartan, their habits cleanly, their bearing martial. Moreover, the Japanese soon showed a disturbing ability to absorb western ideas – about clothes, about trade, about politics, even about war. One cultural bonus of trying to drum these things into Asiatics had always been the satisfaction of demonstrating that they were too dense – and different – to produce anything but a risible imitation of them. Now Japan was disproving this, and in the process seemed to be claiming a kinship with Europe which put at risk the sacred boundaries between east and west. 'Our deadliest enemy in the Far East', wrote T. W. H. Crosland in 1904, 'is not Russia but Japan, for she openly and avowedly set herself out to be the England of the Orient. We do not require any Englands in the Orient.'[5]

This sense of Japan as something of a hybrid has never disappeared. Seventy years after Kipling visited Japan, Arthur Koestler echoed both his sentiments and a line of his poetry in this couplet:

> If East is East and West is West
> Where will Japan come to rest?

The rhyme serves as an epigraph to Koestler's section on Japan in *The Lotus and the Robot.* The title of his book is one of several which suggest the difficulty of keeping Japan within conventional western categories. *Land of Butterflies, Land of War; The Chrysanthemum and the Sword; Saints and Samurai; Samurai and Silk; Samurai and Cherry Bloosom* – all of them reflect the tendency to package Japan in terms of paradox and contradiction. They point to the strange cultural mixture that westerners continue to find there – of tradition and technology, refinement and brutality, east and west. Much the most influential of these books has been Ruth Benedict's *The Chrysanthemum and the Sword.* At the beginning she lists what she takes to be the nation's salient characteristics:

> The Japanese are, to the highest degree, both aggressive and unag-gressive, both militaristic and aesthetic, both insolent and polite, rigid and adaptable, submissive and resentful of being pushed around, loyal and treacherous, brave and timid, conservative and hospitable to new ways. [...] Their soldiers are disciplined to the hilt but are also insubordinate.[6]

For many, these powerful contradictions have left a more last-ing impression than Benedict's attempt to explain them. In one form or another they are still the starting point for almost every book that sets out to introduce Japan to the west. 'Here come the Japanese,' writes Peter Tasker in *Inside Japan* (1987). 'They are the most innovative imitators, the hardest-working hedonists, the lewdest prudes, the most courteous and cruellest and kind-est of people. Rich and yet wealthless, confident but confused, they have just staged one of the greatest comebacks in history.'[7] The catalogue of paradoxes expands across another couple of paragraphs. Six years later we're still getting the same message in *The Japanese* (1993), where Joe Joseph provides us with a fur-ther sample of 'the dozens of breath-taking contrasts and paradoxes that give Japan its peculiar tang'.[8]

Just how deeply this response is embedded in our way of think-ing about Japan is apparent if we open the Fodor guide. On food, for example: 'Sometimes the contradictions of this intriguing cul-ture – as seen in the startling contrast between ancient traditions and modern industrial life – seem almost overwhelming. Who would ever have thought you could face salad with lettuce, tomatoes, and seaweed . . . or green-tea ice cream?' A couple of pages later we are on to Tokyo. Space, we are told, is the most precious commodity, and yet everywhere it is wasted: 'Begin with that observation, and you discover that the very fabric of life in this city is woven of countless unfathomable contradictions.' This is apparently something Tokyo has in common with Japan's other great tourist destination: 'Kyoto's history is full of contradictions: famine and prosperity, war and peace, calamity and tranquillity'.[9] Any city that has been around for twelve hundred years will have had its share of such things, but in this context they inevitably become an expression of paradox. There is no inkling here that our own angle of vision may account for these contradictions. They arise out of the inherent peculiarity of the culture. (Seaweed in a salad, for heaven's sake.) The Japanese seem, by their very nature, to be creatures of paradox.

This is not something we suffer gladly. Whatever challenges the categories by which we understand the world is likely to make us uncomfortable. It troubles us that ghosts belong neither to the living nor quite to the dead, that hermaphrodites belong neither to the male nor to the female, that substances which are viscous or slimy belong neither to the solid nor to the liquid, and so on. Among the most fearful aliens are those that come in the form of some intermediate state – blobs, growths, slime, or, worst of all, the plants or animals which have transgressed their natural laws and acquired a malign intelligence, enabling them to act in concert against us.

Boundaries are a source of security; we need them in order to define the world. They are, literally, what the business of definition is all about. Without east there is no west, without natives there are no sahibs, without 'them' there is no 'us'. To define what we are, we depend on what is alien. To call Japan a paradox is really to say that it threatens the existing boundaries and therefore our definition of ourselves.

It is for this reason that the language of paradox has always been counterbalanced by a language that reaffirms these boundaries as emphatically as possible. Benedict's honourable attempt to make sense of Japan's paradoxes in terms of 'a system consistent within itself' leads her inexorably towards a model of Japanese society that is based on a series of contrasts with American society: whereas in America we do this, in Japan they do that.[10] It's a way of structuring the western response to Japan which has a long history. Most of the Japanese peculiarities noted by Valignano are taken from a work by one of his colleagues devoted entirely to listing oppositions between Europe and Japan. The *Tratado* of Luis Frois collects some six hundred examples of direct antithesis between the two cultures. European women use artificial means to make their teeth white, Japanese women deliberately blacken them; the doors of our houses are hinged, theirs slide on grooves; in Europe it is effeminate for a man to use a fan, in Japan it would be a sign of lowliness and poverty for him not to use one. Everything is grist to the mill: our lavatories are hidden behind the house, theirs are in front; we pick our noses with the index finger, the Japanese use the little finger; our toothpicks are short, theirs are long.

So it goes on. Not just in Frois and Valignano, but in every kind of account that is rendered about Japan in this first century of European contact. The effect is to create an image of a country at the opposite extreme from Europe; and when contact is renewed two hundred years later, exactly the same pattern emerges. Sir Rutherford Alcock, head of the first British legation in Japan, summarises the most common antitheses, picking up the thread straight from Frois:

> Japan is essentially a country of paradoxes and anomalies, where all – even familiar things – put on new faces, and are curiously reversed. Except that they do not walk on their heads instead of their feet, there are few things in which they do not seem, by some occult law, to have been impelled in a perfectly opposite direction and a reversed order. They write from top to bottom, from right to left, in perpendicular instead of horizontal lines; and their books begin where ours end, thus furnishing good examples of the curious perfection this rule of contraries has attained. Their locks, though imitated from Europe, are all made to lock by turning the key from left to right. The course of all sublunary things appears reversed. Their day is for the most part our night; and this principle of antagonism crops out in the most unexpected and bizarre way in all their moral being, customs, and habits.[11]

9

At which point we are launched into another list of anomalies. Western writers have never quite got over the perversity of a country that has chosen the opposite path to the west in so many of the trivial actions of daily life. 'It is such a queer, contradictory, upside down sort of country,' declared Douglas Sladen in 1892.[12] Regardless of the sympathies of the commentator, this theme seems inescapable. 'Further acquaintance with this fantastic world will in nowise diminish the sense of strangeness evoked by the first vision of it,' writes Lafcadio Hearn. 'You will soon observe that even the physical actions of the people are unfamiliar – that their work is done in ways the opposite of Western ways. [...] Mr Percival Lowell has truthfully observed that the Japanese speak backwards, read backwards, write backwards – and that this is "only the *abc* of their contrariety".'[13] The quotation is from Lowell's *The Soul of the Far East* (1888), which opens on a similar note: 'The boyish belief that on the other side of our globe all things are of necessity upside down is startlingly brought back to the man when he first sets foot at Yokohama.'[14]

By the end of the century this upside-down version of Japan was enshrined in the work of even the most eminent Japanologists, to the extent that 'topsy-turvydom' can be given a separate entry in Professor Basil Hall Chamberlain's *Things Japanese* (1890). The phrase 'topsy-turvy' is one that recurs. Thinking back to his return to England after a diplomatic posting in Japan, Lord Redesdale (A. B. Mitford) recalls his shyness about coming home 'from a remote country where everything is strange and topsy-turvy'.[15]

The experience of two world wars did nothing to change the terms of reference. Japan was still being defined in much the same way when *Newsweek* took up the theme in 1945 with an article entitled 'The Topsy-Turvy Mind of the Jap'.[16] Sixteen years later, *Holiday* magazine devoted a complete issue to Japan. No country, the editors remarked, had been more difficult to understand, more demanding of patience, than Japan: 'It *is* remote from our comprehension, it *is* baffling, it *is* topsy-turvy to the eye and mind.'[17] From Marie Stopes to Pico Iyer, from William Plomer to James Clavell, everyone has their list of antitheses. The Japanese way is not just different from the European or American, but the reverse of it. 'The bloody Japs do everything the wrong way round,' a colleague in Tokyo explains moodily to James Bond by way of preface to yet another catalogue of eccentricities.[18]

In part, this is the familiar legacy of orientalism. Listing its principal dogmas, Edward Said notes first 'the absolute and systematic difference between the West, which is rational, developed, humane, superior, and the Orient, which is aberrant, undeveloped, inferior'.[19] The consistent efforts to present Japan in terms of opposition, reversal, topsy-turvydom are primarily attempts to confine it to the oriental half of Said's formula. We prefer what is alien to reinforce our understanding of the world rather than to challenge it. As long as differences are kept in opposition, they strengthen our identity; when they are allowed alongside, they become alternatives and weaken it. Savages can sleep on the floor, blacken their teeth, bathe naked with the opposite sex, do whatever they like; because they are savages, they only confirm our understanding of what it means to be civilised. But when civilised people do these things, we have to start revising our definition of civilisation.

This, I take it, is the problem the Japanese have posed from the start. It is there in Valignano's puzzled acknowledgement of a society that is the reverse of European and yet also the reverse of savage. It is there in Kipling's uneasy recognition that the Japanese is neither native nor sahib. It is there in Benedict's dizzying list of paradoxes and Koestler's whimsical rhyme. The Japanese simply don't fit the categories into which we have divided the world, not even the obvious category of the oriental. As hybrids, they have no clear place in the human (i.e. western) scheme of things. They are alien to it, and alien to us.

In the rest of Part I we look at some of the images which reflect this view. Sooner or later, the effect of them all is to distance what is Japanese from what is human. The first two groups (the subject of Chapters 2 and 3) do this by identifying the Japanese as either subhuman or superhuman; they are animals or they have special powers which put them beyond our reach. Chapter 4 considers the Japanese attitude to death, which for many westerners epitomises the sense that Japan is somehow at odds with fundamental human norms. The final chapter of Part I turns to the whole cluster of images that represent the Japanese as uniform products of a culture more akin to the world of robots and space aliens than to our own sweet humanity.

2. A Marked Resemblance to Monkeys

Nothing simplifies our image of foreigners more ruthlessly than war. In the darkness of the night an apelike soldier crawls out of the jungle and knifes the American sentry. So far so good, but then, in an attempt to lure the other sentry towards him, he makes the mistake of calling him Joe. 'My name ain't Joe,' the American replies and promptly blows him up. It's an easy message to read: the low-browed Japanese is a creature of the dark and of the jungle; his fatal mistake has been to neglect the stubborn individuality of his American enemy.

This classic meeting of the cultures occurs in Raoul Walsh's *Objective Burma* (1945). It is a film to which we shall return, for it offers a good example of the way wartime images of the Japanese tended to differ from those of the Germans. The latter were enemies, and among them were vicious and sadistic individuals, but there was little attempt to indict the German nation, except in so far as it had been perverted by the ideology of Nazism. By contrast, the images of hatred that boiled to the surface during the war against Japan have a virulence which leaves no scope for discrimination. With the Germans we shared a common humanity – there was always room for the concept of 'the good German' – but the Japanese might almost have been a different form of life.

When the dust had settled, D. J. Enright set out, in *The World of Dew* (1955), to analyse contemporary Japanese society. It is a decent, temperate book, but the memories of war were still green. 'The Japanese', he writes, 'may be unique in that their unusually complicated system of behaviour is based not on a recognition of humanity but on a proud and yet pathetic denial of it.' The problem, according to Enright, is that the traditional samurai virtue of absolute self-control is inhuman: 'To show no sign of joy or anger is to be either a god or a beast; and as few of us can persist in godhead for very long it is probably unwise to insist on facing ourselves with this exclusive choice.'[1] As in the medieval Great Chain of Being, there are only two ways to go – up towards the angels or down towards the beasts. Down is easier. Politely but unmistakably, Enright has restated the central premise of wartime propaganda: to be other than human, to be unlike us, is to become a beast. And the Japanese, of course, are more liable to this than the Germans because their purchase on humanity is more precarious. That's what being an alien is about.

The image of the Japanese as subhuman came into its own during World War II, but it had been established well before that. The work of Pierre Loti can serve as an example. Towards the end of the last century his stories of transient romance in exotic parts of the world enjoyed huge success. As the author of *Madame Chrysanthème* (1887), he probably did more than anyone else to shape western images of Japan in the late nineteenth and early twentieth centuries. His novel about a naval officer, stationed in Nagasaki for the summer, who diverts himself by taking a native wife for the period of his stay, spawned a vast number of imitations on both sides of the Atlantic, culminating in Puccini's *Madame Butterfly*. Like his heroes, Loti was a naval officer but, unlike them, he was not a particularly handsome one. A reference in his unpublished diary to his 'repulsive body and long paws' is perhaps a clue to what underlies some of the imagery in *Madame Crysanthème*.[2]

On the whole, Loti disliked both Japan and the Japanese, and the novel gives free rein to his feelings. A typical scene describes the hero spending an evening with four of his brother officers who have also taken local wives. First Loti introduces us to the women: Madame Jonquil who laughs all the time, Madame Bluebell who laughs even more and looks like a young bird, then Sikou-San, about whom nothing is said, and finally the diminutive Touki-San, thirteen years old at most and small as a wellington boot. 'In my childhood,' remarks the hero, 'I was sometimes taken to the theatre of performing animals. One of the great stars there was a certain Madame de Pompadour, a she-monkey decked out with a feather, whose appearance I can still recall. Touki-San reminds me of her.' The narrator watches with amusement as these ill-assorted couples troop into the house he has rented, the girls 'going down on all fours in front of Chrysanthemum, the queen of the house'. Then they set off down the street ('more like a precipitous goat-track') that leads into Nagasaki. Once there, decorum demands that they walk separately. The passage that follows summarises so many aspects of the presentation of Japan with which we are concerned that I quote it at length:

> All five of them hold hands, like little girls out for a walk. And we follow in their wake with an air of detachment. Seen like this from behind, they're very fetching, these dolls, with their hair so nicely done and their tortoise-shell pins so prettily arranged. [...] As with all Japanese women, the backs of their little necks are delicious. And above all they look so funny, lined up like this. 'Our little performing dogs', we call them, and the fact is, that's very much the impression they give.
>
> It's the same from one end to the other, this great city of Nagasaki, where so many rickshaws speed by. Always the same narrow streets, bordered by the same little low houses of wood and paper. Always the same shops, open to the wind, without a vestige of window. [...] And all the vendors, sitting on the ground in the midst of their wares, their legs naked to the waist, almost showing what we keep hidden but modestly covering their chests. And every sort of extraordinary little trade is carried on in full public view with the aid of primitive tools by cheerful-looking artisans.
>
> No horses in the town, no carriages, just people on foot or carried in comic little rickshaws. A few Europeans here and there who've got away from their ships, one or two Japanese (still mercifully few) trying to wear western dress, others who've settled for supplementing their national costume with a bowler hat from which long strands of their lank hair escape.

In the bazaars our girls make lots of purchases every evening. Like spoiled children they want everything – toys, combs, belts, flowers. And then they all give each other presents, with pretty, girlish little smiles. Bluebell, for example, chooses for Chrysanthemum an ingeniously conceived lantern in which shadow puppets, set in motion by a hidden mechanism, dance round and round the flame. In return, Chrysanthemum gives Bluebell a magic fan which can show, according to your inclination, either butterflies flitting among cherry blossom or monsters from beyond the grave chasing one another among black clouds. [...] Everywhere surprising things which seem to be the bewildering creations of brains that work the other way round from our own ...

In the well-known tea-houses, where we round off our evening, the little serving-girls welcome us when we arrive with an air of respectful recognition as one of the groups who are living the high life in Nagasaki. There we chat brokenly, often losing the thread, in miniature gardens lit by lanterns, beside goldfish ponds with little bridges and little islands and little ruined towers.[3]

Dolls, fans, lanterns, butterflies, ingenious toys, Japanese men in absurd western dress, half-naked artisans with primitive tools, respectful little serving-girls in attendance at the tea-house – these are the sorts of image we shall consider in later chapters, but for the moment our concern is with the animals.

This extract gives only a sample of Loti's range. Apart from dogs and monkeys, there are cats, birds, mice and insects all reflecting different aspects of the Japanese character and physiognomy elsewhere in the novel. Loti is not exceptional in this; the same pattern of imagery runs through much that was written about Japan in the second half of the nineteenth century by both Europeans and Americans. 'Of the habits and manners of the Japanese in regard to the sexes, I see little,' wrote Henry Adams in 1886, 'for I cannot conquer a feeling that Japs are monkeys, and the women very badly made monkeys.'[4] Open a travel diary of the period or a book of memoirs, glance at the letters sent home by tourists, diplomats, businessmen, naval officers, and you're as likely as not to find something similar.

Monkeys are without doubt the most popular point of reference. In Loti's novel the image of Touki-San as a little she-monkey is one among many. We are told later that the

Japanese men in their western hats look like performing monkeys ('*singes savants*'), that the old women are '*très singesques*', that the children have '*l'air singe*'. It is an image that one way or another takes in the whole population. At the moment of his departure the narrator can find in himself only 'a smile of mild disdain for this race of teeming, bowing little people [...] tainted with an incurable monkeyishness (*entaché d'incurable singerie*)'.[5]

It is clear from the long passage quoted that for Loti, as for many nineteenth-century writers, the image of the monkey keeps close company with images of children and primitives. Darwin cast a long shadow across European encounters with foreign cultures in the second half of the century, and it is he who provides the unstated link between the three groups of images. The Japanese belong to an earlier stage of development – in evolutionary terms, in human terms and in cultural terms. Their kinship is with the ape, the child and the savage, all of them at a distance from the human norm represented by the perspective of the adult westerner.

The evolutionary model lost some of its immediacy in the early decades of the twentieth century, but the animal imagery it had popularised never dropped entirely out of favour. When Crosland wants to express his indignation at British enthusiasm for 'the plucky little Japs' who have defeated Russia, he has a suitable analogy ready to hand: '... if an army of monkeys were to invade Morocco and achieve a common victory or two, we should throw up our sweaty nightcaps and shout for "the plucky little Simians".'[6] When Chesterton wants to express his distaste for Japanese imitation of what is worst in the west, it is to the same image that he returns: 'I feel as if I had looked in a mirror and seen a monkey.'[7]

Images of this kind carry only a limited range of comparison. No one thinks the Japanese actually *are* monkeys, any more than one would think a gross eater was actually a pig. But once the metaphor is accepted, it becomes that much easier to erase the line between image and reality. This is where the pressures of war come into play. In his excellent book on the Pacific war, John W. Dower unearthed a wealth of material that demonstrates both the range of this imagery and the ease with which it overruns the boundaries of metaphor. The marines who went into battle on Iwo Jima, flame-throwers at the ready, with the words Rodent Exterminator stencilled on their helmets, were merely extending the 'Jap Rat' slogan popular in the United States. How far the image can encroach on people's grasp of reality is suggested by contemporary rumours that the Japanese had accomplished their rapid advance down the Malay peninsula in 1942 by swinging through the jungle from tree to tree. In the general fog of ignorance a cartoonist's fantasy could be taken for literal truth.

The culture from which such a fantasy grew found an able spokesman in Admiral William 'Bull' Halsey, who commented at the start of a naval mission that he was raring to 'get some more Monkey meat'. It's a remark that conveys well enough the tone of a war being fought against 'apes in khaki', 'monkey folk', 'yellow monkeys' and so on. 'We are not dealing with humans as we know them,' declared General Blamey. 'We are dealing with something primitive. Our troops have the right view of the Japs. They regard them as vermin.'[8] In a fascinating memoir of his part in the Burma campaign, George MacDonald Fraser, author of the Flashman books, recalls a lecture by a Highland officer about being taken prisoner by the Japanese: 'Whether you escape or not, don't give up. Remember they're a shower of sub-human apes, and you're better men than they'll ever be.'[9]

Among America's most popular war correspondents was Ernie Pyle, transferred to the Pacific early in 1945. 'In Europe,' he wrote, 'we felt that our enemies, horrible and deadly as they were, were still people. But out here I soon gathered that the Japanese were looked upon as something subhuman and repulsive; the way some people feel about cockroaches or mice.' It was not a point of view he was about to quarrel with. Looking at some Japanese prisoners, he noted, 'They were wrestling and laughing and talking just like normal human beings. And yet they gave me the creeps, and I wanted a mental bath after looking at them.'[10] Pyle was just underlining the message of others who'd gone before. The list of examples collected by Dower goes on for pages and takes in pretty well everyone connected with the war effort – soldiers, politicians, generals, film-makers, newspaper reporters, cartoonists, diplomats, even scientists.

When John Hersey joined a group of marines on Guadalcanal in October 1942, he found the same attitudes. 'I wish we were fighting against Germans,' one of them said to him. 'They are human beings like us. [...] Germans are misled, but at least they react like men. But the Japs are like animals. Against them you have to learn a whole new set of physical reactions. You have to get used to their animal stubbornness and tenacity. They take to the jungle as if they had been bred there, and like some beasts you never see them until they are dead.'

This sense that the Japanese *belong* in the jungle offers powerful support to the animal imagery. As Hersey marches alongside the marines, he comes to share some of their feelings:

> On the way up to the front, we had come through patches of jungle, and it had seemed alien, almost poisonous. The vegetation closed in tightly on either side of the trail, a tangle of nameless trees and vines. It was lush without being beautiful; there were no flowers, and the smell of the place was dank rather than sweet. Each time we came out into the light on the grassy knolls, we breathed deeply and more easily. These open spaces were our natural terrain. They were American; the jungle was Jap.

Alien, anonymous and full of danger, the jungle, with its hint of perverse sensuality, offers a perfect habitat for the Japanese enemy. 'They're full of tricks,' says another marine. 'You'll see that when you go into the jungle after them. They hide up in the trees like wildcats.'[11]

Soon after it was released, *Objective Burma* became something of a *cause célèbre* as a result of British complaints that it showed the war against the Japanese being conducted primarily by the Americans, and more particularly by Errol Flynn. It opens with an aerial shot of the 'Jap-infested jungle' through which Flynn's soldiers will have to trek, first to destroy a radar installation, then to escape the pursuing Japanese. It's important to the meaning of the film that these are not professional soldiers, they are ordinary folk from provincial towns who talk much of football and apple-pie and girlfriends back home. Errol Flynn himself is an architect. They are the normal world standing against the 'evil forces of Japan'. In the nature of things they expect the fighting to be tough – 'when you're dealing with monkeys, you've got to expect some wrenches' – but the moral climax of the film reveals something quite beyond the scope of normal human wickedness. The commando group has split into two patrols, the second of which, led by Flynn's friend Lieutenant Jacobs, is ambushed by the Japanese. Later, in a Burmese village whose inhabitants have been enslaved, the surviving patrol find the hideously mutilated bodies of their comrades. Jacobs, mangled beyond description, lives just long enough to explain that they were tortured to death by the Japanese.

At this point attention turns to the hard-bitten newsman who has gone along to report the raid. He thought he'd seen everything that man could do to man, from the Middle Ages onwards; but this is different. In an impassioned speech he responds on behalf of outraged humanity:

> This was done . . . this was done in cold blood by a people who . . . who claim to be civilised. Civilised! They're degenerate moral idiots, stinking little savages. Wipe 'em out, I say. Wipe 'em out. Wipe 'em off the face of the earth. Wipe 'em off the face of the earth.

Note the smooth transfer of responsibility from a particular group of soldiers to 'a people'. A whole nation has committed these acts. The film was released in January 1945, seven months before Hiroshima.

Little is seen of the Japanese themselves in *Objective Burma*, but when they do appear it is usually to offer visual confirmation of the periodic references to them as monkeys. They move with the jerky robotic motion of a clockwork toy or with an apelike swagger, their helmets low over their eyes – in contrast to the Americans, who tend to wear theirs pushed back to show an expanse of intelligent forehead. In so far as the Japanese have a voice, they speak a chattering language (not, in fact, Japanese) incomprehensible to the western audience. All in all, there is little to link them to the human race.

In other contexts the kinship of the Japanese with animals

offers a basis for reinterpreting actions which would look rather different from a human perspective. Our men sometimes die bravely at their posts, but similar behaviour by the Japanese has another explanation altogether: 'Many of the Japanese soldiers I have seen', wrote the Australian journalist George H. Johnston, 'have been primitive oxenlike clods with dulled eyes and foreheads an inch high. They have stayed at their positions and died simply because they have been told to do so, and they haven't the intelligence to think for themselves.'[12] The image of a herd of cattle acquires a brutal reality; this sub-human species lacks the intelligence even to turn away from the slaughterhouse.

One of the most successful books to come out of the Allied experience of war with Japan – and one of the most rancorous – was by another Australian, Russell Braddon. *The Naked Island* (1951) is a narrative of his capture in Malaya and the years of imprisonment during which he was consigned to the notorious Siam–Burma railway. The image that Braddon's book propagated in the early 1950s (it went through seventeen impressions in two years) was of a yellow race at perpetual variance with the white men of the west, locked into a conflict which had less to do with political realities than with an almost mystical sense of opposition between alien peoples. For the Japanese, as for those who had suffered under them, World War II had been merely an interlude – 'the Hiroshima Incident' they would probably call it. 'But the war itself, of Asia against the white man, that – under one guise or another: in one place or another – still had ninety-five years to go.'[13] War, it seems, is the natural state of things between us and the Japanese. (As we shall see, it would be a mistake to assume that talk of this kind belongs to the past. Michael Crichton's novel *Rising Sun* (1992) takes as its epigraph what it calls a Japanese motto: 'Business is war'.)

Braddon had nothing to learn from America about the simian characteristics of his enemy ('What bastardry were the little monkeys up to now?' the Australians wonder as the sound of tanks approaches), but his portrayal of the Japanese depends on something else. The ultimate superiority of the defeated western forces is established in *The Naked Island* by a tone of voice which refuses to take the victorious Japanese entirely seriously. The conviction that they are not quite human permeates the narrative, and in one particular episode it is reflected in an image that goes to the heart of western sensibilities. If language is one thing that separates the human from the animal, clothes are another. Back in Singapore towards the end of the war, the survivors encounter a more than usually brutal guard:

> Our new guard [...] was a delightful little gentleman called the Ice-Cream Man. He was called the Ice-Cream Man because he was rather less than five feet tall, wore a white topee, which covered most of his face except a chin with a lamentable tendency to recede, sported a white linen coat and white gloves and shouted incessantly. After the first glance the British troops were unanimous – he was the Ice-Cream Man. He was never referred to as anything else. Not, at least, till he came to recognise the sound of those three syllables and to infer, quite accurately, from their contemptuous inflection, that they applied to himself. Then, because if he heard them he bashed the man who uttered them, he became Mr Peters to the Australians and Mr Lyons to the Pommies, which was much the same thing.
>
> The Ice-Cream Man was now in charge of our work on the aerodrome. As a second-class private that was a power he enjoyed. He would assemble our squads each morning in the pinkish light, the Australians, the British and the Dutch, in three separate groups. Then he would announce, 'Nippon Number One. All men say "Mastah"', and point to himself. Then the British squad would shout out all their favourite terms for the Japanese – except Master. And the Australian squad in its turn would be riotous with a clamour of 'Yellow bastards . . . apes . . . galahs . . . and drongos'. [...] 'You syphilitic little monkey', we would roar at the Nip. It was all very noisy and undignified, but gratifying.[14]

The Ice-Cream Man may be a syphilitic little monkey, but he is of a slightly different species from those Admiral Halsey was after. Like Loti's Touki-san, he is a monkey with an ostentatious taste for human clothes. It is the inappropriate linen coat and the outsize white topee that define his place in the scheme of things. Codes of dress have always been a formidable weapon in western, especially English, hands. Nothing divides 'us' from 'them' with such steely precision, nothing defines inferior species so inescapably. Aliens never dress like us, and when they try they always make a mistake. (Too late, James Bond recalls the villain's windsor knot in *From Russia with Love.*)

Early visitors to Japan in the nineteenth century had the double satisfaction of observing a society which on the one hand showed a primitive indifference to nakedness and on the other tried with an outsider's ineptitude to adopt western styles of dress. Strolling through Nagasaki on his first day in Japan, the British diplomat Laurence Oliphant is able to look straight into the houses that line the street:

> . . . Upon the scrupulously clean and well-wadded matting, which is stretched upon the wooden floor, semi-nude men and women loll and lounge, and their altogether nude progeny crawl and feast themselves luxuriously at ever-present fountains. The women seldom wear anything above their waists, the men only a scanty loin-cloth. In the mid-day, during the summer, a general air of languor pervades the community: about sunset the world begins to wash, and the Japanese youth, like copper-coloured Cupids, riot tumultuously.[15]

This is the way natives should be. Oliphant immediately sets his observations within the conventional framework established by travellers to the Pacific in the previous century. What he offers is the familiar image of natives taking their ease in an exotic paradise. And when, a decade or so later, the natives started tricking themselves out in frock-coats and bowler hats, the image was as ludicrous as the king of Tahiti putting on a naval officer's tricorn.

Japanese clothes, from the loin-cloth to the kimono, were an image of the strangeness of Japan itself. It was for this reason that Arthur Liberty sent buyers on a special mission to Japan to study the clothes and bring back exactly the right materials for the first production of *The Mikado*. Gilbert and Sullivan were not much concerned with the reality of Japanese life, but they did want the authentic flavour of its comic peculiarity, and for this the proper clothes were essential.

In general, though, the image of the comic alien was promoted less by the clothes the Japanese were accustomed to wear than by those that were new to them. At about the time Liberty began to think of importing fabrics from Japan, the Japanese themselves, at least among the upper classes, were turning with reckless enthusiasm to western clothes. To foreign observers, the results merely emphasised the gulf between Europe and Japan. Dressed in the fashions of the west, the Japanese were like the *animaux savants* so often mentioned by Pierre Loti, circus animals in human clothes. In one way this image reinforces the perennial uneasiness about category, suggesting hybrid creatures somewhere between the human and the animal, but in another it confirms their non-human status. We may dress up monkeys to accentuate their human characteristics, but we retain a complacent awareness of how inappropriate such clothes really are. A chimpanzee never draws attention to its apishness more sharply than when it is wearing a party dress; the savage is never more blatantly a savage than when he wears a top hat.

Sympathetic observers like A. B. Mitford and Lafcadio Hearn deplored the fashion for western dress as vigorously as anyone. Mitford writes of European garments 'disfiguring into the semblance of apes men who really used to look well in their own national dress', and Hearn prophesies that 'the future demoralisation of Japan is to be effected by Japanese in frock-coats and loud neck-ties'.[16] Both detractors and admirers had one thing in common: they wanted to keep the Japanese different. For both parties, the alienness of Japan was central to its image. East was east, and that was the way it should stay. By trying to step out of its oriental confines Japan had committed the same cultural sin as those westerners who fell into the trap of 'going native'. The phrase is rich in implications. It describes a relationship that is purely oppositional. There is no middle ground, just 'us' on one side of the cultural divide and 'them' on the other. Westerners who respond positively to the alien culture, and therefore threaten the reassuring structure of antitheses, are merely redefined as belonging to the other side. Anything more than a nodding acquaintance with oriental ways can leave one open to suspicion. In *You Only Live Twice* Bond wonders why M hasn't chosen 'a Jap speaker' for the mission in Tokyo, but the answer comes to him at once: 'Orientalists had their own particular drawbacks – too much tied up with tea ceremonies and flower arrangements and Zen and so forth.'[17] Unsound.

(*Plus ça change* . . . The first Englishman to settle in Japan ran into exactly the same sort of objection. Will Adams, the 'Anjin-san' of James Clavell's *Shogun*, reached Japan in 1600 at the end of a voyage which had killed most of his crew and left the remainder exhausted and starving. Favoured by Tokugawa Ieyasu, he found a home there, took a Japanese wife and did what he could to attract British merchants to the country. But when they came, his enthusiasm for things Japanese did not at all answer their notions of an Englishman's proper attitude. After a couple of meetings, John Saris, the clod sent out by the East India Company to establish trade links, concluded with disgust that Adams was a 'naturalised Japanner'. His consequent mistrust and refusal to take Adams's advice about the location of a trading base effectively put paid to Britain's chances of competing successfully against the Dutch and Portuguese.)

In holding the line between one culture and another, clothes are usually a decisive factor. From the early nineteenth century, this received increasing emphasis. A local 'wife' was the sort of amenity that any hard-working trader or administrator might be forgiven, but to start dressing like a native was to indicate a shift of allegiance of a quite different order. Native clothes are signs of the savage. If they are scanty, they express the nakedness of the savage; if they are elaborate and refined, they display the gorgeous plumage of the savage. Either way they are appropriate to their wearers.

European clothes, by contrast, are a sign of civilisation, and for the native to wear them is a form of *lèse-majesté* which emphasises his savagery. The image that underpins the whole equation is that of the animal – the animal in its natural state or the animal dressed in human clothes. The monkeys Loti's narrator sees among the common people of Nagasaki are matched by the upper-class figures Loti himself sees at a ball in Yedo in 1883: 'They're a little too bedecked with gold braid, these numerous Japanese gentlemen – ministers, admirals, officers, officials of one kind or another – all in their party outfits. . . . And then how oddly they wear their tailcoats. No doubt their backs were not designed for this sort of thing. Impossible to say where the impression comes from, but I find that all of them, always, in some elusive way bear a marked resemblance to monkeys.'[18]

When the time came for war with Japan, the image-makers did not have far to look.

3. Strange Forms of Knowledge

L oti's remarks have a malignity all his own, but the supercilious note he strikes is characteristic of much contemporary writing about Japan. Western visitors in the nineteenth century, like early visitors in the sixteenth, found many admirable traits among the Japanese but nothing about the place or its people to excite awe. That was part of its attraction: few nations were so easy to patronise.

In the course of a dozen years, this changed. First, there was the war with China. In 1894 China entered Korea to help crush a rebellion against the king, and this provided Japan with a welcome excuse to intervene. Within nine months she had comprehensively defeated China both on land and at sea. It was the first indication to most westerners that Japan was more than the toy-town country of temples and cherry blossom that western travellers had been promoting for the previous thirty years. Still more devastating was the Japanese victory over Russia ten years later: for the first time a modern eastern nation had defeated a modern western nation. The result was an even sharper revision of contemporary images of Japan.

In 1895, shortly after the defeat of China, one aspect of Europe's changed perception of Japan was encapsulated in a new phrase: The Yellow Peril. Originally the title of a drawing sent by Kaiser Wilhelm to his cousin Tsar Nicholas II, the Yellow Peril was represented by thunderous clouds in the midst of which sat an image of the Buddha surrounded by fire. The threat is not primarily a human one; what overshadows the nations of the west has a potent suggestion of something mystical and superhuman. Later versions of the Yellow Peril have varied the imagery, but the controlling metaphor, whether of a tide or a plague or a swarm, is usually non-human. It is an image of something alien. As the white nations, depicted on the edge of a cliff, look uncertainly towards the cloud-borne Buddha hovering above a peaceful western landscape, we are close to an image from early science fiction.

It struck an immediate chord. All over Europe and America the drawing was reproduced, until its caption became a contemporary slogan. It gives substance to a fear, which has endured to the present, that when confronting the Asiatic enemy the west is never quite on equal terms. The qualities which stamp the yellow man as inferior are what give him an edge when it comes to conflict. Hersey's marines speak of the Japanese in terms that mingle contempt and wonder. The silence of movement, the ferocity, the expert camouflage, the ability to become part of the jungle – all are features of the animal and the savage; but on Guadalcanal they are also features of the superman.

It is through an extension of these attributes that the figure of the ninja has acquired cult status. A renegade exponent of the Japanese martial arts, he exists at the point where perfected technique passes into the realm of magic. When a reproduction 'Sword of the Ninja' was offered for sale recently by a company based somewhat unromantically in Bromley Road, readers of the advertisement were told that it had been 'Recreated in its full size, complete with a dramatic display and all its hidden secrets . . .' Beneath a shadowy illustration of the ninja crouching with drawn sword in front of a full moon, the text made its pitch in approved 'Mysteries of the East' style: 'It was the *Ninja-to*. Sword of the legendary Shadow Warrior of Japan. As silent and mysterious as the Ninja himself. Like him, it had many secrets. For this sword's ingenious design concealed extraordinary things . . .' The sword clearly offers us oriental secrets of a kind that wouldn't normally come our way in

Bromley Road. It is a taste of what is hidden behind the veil. Even in Japan its production is 'virtually forbidden these days'.

The man who has done more than anyone else to bring these mysteries to a wider public is Eric Van Lustbader, whose series of ninja novels tells the story of Nicholas Linnear. Born of a Japanese mother and an English father, Linnear is the ninja in the title of the first of them, and his life provides a perfect excuse for deploying Japanese stereotypes. For hundreds of years the art of the ninja has flourished in secret, conferring on its adepts superhuman skills which leave western technology far behind. The first victim dies in the night when a metal star flashes into his chest: 'His arms and legs felt as if they were full of lead and the air seemed to have run out of oxygen just as if he were lost on an alien planet without the protection of a spacesuit.'[1] The image from science fiction is altogether appropriate to the activities of this oriental assassin. Like a shadow, he glides over to the corpse and recites the *Hannya-Shin-Kyō*. (We aren't told what this is, but it's clearly something very Japanese indeed.) Then he stands up again:

> The corpse seemed as light as air in his arms. With barely any discernible motion or effort, he launched the corpse out into the night, over the edge, far enough out so that it fell squarely into deep water. Immediately the strong current took it.
> Within seconds the shadow had disappeared, having become one with the darkness and having left no trace of its ever having existed.

When the corpse is discovered, it is left to Nicholas Linnear to inform the sceptical police chief what they are dealing with: 'There is a ninja abroad here and in all the world there is no more deadly or clever foe. You must act with extreme caution. Modern weapons – guns, grenades, tear-gas – will give you no security against him, for he knows of all these things and they will not deter him from destroying his intended target and escaping unseen.'[2] The other member of Linnear's audience, Doc Deerforth, has reason to take him seriously, having come across a ninja during the war. He tells Linnear how he woke one night in the Philippines to find a disembodied face hovering over him.

It reminded him of the face of a madman he had once seen in hospital. The description that follows shows just how easily the images current during the war can be repackaged for a modern audience.

> 'This man had reverted. He was certainly no longer human but had returned to the animal state of his ancestors. There was no hint of what we might term "intelligence" in his eyes; at least not as modern man defines intelligence. But I saw cunning there, of a kind and in a strength which terrified me. For a moment I fantasised what it would be like having this man loose in the world. Richard Speck? Gary Gilmore? Jack the Ripper? It was beyond imagining. For this was a man who was clearly beyond morality.
>
> 'Now you know some of what I saw in the eyes hovering above me that night on Leyte. But not all. To call this "madness" would be to seriously underestimate it, for it was far more. Ours is a world of order, ruled by laws. From science to morality there are parameters within which we all live. This man did not. He lived outside time as if residing within chaos. I don't know how to describe it better, but seeing him thus in the flesh only underscored the fact rather than the fiction of his supernatural origins.'

Whisked up by this black-clad figure and slung over his shoulder, Deerforth finds himself at the mercy of a man who would clearly have been at home with the jungle-loving Japanese Hersey never quite encountered on Guadalcanal:

> 'Even upside down I could see well enough to know that he was a magician. No one I knew could possibly have got in and out of our encampment totally undetected as this man had. [...] He ran with such fluidity that there was no up-and-down motion, merely the sensation of forward movement.
>
> 'We were in the jungle now, travelling extremely quickly. In fact, even though the way was now more choked with foliage and underbrush, our speed actually increased. His strength and endurance were exceptional.'[3]

The image is of a creature who does not conform to our laws, either moral or scientific. He is both less than human and more than human, a focus equally for our fears of evil and our dreams of power. The negative images of a primitive, monkeylike people have their obverse in this fantasy of superhuman abilities which derive from recovering the physical empire of the animals.

At the same time it is suggested that the physical powers of the ninja are by-products of a training which is essentially spiritual. When, in the third volume, Linnear has come to the end of the line, hopelessly outgunned by the powers of the evil Omukae, he returns to his teacher Kansatsu, assumed to be long dead but in fact withdrawn to a mountain fastness in northern Japan. In a scene that takes us straight back to the tradition of *Lost Horizon*, Linnear sets out to scale the treacherous peak known as the Black Gendarme and is rescued from death in the snow by his teacher, who takes him to the stone house in which he lives on the mountain. 'Think of it as a monastery, a holy place of serenity and of strength,' he tells Linnear, who in due course recovers to fight another day.[4]

The peculiar arts that flourish in the east are usually identified by Japanese tags which define them as outside our western compass. In the normal way of things Linnear relies heavily on what is called *Getsumei no michi*, the Moonlit Path, but in this volume the ultimate source of power is *Kokoro*, the heart of things. By drawing on its energy, the adept can achieve supernatural feats of strength, endurance, self-healing and the like. Hard for the western mind to grasp? That is because the east has access to truths beyond our comprehension.

From this point of view, it's less surprising that the Buddha should figure so prominently in the original image of the Yellow Peril. The west has always regarded Asian religions with a certain ambivalence: on the one hand, they are undeniably heathen, blessed with none of the clear light of Christianity, but on the other, their very obscurity exercises a fascination of its own. Lurking among the monstrous shadows may be secrets unguessed by the stolid philosophers of the west, kinds of knowledge denied to our ordered and rational procedures.

Like many of the images we are concerned with, it's a notion that ranges promiscuously across the countries of Asia – Tibet one year, India the next, China or Japan (the two are so easy to confuse) the year after. In *The Razor's Edge* (1944) Somerset Maugham gave renewed popular authority to the idea that if you were a spiritual seeker Asia was the place to go. Enmeshed by the complex trivialities of western life, his hero turns to India for release. After a period of study under an Indian guru, he sits one night in the mountains, until the darkness fades and the rising sun brings his moment of enlightenment: 'I had a strange sensation, a tingling that arose in my feet and travelled up to my head, and I felt as though I were suddenly released from my body and as pure spirit partook of a loveliness I had never conceived. I had a sense that a knowledge more than human possessed me, so that everything that had been confused was clear and everything that had perplexed me was explained.'⁵

Isolated for so long, Japan came late to this tradition, and its commitment to industrial progress has been a further handicap. It is a culture that offers little in the way of naked holy men or suffering masses, but for the western world its credit is redeemed by one outstanding resource. In the twentieth century Zen Buddhism has given a spiritual lustre to western images of Japan that is unmatched anywhere outside India and Tibet. Popularised by the work of D. T. Suzuki and Alan Watts, Zen first became fashionable in the west in 1950s America. These were the years when Jack Kerouac's Dharma Bums recited *haiku* to one another as they walked the California mountains in search of enlightenment, and the *Chicago Review* could publish nine articles on Zen in a single issue. 'Zen Buddhism', claimed *Time* magazine in 1958, 'is growing more chic by the minute.'⁶

Since then, the way of Zen has been a recurring element in popular representations of Japan. Echoes of Eugen Herrigel's *Zen in the Art of Archery* (1953) are not hard to discern in this passage from James Clavell's *Shogun*. The brutish Buntaro has undertaken to shoot at one of the hero's gate-posts, which are forty paces away, shrouded in darkness and on the other side of a paper screen. In a trance he draws back the bowstring and releases an arrow 'with savage, almost poetic liquidity'. It disappears through the screen:

Another arrow was launched almost before the first had vanished, and then another [...] a fourth arrow and then a last. The silence was filled with the echo of the twanging bowstring. Buntaro sighed and came back slowly. He put the bow across his knees.

Mariko and Fujiko sucked in their breaths and smiled and bowed and complimented Buntaro and he nodded and bowed slightly. They looked at Blackthorne. He knew that what he had witnessed was almost magical. All the arrows had gone through the same hole in the shoji.[7]

Blackthorne finds them neatly – miraculously – grouped in the distant gate-post.

It is this element of magic that the Japanese warrior owes to his eastern origins. Even though Japan is now thoroughly modernised and full of men wearing dapper western suits, there is a lingering suspicion that it harbours oriental secrets of a kind likely to put the west at a disadvantage. Somehow the Japanese can do things we can't. 'In 1975,' writes Ezra Vogel in *Japan as Number One* (1979), 'one Japanese worker could produce about one thousand English pounds worth of cars every nine days, whereas at Britain's Leyland Motors, to produce the same value a worker took forty-seven days.'[8] The title of the chapter is 'The Japanese Miracle'.

A recent television programme set out to analyse the success of Japanese manufacturers in the luxury-car market. It did this partly by intercutting shots of the assembly line with a series of images of the traditional tea ceremony. The suggestion that Japanese success is intimately linked to its alien culture was made explicit by the programme's title, *Zen on Wheels*. It drew on the same imagery as an advertisement for the Toyota Supra put out a few years ago, showing the car positioned in the centre of an immaculately raked Zen garden with the first rays of the Rising Sun glowing on its bodywork. The Supra, we learnt, was the product of 'a way of looking at things that owes much to Zen'. Among other achievements, its engine noise had been suppressed in an 'effort to achieve the sound of one hand clapping'. This was technology raised to a higher plane: for the awe-struck westerner, one more example of the mysteries of the east.

It is a cultural model that retains considerable authority. As part of the 1991–2 Japan Festival, the Victoria and Albert Museum mounted 'Visions of Japan', billed as 'the most ambitious exhibition focusing on a single country ever to be staged in Britain'. Divided into three rooms – Cosmos, Chaos and Dreams – it took the visitor first into Cosmos, a room devoted to a celebration of Japan's spiritual heritage, in particular to aspects of Buddhism and the tea ceremony. The second room, Chaos, presented contemporary Tokyo as a huge, machine-dominated game palace; the third, Dreams, was a vision of a future world shaped by information technology. Overall, a third of the space had been given to the spiritual elements of Japanese culture.

It would be hard to imagine a comparable exhibition on Britain or America. If, as we used to be told, Protestantism helped to make us great, it did so by stressing the earthbound virtues of self-reliance, hard work and a clear conscience. By contrast, the spiritual legacy of the east comes to us veiled in mystery. As we move from Cosmos to Dreams or struggle to make sense of the juxtaposed images of car production and the tea ceremony, the conviction grows that these people have found a short-cut: there must be a connection between the compact, precise gestures of the tea ceremony and the ingenuities of the car designers which we can only guess at. Behind the bland faces of our Japanese competitors are strange forms of knowledge.

4. Glorious Death

To the westerner there's nothing quite so characteristic of the Japanese as their enthusiasm for death. And nothing quite so alien. Reflecting on the essential difference between east and west, Lustbader's Doc Deerforth contemplates the kamikaze flights of the Second World War:

> The cultural chasm between East and West could be summed up by those aircraft, Doc Deerforth had always thought. The Japanese name for them was *Ōka* – the cherry blossom. But the Americans called them *baka* – the idiot bomb. Western philosophical thought had no place for the concept of ritual suicide inherent in the Japanese samurai of old. [...] Doc Deerforth would never forget the *haiku* which, so the story went, had been written by a twenty-two-year-old kamikaze pilot just before his death; this, too, was tradition: 'If only we might fall / Like cherry blossoms in the spring – / So pure and radiant!' And that, he thought, was how the Japanese felt about death. The samurai was born to die a glorious death in battle.[1]

Doc Deerforth's own feelings could not be in sharper contrast: 'And all I wanted was for the war to end with my skin intact and my mind unbent.'

It seems so fundamental, this apparent disagreement about the value to be put on life. Nothing has lent more weight to western suspicions that the Japanese lack some crucial component of what goes to make up a human being. It was noted from the start that they were peculiarly cavalier about both their own and other people's lives. Reports from merchants and missionaries are full of accounts of execution and suicide, deaths inflicted and endured for what to the western eye were the merest trifles. 'And in my time', wrote the Italian traveller Francesco Carletti, 'many suffered crucifixion on the slightest pretext, such as theft of a radish or some similar trifle, in no way calling for capital punishment. But they pay no more heed to the death of those who suffer in this way than we should to the killing of a fly.'[2] One of the few accounts of Japan written during the years of exclusion, Engelbert Kaempfer's history, accepts as a matter of general agreement that the Japanese were 'regardless of their own lives'. 'All contemplate death with indifference and speak of it with levity,' wrote John Tremenheere in 1863.[3]

Suicide was as commonplace as it was grisly. 'To cut the belly in this way', noted Valignano, 'is so common in Japan that it sometimes happens that very small children do it in front of their parents when they are angry with them.'[4] By the time the country closed its doors in 1637, accounts of *hara-kiri*, or more properly *seppuku*, had worked their way firmly into the western consciousness, and the fascination at once reasserted itself when Japan came back into view in the nineteenth century. Both A. B. Mitford and Ernest Satow wrote detailed accounts of the death of Taki Zenzaburo, who was forced to commit *seppuku* in 1868 for having given the order to open fire on foreigners in Kobe. The scene, which takes place in a temple at night, has a strong flavour of the exotic. The fires in the temple courtyard 'threw a dim flickering light over the heavy eaves and quaint gable-ends of the sacred buildings', while inside the hall of the temple 'tall candles placed at regular intervals gave out a dim mysterious light'. Taki himself, Mitford tells us, looked at the dagger 'wistfully, almost affectionately' before the final act.[5]

What is absent from Mitford's description is any suggestion of fanaticism. The episode is deeply coloured by a sense of its remoteness from the west, but Taki is acknowledged to be 'a brave and chivalrous man'. Later, when Japan had acquired the power to pose more of a threat to the west, there were commentators quick to point a different moral. Writing of the

Russo-Japanese war, T. W. H. Crosland sets this supposed indifference to death in a more familiar framework: '[Japan] beats Russia because her ranks are packed with men who would rip themselves up rather than suffer defeat, and to whom life is not a matter worth a moment's consideration. They are men, in fact, who believe themselves to be without souls.'[6]

Crosland's conviction that we are dealing with something quite foreign to our comprehension is a recurrent feature of western attitudes. Observers who praised the readiness of Japanese martyrs to die in the name of Christ did not find the readiness of other Japanese to die in the name of the emperor in any way comparable. Responses during the Pacific war followed the same pattern. In his autobiography Admiral Halsey remarks that, in spite of Intelligence reports, the Americans could not believe that Japan's kamikaze strategy would materialise: 'The psychology behind it was too alien to ours; Americans, who fight to live, find it hard to realize that another people will fight to die.'[7] The difference between them and us in this matter is crucial; it was an article of faith for everyone from American admirals to British housewives. When the Mass Observation panel collected popular reactions to Japan in December 1941, they came up with a string of similar comments. 'We don't go in for that sort of thing,' said one woman about Japanese suicide raids. 'We are willing to take risks, but not suicide like that. I suppose we have something to live for, that's what it is.' 'The Japanese are dreadful fighters,' declared another; 'they don't care if they die in battle – in fact, they prefer to.'[8]

In 1957 John Marquand's *Stopover Tokyo* spent three months on the American bestseller lists. Its hero, Jack Rhyce, had killed plenty of Japanese during the war, but he is unable to say exactly how many. 'You can't always tell everything that a machine-gun or a hand grenade does,' he explains to the heroine. 'And you see, most of them preferred to die.'[9] Even now, half a century after the end of the war, it is still difficult for us to see the kamikaze flights as anything other than a bizarre expression of the suicidal impulses that are central to western images of Japan.

Yet in our own legends of war, those who knowingly accepted certain death for the sake of comrades or country stand high in the heroic pantheon. We need not go back to Regulus or Roland; half the poems I learned in childhood seemed to be about someone or other taking on death with a smile: 'Shall we fight or shall we fly? / Good Sir Richard, tell us now, / For to fight is but to die!' Sir Richard, of course, answers with a laugh, and the little *Revenge* runs on sheer into the heart of the foe.

It seemed altogether right that the 17th/21st Lancers should be called the Death or Glory Boys; these poems were obsessed by the subject. 'When can their glory fade?' we asked of the Light Brigade as they charged into the valley of death – 'Theirs not to reason why / Theirs but to do and die.' The soldiers at Hohenlinden seemed only too keen to confront death: 'The combat deepens. On, ye brave, / Who rush to glory, or the grave!' Casabianca went the same way, but no one suggested that he should have hopped off the burning deck while he had the chance.[10]

It was not just a question of death before dishonour. Well into the twentieth century a soldier's death could be seen as a kind of fulfilment. 'But I've a rendezvous with Death,' wrote Alan Seeger in the early stages of the First World War,

> At midnight in some flaming town,
> When Spring trips north again this year,
> And I to my pledged word am true,
> I shall not fail that rendezvous.[11]

He died in 1916, the year after Julian Grenfell, who himself had died shortly after writing 'Into Battle':

> And life is colour and warmth and light,
> And a striving evermore for these;
> And he is dead who will not fight;
> And who dies fighting has increase.

It's not an attitude we have much sympathy with today, but it took the First World War to make us repudiate it. (Just as, perhaps, it took the Second World War to make the Japanese do the same.) Only cultural amnesia could explain the popular notion that while the Japanese soldier carries on a semi-mystical love affair with death, his western counterpart is doing all he can to avoid it. We too have our suicide missions, but the phrase is purged of negative implications. To put it crudely, our suicides are heroes, theirs are maniacs.

This is not to suggest that the attitude reflected in those scraps of verse is the same as that of the Japanese; given the differences of culture, it would be odd if it were. I merely want to question the idea that the western attitude is necessarily the *opposite* of the Japanese. What underlies this assumption is the same structure of antithesis that we looked at in the opening chapter and that has shaped western observations of Japan since the first Europeans arrived there. As far as possible, everything must be set within a framework of oppositions. The search is for ways of defining difference rather than similarity. So kamikaze pilots in the Pacific or suicide charges on the beaches of Okinawa are seen not in terms of comparable acts by Allied airmen and soldiers, but as a stark opposition between noble self-sacrifice (*'Dulce et decorum est . . .'*) and demented fanaticism.

The popular conviction that suicide is something of a national hobby in Japan is unshakeable by any evidence to the contrary. Since Madame Butterfly kissed the blade of her father's dagger (with which he had ended his own life) and retired behind a screen to stab herself, there have been few popular novels about Japan without at least one honourable suicide. At the time of James Bond's adventure, there were some half a dozen western countries with higher suicide rates (including Austria, Denmark, West Germany, Sweden and Switzerland),[12] but it would have taken more than this to blow Fleming off course. In the grounds of a castle near Fukuoka the villain has constructed a 'Garden of Death'. Filled with snakes, scorpions, poisonous spiders, poisonous fish, poisonous vegetation and a sprinkling of lethal fumaroles, it proves an irresistible lure to the suicidally inclined Japanese. Such are the numbers flocking to it that the head of the Japanese secret service, who himself trained as a kamikaze pilot, decides that the place must be destroyed. This is where Bond comes in. He finds it all rather hard to understand. When told of a student who has killed himself because he failed his exams, Bond protests that the boy could have tried for a lower grade of college: 'As you know, we say "Blast!" or perhaps a stronger word if we fail an examination in Britain. But we readjust our sights, or our parents do it for us, and have another bash. We don't kill ourselves. It wouldn't occur to us.'[13] *Have another bash* . . . the pragmatic British alternative says all that needs to be said about the gulf between the two cultures.

In their mixture of fascination and bewilderment the British and Americans are at one. Nathan Glazer remarked in 1972 that the only event in recent Japanese history to be widely covered by the American press had been the death of the writer Mishima Yukio. On the morning of 25 November 1970 Mishima drove with four cadets from his Shield Society to the headquarters of the Self-Defence Force in the centre of Tokyo. There they took the commandant prisoner at swordpoint and held him while Mishima addressed the men of the 32 Regiment from the balcony outside the commandant's office. Mishima wanted to tell them that Japan had betrayed her history and traditions, that she had sold her soul for material prosperity; but his voice was drowned by shouts and jeers from below and the noise of circling helicopters from above. After seven minutes he ended with a futile call on the soldiers below to join him. He and his most trusted cadet shouted three times '*Tennō Heika banzai*' ('Long live the Emperor') and then returned to the commandant's office, where they committed *seppuku*. Another cadet completed the ritual by beheading them.

To most Japanese this action seemed, as Mishima knew it would, an image of lunatic eccentricity, but to the west it epitomised a cardinal element of the Japanese character. *Newsweek* summed it up a couple of weeks later: 'He was a living example of the contrast between two historic Japanese forces – the spiritual and the worldly, the aesthetic and the martial. And it was his attempt to put aside the chrysanthemum and bring back the sword that led to his doom.'[14] The Chrysanthemum and the Sword – Mishima becomes a perfect image of the contradiction by which Benedict's book had defined Japan for modern Americans.

Stereotypes of one sort or another are inevitable, as are the distortions they involve. How else but by rough categorisation can we understand anything at all about an infinitely diverse world? The problem, as I argued in the Preface, is not so much that stereotypes are inaccurate as that they are partial. In the interests of a simplified and more manageable reality, they ignore conflicting evidence and invite us to take the part for the whole. Experience counteracts this. If we live in England, we're likely to learn for ourselves that the Scots aren't all mean and the Welsh aren't all good singers; familiarity undermines the stereotype. But where there is no familiarity, the stereotype remains unchallenged, and the consequences can be far-reaching. In the case of Japan, we glimpse them perhaps when we turn to some of the nightmares of the last war – to Hiroshima and Nagasaki and the fire storms that obliterated Tokyo, killing more than 80,000 people within a few hours. To what extent were these military triumphs made possible by a series of stereotypes which had not only suggested that the Japanese were pretty keen on dying anyway but had gone a long way towards denying that they were human at all?

This happens in war, though when fighting had to be done in sight of the enemy, with pikes and swords and arrows, it was probably a little more difficult. As recently as 1914, soldiers of the opposing armies could meet at Christmas between the trenches and exchange drinks and photographs and reminiscences of home. The High Command was not amused; for soldiers to see the opposing side as human beings might complicate the business of killing them. There was no repetition of the Christmas truce. Even so, the propaganda which worked effectively at home to transform Germans into one undifferentiated alien entity – the Hun – made relatively little headway in the trenches, where soldiers tended to be cynically aware of their common cause with the 'enemy'.

As warfare came to be conducted at increasingly long range, this problem diminished, but there was always the possibility that the enemy might show itself human at an awkward moment. In *Homage to Catalonia* George Orwell describes his inability to snipe at a half-dressed fascist soldier who was running along the top of the trench in full view, holding up his trousers with both hands: 'I had come here to shoot at "Fascists"; but a man who is holding up his trousers isn't a "Fascist", he is visibly a fellow-creature, similar to yourself, and you don't feel like shooting at him.'[15]

Japan presented few difficulties of this kind, for it had no voice in our societies. Those individual Japanese who had found their way to the west were segregated and silenced. That the treatment of Japanese-Americans during the last war was unjust is not in doubt, but its motivation was more complicated than is usually acknowledged. The ostensible reason for rounding up over 110,000 Japanese-Americans and herding them into camps in the middle of nowhere, regardless of their loyalties, was to cut off a potential supply of spies, saboteurs and fifth columnists. No doubt this was a genuine fear in the months after Pearl Harbor, but packing off all available Japanese to the desert also served another purpose. They were no longer around to contradict, by the trivialities of their daily lives within the community, the image of Japan and the Japanese that propaganda demanded. The more Japanese there were in view, the less alien they would seem, and the less alien they seemed, the less satisfactory they would be as an enemy. A Japanese buying groceries in the local store would have been all too likely to remind you that he was, in Orwell's words, 'visibly a fellow-creature, similar to yourself'.

Among other things, it would have become more difficult to kill civilians. At the start of the war President Roosevelt had condemned the bombing of civilians in uncompromising terms:

> The ruthless bombing from the air of civilians in unfortified centres of population during the course of the hostilities which have raged in various quarters of the earth during the past few years, which has resulted in the maiming and in the death of thousands of defenceless men, women and children, has sickened the hearts of every civilised man and woman, and has profoundly shocked the conscience of humanity.[16]

In other words, there was considerable ground to be made up before America itself could turn its attention to the defenceless men, women and children of Tokyo, Hiroshima and Nagasaki. The terrible cruelty with which many of the Japanese waged war made this less difficult, but so also did the manipulation of certain dominant images of Japan. The notion of the Japanese as an indistinguishable mass, unmoved by the emotions that govern the lives of the rest of us, made the usual discriminations between soldier and civilian that much easier to abandon. Moreover, these were people to whom death was meat and drink; they didn't react to it in the same way as you and I: they didn't *mind* it.

And the Japanese-Americans whose ordinary anxieties and griefs might have challenged this assumption were safely stowed in Arizona.

Part of what makes Hiroshima such an indelible image is the godlike detachment of the act. The gap between cause and effect, between the solitary plane passing high overhead and the grey waste of a whole city incinerated underneath, is almost too much for the mind to grasp. What happened to Tokyo was in some ways just as terrible, but the waves of planes and the endless clusters of bombs make it easier to hold on to the necessary connections. Hiroshima is the ultimate product of alienation.

The achievement of John Hersey's *Hiroshima* was to bring home to people the reality behind the stereotype. These victims had thoughts, feelings and histories, all different, all individual – they *did* mind. Hersey organised the book as a record of how the bomb affected the lives of six people who were in Hiroshima at the time. Five were Japanese and one a German missionary. The account begins with an image of what each of the six was doing at the moment of the explosion:

> At exactly fifteen minutes past eight in the morning, on August 6th, 1945, Japanese time, at the moment when the atomic bomb flashed above Hiroshima, Miss Toshiko Sasaki, a clerk in the personnel department of the East Asia Tin Works, had just sat down at her place in the plant office and was turning her head to speak to the girl at the next desk. At that same moment, Dr Masakazu Fujii was settling down cross-legged to read the Osaka *Asahi* on the porch of his private hospital . . .[17]

And so the account continues. What Hersey did was to undermine the comfortable sense of remoteness which had insulated most of his readers from the events described. His narrative insisted that these things had happened to human beings.

Was Ishihara Shintaro right when he suggested in *The Japan That Can Say No* that America felt able to drop the atom bombs on his country for reasons of race – 'because we are Japanese'?[18] Perhaps. Could the bombs ever have been dropped on Germany? Probably, in the end. After all, we managed to take Dresden in our stride. And as Germany itself was demonstrating, if enough effort is put into convincing you that your next-door neighbour is subhuman, an enemy of all you hold dear, a cancer in the social body – a Jew, to use the shorthand of the time – there's really nothing you won't do, or at least allow to be done. The bomb could have been used on Germany, or anyone else, given time to prepare the ground. But the fact that it was used on Japan is an indication of how well the ground had been prepared already in that part of the world, prepared by all the images that said implicitly or explicitly that the Japanese are not the same as us, that they're not quite human, that the same standards don't apply, that death doesn't mean the same to them as it does to us – that they're aliens.

If all this seems a long way off, consider the words of a television compère (not Clive James on this occasion) introducing yet another clip from the Japanese game show *Endurance*: 'Yes, it's those jolly Japanese again, trying to prove that life can be so much sweeter if it seems likely to end at any second.'

5. An Unfathomable Planet

In the Victorian age European eyes seem always to be observing Japan from a great height. Its diminutive scale didn't make such an impression on the travellers of the sixteenth century, probably because the disparity of size was not then so great, but to the big Victorians it was a Lilliputian world. They were endlessly fascinated by how small the people were and how compact their lifestyle. It is a perspective that can lend the scene a certain toy-town neatness which is not without charm. The formidable Isabella Bird, arriving in Yokohama in 1878, had taken the measure of the place before she was well off the ship:

> The first thing that impressed me on landing was that there were no loafers, and that all the small, ugly, kindly-looking, shrivelled, bandy-legged, round-shouldered, concave-chested, poor-looking beings in the streets had some affairs of their own to mind. At the top of the landing-steps there was a portable restaurant, a neat and most compact thing, with charcoal stove, cooking and eating utensils complete; but it looked as if it were made by and for dolls, and the mannikin who kept it was not five feet high. At the custom-house we were attended to by minute officials in blue uniforms of European pattern and leather boots; very civil creatures, who opened and examined our trunks carefully, and strapped them up again, contrasting pleasingly with the insolent and rapacious officials who perform the same duties at New York.[1]

'Very civil creatures' – the phrase nicely conveys the benign distance that separates her from this promising new species.

In other circumstances the neatness and discipline of Japanese life could excite either contempt or deep suspicion. 'Above all,' wrote Loti in 1889, 'one gets bored with the endless monotony of the little Japanese streets, with the thousands of identical little grey houses, all of them wide open as though to show off their identical interiors, the same little white mats, the same little smoke-boxes, the same little ancestral shrines.'[2] Such uniformity is disagreeable to the western observer. The feeling persists that there is something faintly – one cannot escape the word – inhuman about it. It's a feeling that is never far away when reference is made to the normal conditions of daily life in Japan. The crowded subway trains, the rabbit-hutch flats, the capsule hotels, the mass of humanity seething through Shinjuku station, the armies of obedient salarymen, the ranks of neatly dressed schoolchildren: all of them are part of the same antlike world which seems to lack those elements of irregularity, unpredictability and individuality which for us are the hallmarks of the human.

In July 1991 the French prime minister, Edith Cresson, remarked to an interviewer that the Japanese 'work like ants'. Blithely she went on, 'We cannot live like that. I mean, in those tiny flats, with two hours of commuting to get to work . . . We want to keep our social security, our holidays, to live like human beings as we have always lived.'[3] As usual, the west lays down the terms which define life as a human being. Cresson's reference to the Japanese as ants was explicit enough to cause a diplomatic stir, but she was merely reflecting the standard western assumption that we are more fully human as individuals than as members of a group.

In *A Circle Round the Sun* (1992) Peregrine Hodson, working for the Tokyo branch of a western bank, summarises the attitude of his head office towards the Japanese: 'They're all the same, like ants or robots, and they have no individuality.'[4] It's a belief ingrained in our culture, and one that's reinforced every time we see yet another picture of a capsule hotel or a white-gloved functionary cramming commuters into a railway carriage. Pachinko parlours, the reporter tells us on Channel 4's *Travelog*, provide relaxation 'for the vast army of salarymen, the tireless drones of this buzzing society'. And again we congratulate ourselves on belonging to the individualistic west, where life does not have to be lived to the rhythm of the anthill or the beehive.

This individuality is a source of pride, but our satisfaction in contrasting it with the uniformity of Japanese life is touched by fear. As the horror films show, practically any species can be dangerous if its members act in concert – birds, ants, even rabbits, not to mention creatures from another planet. It's not accidental that our fantasies of invasion from outer space almost invariably depict alien groups who have a single shared intelligence. We're never invaded by other individualists – other humans. Often the invaders take human form, but they are a different order of being. The Midwich Cuckoos, who threaten the life of a quiet English village in John Wyndham's novel, or the Body Snatchers, who invade small-town America in Don Siegel's film, are well-known examples. What disturbs us most about these creatures is that any appeal to individual judgement, to personal loyalties or obligations, will certainly be futile against the imperatives of the group. This is the horror at the heart of the Quatermass stories: it's as though the individual's past, with its unique pattern of emotional and intellectual impulses, has been wiped clean. The people we are left facing are the dehumanised agents of an invisible and alien power.

That is precisely the fear expressed in Michael Crichton's *Rising Sun* (1992). To move against one Japanese is to find yourself pitted against all the others, who operate like the tentacles of a remote intelligence in the background. Individual Americans are powerless against the concerted might of Japanese interests which have embedded themselves in the fabric of society:

> 'You must understand,' Connor said, 'that there is a shadow world – here in Los Angeles, in Honolulu, in New York. Most of the time you're never aware of it. We live in our regular American world, walking on our American streets, and we never notice that right alongside our world is a second world. Very discreet, very private. Perhaps in New York you will see a Japanese businessman walking through an unmarked door, and catch a glimpse of a club

behind. Perhaps you will hear of a small sushi bar in Los Angeles that charges twelve hundred dollars a person, Tokyo prices. But they are not listed in the guidebooks. They are not a part of our American world. They are part of the shadow world, available only to the Japanese.'[5]

There is nothing specific to the Japanese about this fantasy – forty years earlier the unmarked door would have opened on to a meeting of communists – but it can accommodate the Japanese so easily because they have already been constructed as aliens, a focus for everything which makes our familiar world insecure. In spite of its contemporary gloss and its battery of well-researched statistics, Crichton's novel is at heart just another variation on the theme of the Yellow Peril. What Connor says about the Japanese businessman in the 1990s is almost indistinguishable from what Nayland Smith was saying about Fu Manchu in the 1930s: 'We in the West follow our well-trodden paths; no one of us sees more than the others see. But under the street along which we are walking, at the back of a house which we have passed a hundred times, beyond some beach on which we sun ourselves, lies something else – something unsuspected.'[6]

Although no one quite says that the Japanese belong on another planet, the imagery which suggests it has a long tradition. Loti's distaste for Japanese uniformity was balanced by a fondness for Japanese art, but he recognised in it the forms of a different world. 'Here,' he remarks of a temple in Nikko, 'the smallest sketch, the merest line is profoundly alien to us, as much as if it had come from some neighbouring planet that had never been in communication with our side of the earth.'[7] Even the friends of Japan have found themselves disorientated by the depth of its strangeness. Lafcadio Hearn's account of Japanese peculiarities ends on a note of bafflement: 'These and other forms of unfamiliar action are strange enough to suggest the notion of a humanity even physically as little related to us as might be the population of another planet.' He is equally pessimistic about our chances of coming to grips with the language: 'Experience in the acquisition of European languages can help you to learn

Japanese about as much as it could help you to acquire the language spoken by the inhabitants of Mars.'[8]

The jets that now link Tokyo to the cities of the west in a matter of hours seem to have left this feeling untouched. 'The world outside Japan is another universe, with a different language,' writes Hodson in *A Circle Round the Sun*,[9] and the paperback cover carries a quotation from the *Sunday Telegraph* to confirm it: 'Half travel book, half existential thriller . . . Life lived on the rim of an unfathomable planet'. A year earlier, Pico Iyer's *The Lady and the Monk* (1991) had taken readers to the same unfathomable planet. 'In Brazil, in Italy, in Thailand,' remarks the narrator's friend, 'I never had any trouble meeting people. But this place is like another planet.' He is simply endorsing what the narrator himself has discovered in a passage that brings together a familiar network of images:

> It was not just that Japan occupied a different kind of universe, which rarely made contact with our own; but, more, that this island was – by choice as much as circumstance – psychically as well as physically removed from the world at large. The analogy here was not so much with Gulliver as with Alice; in Japan one felt as if the world had been turned upside down and inside out, all its values and assumptions turned on their heads – as if, one might say, the force of gravity had been so radically altered that one had ended up on another planet.[10]

The Lady and the Monk is an engaging book which looks at Japan with a friendly eye, but it's not difficult to see how, from a less sympathetic perspective, this strand of imagery could nourish our suspicions of a people so impenitently different from ourselves.

Today, the blank uniformity which so often betrays alien species that try to pass themselves off as human takes a form that modern Japan has made peculiarly its own. Towards the end of the war, the American army's *Infantry Journal* warned its readers against thinking of the average Japanese as 'a buck-toothed, near-sighted, pint-sized monkey' and suggested that a more accurate image might be 'a robotlike creature'.[11] It was a prophetic shift of clichés. Out of the devastated husk left by the war Japan has emerged as the most technologically advanced society in the world. In 1960 Arthur Koestler characterised it as a mixture of Lotusland and Robotland. The past thirty years have swung the balance decisively in favour of the robots: Japan is their natural home. It's a doubtful accolade. Behind much of the enthusiasm for Japan's industrial achievements – her miraculous deployment of machinery, her technological ingenuity, her clockwork efficiency – lurks the half-spoken belief, anticipated by the *Infantry Journal*, that this is possible because the Japanese are a bit like machines themselves. They don't just make robots, they live like robots.

Once again, the seeds of this image go back to the nineteenth century. Isabella Bird's observation that the restaurant she sees on landing at Yokohama 'looked as if it were made by and for dolls' was far from original; it was repeated with wearisome frequency by nineteenth-century visitors to Japan. Often it's no more than a reflex cliché, but the sense of something contrived, mechanical, non-human, can easily be drawn into the foreground. To Henry Adams the whole of Japan was merely a toy world which offered a clever imitation of life. 'The imitation is not perfect,' he adds. 'Especially the women are wooden, jerky, and mechanical; evident dolls badly constructed.' Sir Edwin Arnold had a similar reaction to the babies he saw carried on their mothers' backs – 'so like to dolls that you almost look for the wire wherewith to make them wink and squeak'. 'Automata' was Loti's verdict on the Japanese women he danced with at the ball in Tokyo – 'if they get out of step, you have to stop them and set them going again, otherwise they would just keep on.'[12]

Comments of this kind do little more than reflect a general sense that the Japanese hadn't altogether mastered the business of being human. Whereas the monkey image was underpinned by popular notions about evolution, the image of the machine, at least as it is used of Japan, had no comparable structure to sustain it. It had to wait for the twentieth century before its application became clear. Today it is probably the dominant image of Japan, and it carries an unmistakable element of menace.

In the 1950s and 1960s aliens in human form, once exposed, used to dissolve into some sort of disgusting vegetable matter, or else, like vampires, shrivel into nothing, but now when the human skin is peeled back it more often reveals the gleaming tendons of a machine. This is what explains the dark behaviour of the science officer in *Alien* or the frightful invulnerability of *The Terminator*. Scratch a Japanese from a popular novel and you can often find much the same thing. 'Robots without values or personality' is how, according to one reviewer, Crichton depicts the Japanese in *Rising Sun*.[13] In Fred Hiatt's *The Secret Sun*, another successful thriller about Japan which also came out in 1992, the hero reflects that what Americans want to hear about the Japanese is that they are 'repressed, robotic monsters who led inferior lives'.[14]

In part, it is Japanese efficiency that provides a focus for western suspicions; we've always been uneasy about people who make the trains run on time. Human beings, we feel, are by nature more baggy and imprecise, more Wodehousian in their disposition of affairs than this split-second stuff allows them to be. Our use of the word 'machine' in human contexts has a certain ambiguity. We talk readily of people as part of a war machine or a military machine, and a character in a popular novel might well be referred to as a perfect fighting machine, but to talk of someone as a machine for writing books or painting pictures or making love would have quite different implications. The most distinctively human concerns seem less amenable to group discipline; they are matters of individual judgement and response. In the first category of activities a mechanical performance is more than human; in the second it is less than human. The feeling that Japan has allowed the machine into areas where it does not belong is reflected in a range of images that portray Japanese life as a product of the conveyor belt: mechanical, standardised, monotonous. The age of the machine has given us a new metaphor for the clichés Loti was trotting out a hundred years ago.

The benefit of this, from a Japanese point of view, is the confidence it inspires in their technology. When we buy their cars and computers we are getting them, as it were, from the robot's mouth. To the average human, the natural kinship of the Japanese with machines is a convincing guarantee that they know what they're doing. On the downside, the Japanese taste for uniformity gives them, to the western eye, something in common with the old enemies of the Cold War period. One of the aspects of Russian and Chinese communism picked on most eagerly by the west was the drab sameness of their dress. To the westerner it has a flavour of the penal institution, which Japan, at the opposite end of the political spectrum, in some ways seems to share. It's a country that goes in for uniforms – from the military-style uniforms of the high-school students to the shiny suits of the salaryman and the overalls worn by factory workers and their bosses.

The point was bluntly made by a television comedy sketch a few years ago when Japanese car manufacturers first began to set up plants in Britain. The sketch took place in one of the new factories, but the factory setting had been transformed into a Japanese prisoner-of-war camp. Although Japanese investment in Britain is on the whole viewed kindly – it creates jobs, stimulates the economy and so forth – positive reactions are held in check by a stock of negative images which can be continually redeployed. In this case the inhuman cruelties of the POW camp were seen to have a comic equivalent in the inhuman (over-rigid, over-regulated) arrangements of the factory. New circumstances can simply be plugged into the old image banks.

The great advantage of this is that it spares everyone the need to think; the normality of our ways is automatically confirmed. By selecting obvious aspects of Japanese conformism to do with dress, hierarchy, routine and so on, and by associating these with the repetitive, unconscious actions of the robot or the zombie, the imagery sets up an opposition between us and them that leaves our own sorts of conformism invisible. We westerners, reassuringly situated on the side of life, humanity and the individual, can close the book or leave the cinema with the ideological implications of our position unquestioned.

For years now, it has been difficult for anyone to write a book on Japan without quoting the west's best-loved Japanese proverb: the nail that sticks up must be hammered down. It's quoted not just because it illustrates something about Japanese society but because it invites us to recognise with a shiver of relief how different is our own society. Once again, it is as though a perception about Japan can have meaning for us only if we set it in direct opposition to a contrasting version of the west – Japanese conformism on one side, western individualism on the other. Most western societies probably are less conformist than the Japanese, and the distinction is an important one, but it's a question of degree not of absolute opposition. We don't talk about hammering down nails, but we do talk about being out of line, or, even worse, way out of line. The implications of such phrases are easy to forget as we marshal our armies of opposing stereotypes.

Even when an attempt is made to strike a balance, the scales are weighted. One example was the American film *Gung-Ho* (1987). Like the comedy sketch, it took its lead from the Japanese factories that were being set up in the west. It deals with the efforts of a Japanese car manufacturer, Assan (ass/arse = joke), to operate a factory in the ailing town of Hadleyville. (Filmgoers will recognise the symbolic setting of Fred Zinneman's *High Noon*.) The opening shot presents, without explanation, a room full of Japanese, all in identical uniforms, screaming like madmen. After a sequence in which the American hero is driven to the airport, we return to the Japanese, now kneeling on the floor in front of a man who shrieks at them from a podium in the voice of a demented prison-camp commandant, while another walks round with a long pole which he cracks down on the shoulders of selected victims. Subtitles to the shrieking at last tell us that the men are there because their bosses have found them lazy and lacking in confidence. It is part of a Management Training Programme – more nails being hammered down.

As the credits come up, we are shown images of the American's first encounter with Japan: neon lights, a capsule hotel, the bullet train, strange food juxtaposed with a flash of McDonald's, confused bowing, and finally an image of the hero lost in the middle of a rice-field. His presentation to a board of utterly humourless Japanese is a disaster, and after a brief shot of him sitting baffled in a temple we see him arriving back, with immense relief, in the United States. It turns out, however, that, contrary to all appearances (who knows what goes on in the minds of the Japanese?), the presentation has been successful, and the Japanese duly turn up in Hadleyville. Their arrival at the airport cues a number of standard jokes: the team leader takes off his shoes to walk along the red carpet, the microphone is too high for him, he can't speak proper English ... It's a good-natured film which tries to make it clear that there are faults and virtues on both sides, but by the time it gets to its main concern it is hopelessly mired in its own clichés.

The trouble is that the apparent even-handedness is a fraud. The faults on the American side are basically superficial – the factory employees are resting on past laurels and not working hard enough to be competitive – whereas those of the Japanese are central to the values of their culture. 'How's your family like America?' someone says to the team leader after he has been in the country some time. 'I didn't ask,' he replies. When one of the Americans wants the afternoon off to be with a son who is having his tonsils out, the Japanese tell him dourly that it will count against him. There is a lack of humanity in their relentless devotion to work, and towards the end the Japanese team leader begins to realise this. He berates his colleagues for attaching too much importance to work: 'Our friends, our family should be our life. We have things we can learn from Americans.' Other members of the team gradually see the light. Ito-san, fat and potentially jolly, who earlier had been cowed into agreeing that he wanted to stay at work rather than join his wife who was in labour, bounces forward at the end to say that she has given birth to a daughter. The Japanese have learned humanity. By comparison, the American lessons are trivial. What presents itself as a humorous conflict of cultures is, in fact, a celebration of American culture. And though the Japanese can be humanised through exposure to the American way, it's clear that their society as a whole, unleavened by association with the west, is humourless and robotic.

We have not after all moved far since Fr Valignano sent back his report to Jesuit headquarters in 1583. The Japanese are like this; we're like that. The Japanese do this; we do that. This same structure of antithesis governs every perception of the relationship, even in more sophisticated representations of modern Japan. The images we are offered are images of difference, and culturally we are fine-tuned to pick them out. Massive areas of interest and response that we have in common are passed over so that we can concentrate on the fact that they read from right to left rather than left to right, that their toothpicks are long whereas ours are short, and so on.

The terms of the relationship are written in stone. When Clive James sets out in *Brrm! Brrm!* to wrench the perspective around and observe the oddities from a Japanese point of view, the result is an elegant and appealing novel but one that does nothing to challenge the standard patterns of response. To point out how strange the English look when seen through Japanese eyes is an advance on repeating how strange the Japanese look when seen through English eyes, but it leaves the basic formula untouched. The novel mocks familiar western stereotypes ('KARATE POET', 'Gettin' a bit of bowin' practice, are we, Akira?' etc.) but then constructs its hero out of the same stereotypes. Suzuki *is* a karate expert, he *does* write a poem about cherry blossom, he *is* overpoweringly polite. It's to James's credit that he manages to shift the conventional balance of sympathies towards Japan, but in the end, though the adjectives may have changed, we're left with the same old pattern of antithesis: England – coarse, rude, messy, anarchic; Japan – refined, polite, neat, disciplined. At no stage do we relinquish our obsession with difference and catch sight of the points of contact.

We do not want to do this, for it would mean losing our myths. Even the most commonplace perceptions of Japan are still determined by our relentless search for the extraordinary. 'Mari Tanaka is 25. Every month she takes her mother's credit cards and spends £1000 on clothes. In Tokyo this is not considered at all unusual.' These words on the cover of the *Daily Telegraph* magazine announce a special report on consumer spending in Tokyo.[15] The article describes young people drinking sake 'laced' with gold and eating salads sprinkled with gold flakes; they have their bodies massaged with gold and brush their teeth with toothpaste 'laced', yet again, with gold. No doubt all this has happened, but one could spend a long time in Tokyo without bumping into anyone who'd done it. The point, however, is to preserve an image of what is exotic and different in what is actually a context of increasing similarity. As the article makes clear, these young people are consuming the products of the west: their clothes come from Paris and Milan, their cars from Britain and Germany. Wearing Armani suits, driving Mercedes and BMWs, making a living out of western pop music, they speak eloquently of the links between east and west. But this is not what we want to hear; we require Japan to be different.

Nowhere is this more apparent than in Joe Joseph's *The Japanese* (1993), ominously subtitled 'Strange but not Strangers'. Written with considerable panache by a former Tokyo correspondent of *The Times*, it exemplifies most of the responses we've been looking at. This is Japan as freak show, an endless parade of bizarre (one of Joseph's favourite words) eccentricities. The Japanese to whom he introduces us are the people who'll spend £50 on a musk melon, buy a toothbrush for their dog and a mink seat cover for their lavatory; who are obsessed by golf but never get on to a golf course; who have such an array of televisions they can even fit one in their filofax; whose whole perspective on life is a sustained affront to normality.

The reader, by contrast, is positioned alongside Joseph as an average, sane sort of westerner peering across the gulf that separates us from them: 'One typical incident highlights just how rich and how different from you and me the Japanese have become . . .'; 'But can you imagine a British or American businessman spending Sunday afternoon . . .'; 'Most westerners might think that . . . But . . .'; 'You might think that . . . Think again'; 'You and I might think . . . Not the Yokoyama family'. The ways of the Japanese are beyond comprehension: 'Imagine if you had just picked up a good degree from a top university, landed a high-flier's job in a blue-chip bank and were then told by your new boss to spend your first week on the job ironing crumpled £5 notes, or standing outside in a slashing downpour polishing the bank's brass nameplate.' Just another of the 'bizarre induction rituals' endured by the 'millions of corporate warriors who spread like ants from subway exits every morning towards desks in overcrowded offices'. As the subtitle warned us, these people are Strange. The only possible reaction is frank bewilderment. And that, we're told, is the essential difference between recent arrivals in Tokyo and long-term foreign residents: 'the recent arrivals look as though they've been in a state of bewilderment for the past two days. Long-term foreign residents have been bewildered for years.'[16]

Bewildered about ironing crumpled banknotes, about reading from right to left, about using the wrong size of toothpick, about eating seaweed, about doing all the other unfathomable things that put Japan on the far side of the universe. But do these things have to be so bewildering? Over the past few years the Japanese have become tourists. The taste for foreign travel is one of many ways in which they have begun to assimilate western perspectives, or so you might think. Think again, as Joseph would say. What we see in the mass media are coachloads of identical, camera-laden little chaps trooping on and off the bus to take group photographs of themselves grinning inanely in front of some cultural monument before hurrying on to empty the shelves of Fortnum & Mason. It all looks so different from our own freer, more anarchic, more individual way of doing things. And yet the differences, compared to the similarities, are nugatory.

In his book on Victorian attitudes to Japan, Yokoyama Toshio noted that in the 1870s, at just the time when Japan was drawing closer to Britain in terms of its institutions and technology, the general response among British writers was to give increasing stress to its remoteness. The parallel is striking, and it points yet again to a deep-seated need to define Japan by its otherness. ('We do not require any Englands in the Orient.') When western travellers first set foot in Japan, they found strange beings who deliberately blackened their teeth; when western journalists set foot in Japan today, they find strange beings who have their bodies massaged with gold. Valignano told with amazement how noblemen would spend a fortune on articles of common clay for the tea ceremony; the modern journalist writes with similar wonder of the businessman who spends a fortune to buy a Rodin for his yard. The emphasis has scarcely changed. These people are an alien nation.

PART II

Aesthetes

6. A Realised Fairyland

The alien is not always undesirable. It can give us nightmares, but it can also, when we call it the exotic, fuel our fantasies. In 1993 over a million European and American tourists landed at Narita airport. What were they hoping to find?

In a brave effort to humanise one of the long corridors of the university where I teach, someone has tacked up a poster advertising Qantas flights to Japan. The top half consists of four photographs: a geisha playing the koto, a dancer at the Ise shrine, Mount Fuji touched by winter sunlight, and a view of Ginza by night. The bottom half is a large picture of Kyoto's Katsura Rikyu garden in which a hesitant girl, wearing kimono and geta, holds a parasol over her head. These five images encapsulate the main ingredients of Japan's appeal to the west. They offer a version of the country that is both feminine and artistic; it has been filtered of all impurities – including ordinary Japanese. What is left is an aesthetic wonderland, a place to be viewed. Modern Japan is represented by the single image of a blaze of neon along the Ginza. All that can be seen of the cars are streaming lights – no people, no problems, just a hint of hi-tech excitement. Even here the guiding principle is aesthetic.

That this is the hallmark of tourist Japan can be confirmed by a glance at Fodor. Each of its fifteen chapters is prefaced by an illustration. Together they present us with a timeless world of rock gardens, mountain peaks and tranquil lakes. A spray of bamboo stands in front of the mountains, a lone rock with a single pine breaks the surface of the lake. This is the way it has always been. When people appear, they are part of the same eternal picture: three figures, their heads more or less hidden by coolie hats, pick tea on a hillside; a bunraku puppeteer manipulates a puppet on the stage; a monk, whose features are invisible, kneels over a piece of calligraphy; a woman in traditional dress performs the tea ceremony; two apprentice geisha at the edge of a lake stand under a parasol. These are the only human figures. Like the world of the Qantas poster, this is a Japan refined to its mythical elements, purged of modern Japanese and of all the other unwelcome realities of the present day – modern buildings, modern clothes, modern cars, modern technology. A single illustration concedes that we are in the twentieth century: the bullet train speeding past Mount Fuji. Like the lights of Ginza, this is an icon of modernity or, more precisely, a meeting of two icons representing modernity and tradition, the new Japan and the old; it brings us no closer to the lives of those who are ranged inside the streamlined carriages. The pure lines of Mount Fuji rise upwards and the pure lines of the bullet train intersect its base, composing themselves into a perfect aesthetic image.

The Qantas poster and the Fodor illustrations are typical. They highlight three aspects of Japan: its women, its landscape and its art. Representations of the Japanese woman will be considered later; here we are concerned with the other two, which together make up the image of aesthetic Japan. We'll look first at Japan as picturesque fairyland, a world inhabited by figures from the silk screen and the picture book. In the next chapter I argue that this apparently timeless image has been deployed according to a clear political agenda. Chapters 8 and 9 suggest how it reflects both the insecurities of the west and the ingrained conviction of western superiority. In the final chapter I focus on those aspects of the aesthetic image that pull it away from the exotic and back towards the alien.

On 8 September 1862 a young Englishman stood at the rail of the steamer *Lancefield* as it made its way up the bay of Yedo past the line of irregular hills overshadowed by the flawless cone of Mount Fuji. Ernest Satow was arriving in Japan to take up the post of student interpreter at the British Legation. He later became British minister and one of the great Japanologists of the nineteenth century, but the impulse that had brought him to Japan was neither political nor academic. A year or two earlier he had picked up Laurence Oliphant's account of Lord Elgin's mission to China and Japan in 1857–9. The book 'inflamed my imagination with pictures verbal and coloured of a country where the sky was always blue, where the sun shone perpetually, and where the whole duty of man seemed to consist in lying on a matted floor with the windows open to the ground towards a miniature rock-work garden, in the company of rosy-lipped black-eyed and attentive damsels – in short, a realised fairyland'.[1]

These are images straight from the travel brochure, direct precursors of the ones we are familiar with today. And as we read Oliphant's account of his first sight of Japan it is easy to see how Satow got hold of them. The ship glides into Nagasaki bay past the native fishing boats, 'their sails "folded like thoughts in a dream"'. From the deck Oliphant can make out the barracks and gardens on shore, where people in brightly coloured clothes impart a 'gay and almost fairy-like aspect to the scene'. The Japan he sees from the ship is a postcard picture of terraced rice- fields, shady groves and thatched cottages. Once ashore, he is struck by the manicured quality of the landscape:

> We were filled with astonishment and delight at the exquisite taste displayed in the gardens and cottages upon the roadside. These charming little cottages, raising their thatched roofs amid the fruit-trees and creepers which threatened to smother them in their embraces, were surrounded by flower-beds tastefully laid-out, resplendent with brilliant hues, and approached by walks between carefully clipped hedges.

When they pause at a tea-house for a 'picturesque picnic', Oliphant notes the hanging woods and gardens, 'tastefully laid out with rock-work', which fringe the bank of the river 'to the point at which it entered the grounds in a picturesque cascade'.[2]

This is Satow's realised fairyland. Even before we hear about

the blithe indifference to nakedness on the part of the inhabitants, it is clear that in this other world, which has left 'not a
single disagreeable association to cloud our reminiscences', we
are on the margins of paradise. In 1892 Kipling returned to
Yokohama and in his first letter for *The Times* painted an idyllic
picture of himself in the garden of the old French Legation. It
can be quoted in place of all the less colourful prose devoted to
similar descriptions in the closing decades of the Victorian era:

> We, being wise, sit in a garden that is not ours, but belongs to a
> gentleman in slate-coloured silk, who, solely for the sake of the
> picture, condescends to work as a gardener, in which employ he
> is sweeping delicately a welt of fallen cherry blossoms from under
> an azalea aching to burst into bloom. [...] Half-a-dozen blue-black
> pines are standing akimbo against a real sky – not a fog-blur nor
> a cloud-bank, nor a grey dish-clout wrapped round the sun – but
> a blue sky. A cherry tree on a slope below them throws up a wave
> of blossom that breaks all creamy white against their feet, and a
> clump of willows trail their palest green shoots in front of all. [...]
> Outside, beyond the foliage, where the sunlight lies on the slate-
> coloured roofs, the ridged rice-fields beyond the roofs, and the
> hills beyond the rice-fields, is all Japan – only all Japan; and this
> that they call the old French Legation is the Garden of Eden that
> most naturally dropped down here after the Fall.[3]

The Japanese garden is both a natural paradise and a work of
art. As such, it links the two central aspects of aesthetic Japan.
Kipling's silk-clad gentleman who condescends to act as a gardener 'solely for the sake of the picture' is fulfilling an important
role. For the generation of travellers who followed in Oliphant's
wake, there was one adjective that came to the pen more easily
than any other. Above all, Japan – its tea-houses, its gardens, its
villages, its people, its customs – was picturesque. And by
picturesque they didn't just mean pretty, they meant, quite literally, like a picture. Japan was a living embodiment of its own
art. Many travellers had scarcely set foot on shore before they
began to make comparisons with screens, fans, plates, tea-
caddies and so forth. In some cases they didn't even wait to get
off the boat: 'We are coming in; it is like the picture books,' wrote
the artist John La Farge on the cover of a letter he mailed from
the steamer. 'Anything that I can add will only be a filling in of

detail.'[4] He was arriving at Yokohama with Henry Adams in the summer of 1886. Soon his travelling companion was echoing his sentiments. 'All like the pictures that one sees on plates', he wrote the following month, when he and La Farge were established in a house in Nikko. And to another correspondent, '. . . the country still keeps to me its first peculiar aspect of a toy-world, where all the picture books and tea-cups of childhood are animated with a clever imitation of life'.[5]

Travellers as different as Pierre Loti and Isabella Bird were equally struck by the truth of the image. The woman who gets into the train with Loti at Kobe 'seems to have escaped from a screen with figures on it'. And Bird, looking at the mass of humanity in Shinbashi station, reflects, 'I feel as if I had seen them all before, so like are they to their pictures on trays, fans, and tea-pots.' To imagine Tokyo, suggests Baron de Hübner, you need only think of a line of rickshaws filled with 'Japanese exactly like the pictures you have seen a thousand times printed on vases, screens, or rice-paper'. The image turns up everywhere from Murray's Handbook to the memoirs of Lord Redesdale – the same Redesdale (A. B. Mitford) who advised Gilbert and Sullivan about the Japanese aspects of *The Mikado*. 'On many a vase and jar – / On many a screen and fan, / We figure in lively paint,' sang the nobles when the curtain rose. By then they were expressing a commonplace perception of Japan.[6]

From here it is a short step to apprehending the whole country as a series of pictures composed for the spectator's benefit. In his final letter for *The Times* in 1892, Kipling transforms the memories of his trip into a gallery of paintings which he presents to the reader one by one. A Tokyo street scene after dark becomes an elaborate pictorial display in which the indigo of the people's clothes and the blood-red of the paper lanterns mix with the colours of the flowers and shrubs and the glow of the street-lights rising into the darkness. 'That was a superb picture,' he concludes, 'and it arranged itself to admiration.'[7]

A hundred years after Kipling, Pico Iyer begins *The Lady and the Monk* by describing a brief stopover in Japan on the way to Southeast Asia. With a few hours to spare, he takes a bus from the airport to the local town, Narita: 'As I began to walk along the narrow lanes, I felt, in fact, as if I were walking through a gallery of still lifes. Everything looked exactly the way it was supposed to look, polished to a sheen, and motionless.'[8] It has to be motionless because motion would imply change, and the essential attraction of this picture is that it can be relied on not to change.

To step into a work of art is to step out of the flow of time. Fodor's geisha would be as much at home on a nineteenth-century screen as Gilbert and Sullivan's nobles. Replace Ginza's neon with Kipling's paper lanterns, and there's nothing in the Qantas poster that Kipling himself couldn't have seen a hundred years earlier. Or consider what Nikos Kazantzakis produces when he tries to imagine the newly reopened Japan that greeted westerners in the previous century: 'And then there was presented to the enchanted eyes of the whites that superb spectacle: forests of blossoming cherry trees in springtime, thousand-coloured chrysanthemums in autumn, gentle, diminutive women, silks, fans, strange temples, statues, paintings, an unexpected world full of joy and grace.'[9] It is a world where the women will always wear kimono and the cherry trees will always be in blossom. Like the frieze on Keats's Grecian Urn, its beauty is immune from time.

Central to the idea of picturesque Japan is the belief that its people are not just figures in a work of art, they are themselves artists, super-sensitive to the aesthetic resonances of everything around them. 'Throughout the length and breadth of the land, and from the highest prince to the lowest peasant,' wrote Percival Lowell in The Soul of the Far East, 'art reigns supreme.'[10] Back in 1876, Charles Dilke, remarking on their 'inborn sense of art', pointed out that 'Japanese are not like other dwellers in picturesque places, unaware of the beauties that surround them. They love the picturesque; they are the only people who plant in their fields double fruit trees for the beauty of their bloom.'[11]

Dilke's fruit farmers would have understood the grain dealer Kipling meets in Nagasaki who has decorated his spotless house with a dwarf pine in a green glazed pot beside which is a branch of azalea: 'The *bunnia* [grain-dealer] has put it there for his own pleasure, for the delight of his eyes, because he loves it. The white man has nothing whatever to do with his tastes, and he keeps his house specklessly pure because he likes cleanliness and knows it is artistic.'[12] The contrast with Europe, particularly the European peasantry, had been noted by numerous travellers. 'A taste for the fine arts is common among the very lowest classes,' wrote Baron de Hübner in 1871, 'and to a degree which is not found in any country in Europe. In the humblest cottage you will find traces of this . . .' Among the Japanese, 'the sense of beauty is innate'.[13]

By the time Marie Stopes arrived in 1907, this perception had become one of the clichés about Japan. 'There is a phrase which seems to hover over every conversation on Japan,' she remarks. 'It is, "Of course everything in Japan is so artistic!" It sometimes appears in the alternative form, "The Japanese are a nation of artists".'[14] She goes on to claim that western influence has now so far undermined the old artistic traditions that this is no longer true. If she was right, the point has been lost on most of the writers who came after her. The image of Old Japan dies hard. Almost all the figures who appear in the Fodor illustrations, as in the Qantas poster, are connected in one way or another with the nation's traditional arts, and the text carries the same message. 'In the world of Japanese cuisine,' we are told, 'there are colors to delight in and shapes, textures, and flavors are balanced for your pleasure. Naturally, the aroma, flavor, and freshness of the foods have importance, but so do the dishware, the design of the room, the sound of water in a stone basin outside.'[15] Guidebooks will usually tell us something about the national cuisine, but it's not often that we're alerted to the sound of water in a stone basin outside the restaurant.

These are the artistic Japanese who can't see a blossom fall without composing a poem about it. 'When it rains,' said a commentator previewing a BBC radio programme, 'we reach for our umbrellas. The Japanese start wondering what is the right word to describe it.' The people who delighted Pico Iyer by decorating their telephone cards with images of rock gardens or Hokusai mountains and selling them in neat little bags – 'the perfect world gift-wrapped' – are cast in the same mould.

And all of them owe a debt to Lafcadio Hearn. Not many writers on nineteenth-century Japan failed to contribute to the image of an artistic fairyland, but it was he who did most to define it for the west. A shy, difficult man, who was over forty before he set foot in what became his adopted country, he was vividly responsive both to the qualities of its landscape and to the subtleties of its decorative art. His work fuses them into an aesthetic vision which has exercised enormous influence over twentieth-century images of Japan. In an early essay he describes the feelings of the stranger, newly arrived, who has eyes only for Old Japan:

> It then appears to him that everything Japanese is delicate, exquisite, admirable – even a pair of common wooden chopsticks in a paper bag with a little drawing upon it; even a package of toothpicks of cherry-wood, bound with a paper wrapper wonderfully lettered in three different colours; even the little sky-blue towel, with designs of flying sparrows upon it, which the jinrikisha man uses to wipe his face. The bank bills, the commonest copper coins, are things of beauty. Even the piece of plaited string used by the shopkeeper in tying up your last purchase is a pretty curiosity.[16]

It is an aesthete's dream, a world packaged with supreme artistry down to the smallest detail. Hearn stayed long enough to see this vision take on the sadder aspect of a 'beautiful illusion', but it has remained a potent source of imagery for the west.

Those modern Japanese who listen for the sound of water outside the restaurant or seek to discern the quality of the falling rain are fitting descendants of the picturesque figures observed by our Victorian ancestors. In 'The Decay of Lying', Oscar Wilde casts a quizzical glance in their direction:

> Now, do you really imagine that the Japanese people, as they are presented to us in art, have any existence? [...] The actual people who live in Japan are not unlike the general run of English people; that is to say, they are extremely commonplace, and have nothing curious or extraordinary about them. In fact, the whole of Japan is a pure invention. There is no such country, there are no such

people. One of our most charming painters went recently to the Land of the Chrysanthemum in the foolish hope of seeing the Japanese. All he saw, all he had the chance of painting, were a few lanterns and some fans. He was quite unable to discover the inhabitants, as his delightful exhibition at Messrs Dowdeswell's Gallery showed only too well. He did not know that the Japanese people are, as I have said, simply a mode of style, an exquisite fancy of art.[17]

It would be rash to dismiss Wilde's comments as merely facetious. When the London *Evening Standard* wanted a photograph for a recent feature on the Japanese in London, it produced an image which could have come straight from a book of nineteenth-century travels. The picture shows a model, once again in kimono and *zori*, standing with a fan in front of the waterfall in the Kyoto Garden in Holland Park.[18] The article was actually about something quite different – the commercial impact of the Japanese on London – but the lure of traditional imagery was too strong to resist. Created out of myth, the picture exists in splendid detachment from its text, a triumphant image of quintessential Japan – the Japan that is 'simply a mode of style, an exquisite fancy of art'.

The girl in the garden, whether she turns up on nineteenth-century porcelain or a Qantas poster, in the letters of Kipling or the pages of the *Evening Standard*, is a perfect example of that style. She is the archetypal inhabitant of the aesthetic fairyland offered by the travel brochures. Reality falls away, as it did for Oliphant sailing into the bay of Nagasaki: 'Well might we imagine ourselves gliding across these solitary waters to some dreamland, securely set in a quiet corner of another world, far away from the storms and troubles of this one.'[19] Oliphant's destination is outside time, which is why it remains as available today as it was to Victorian travellers over a century ago.

7. Force of Circumstance

In April 1952 Japan became a sovereign state again rather than an occupied country. This political change was accompanied by an equally drastic change of image. After the eclipse of the 1940s, the aesthetic fairyland was back in favour. Wartime images did not disappear, but they were no longer unopposed.

Just four months after the official end of the occupation, the August issue of *Holiday* magazine ran a lavishly illustrated feature on Japan by James A. Michener.[1] The editor billed it as 'a double-length report on our recent enemies by a man who fought them in the Pacific and·who has just revisited them to give you this intimate, colorful and surprising picture'. Intimate, colourful, surprising – the adjectives already indicate that the recent enemy is going to be repositioned. This is the private and individual face, not the public and collective one; it is a colourful rather than a uniform Japan; it is different from what we have come to expect. The emphasis at once becomes apparent. Americans lucky enough to visit this new Japan will discover something as remote from the wartime newsreels as could well be imagined. The brutal aggressor has vanished; the language now is all of delicacy and cultivation:

> If you are one of the lucky ones, you will find in Japan a land of exquisite beauty and a people dedicated to its cultivation. [...] In the cities, where the ways and comforts of the West are at your disposal, you will be captivated by the gaudy colors and the

work of 1952, Vern Sneider's *The Tea-House of the August Moon*. With the help of a stage play and then a film starring Glenn Ford and Marlon Brando (Brando in the unlikely role of Japanese interpreter), it became one of the most popular representations of Japan in 1950s America. Set in the 'emerald-green hills' of Okinawa, the Japanese island where some of the cruellest fighting of the Second World War had taken place, it concerns the attempts of the American forces to organise and control the local population. The Okinawans are categorised as 'enemy civilians' and duly expected to cut communication lines, blow up supply dumps and commit all the acts of sabotage that a fanatical enemy usually goes in for; but the opening pages of the novel quickly displace the old image of the Japanese samurai. Communication lines are cut, but by peasant farmers who don't know what a telephone is and use the wire to hold together their rickety horse-drawn carts; trucks are waylaid, but by children who want chewing gum and chocolate.

Far from being the slit-eyed savages of the war films, the Okinawans turn out to be simple people with childlike wants and squabbles. The amiable Captain Fisby, sent by his gung-ho colonel to bring American civilisation to the benighted natives of one particular village, finds himself increasingly seduced by the traditional Japanese values and lifestyle to which he is introduced by a pair of geisha girls. The military priorities of drainage, education and democratisation soon take second place to digging a lotus pond which the geisha require for their tea-house. In the stage play the natives abandon a meeting about democratic government because it's 4.45 p.m: 'They not like to miss sunset. This is time of day they sit in pine grove, sip tea and watch sun go down.'

Before long the American captain, now wearing native wooden sandals, has acquired a new outlook on life. He is entranced by the beauty of the paper lanterns strung among the pine trees around the tea-house, 'casting their soft glow on the arched bridges and the still water of the lotus pond'. At the insistence of First Flower, one of the geisha, he takes up meditation and even begins to revise his ideas about food. The interpreter explains First Flower's feelings: 'She say when she eats, she likes to see the seasons of the year there on the dishes before her. In the spring she likes to see the little green peas, and they make her think of the whole earth coming to life, and the birds singing in the blossoming cherry trees . . . And boss, when the purple grapes are there before her, she sees the October moon high and white in the heavens . . .'[2] And much else along the same lines.

This is all new to Fisby. Previously he ate food to get it over with, 'but now he rather liked First Flower's way of thinking'. Later he is initiated into the mysteries of the tea ceremony. By the end of the book, the cultural lines have been firmly drawn. The villagers need American help to get the local economy going, but when it comes to taste and sensibility the balance is heavily on the side of Japan. And this is where it remained for the next two decades, until fear of Japan's economic dominance began to tilt the scales once again in a more hostile direction, giving rise to the series of Yellow Peril productions considered in Part IV.

By presenting Japan in aesthetic rather than military terms, Sneider's novel, like Michener's article, reflected the political requirements of the early 1950s. The new enemy was communism, and the battleground was Korea. Behind the efforts of North Korea to take over the South was the huge shadow of communist China. Japan was now a valuable source of military bases and equipment; political circumstance had turned it with striking rapidity from foe to friend. Not that we heard much about this military usefulness at the time. The emphasis was on cherry blossom and contemplation rather than on steel plants churning out war material, but it was nonetheless the political situation that determined the aesthetic focus.

That the 1950s should have returned to a version of Japan similar to that presented by Oliphant is not particularly surprising; he too was looking for a contrast with hostile China. When he sailed into Nagasaki harbour with Lord Elgin, they had just left behind the messy circumstances of the second Opium War. Throughout his narrative it is clear how much the image he creates of Japan owes to his distaste for China, and he admits that the contrast was so great that he found it difficult not to colour Japan too brightly. In China decorative detail becomes grotesque, in Japan it hits the happy medium; Chinese words 'consist generally of a gulp or a grunt', the sounds in Japanese 'are musical, and not difficult to imitate'; the Chinese show the least attractive features of their Mongol ancestry, but the Japanese 'differ essentially', having noses less broad and eyes less oblique – 'altogether, the cast of countenance is far more agreeable'.[3]

One after another, writers of the period strike the same note. Sherard Osborn, captain of the ship which brought Oliphant and Lord Elgin to Japan, writes of their stay as 'a bright oasis in the desert-like monotony of our existence in China', and dwells on his reluctance to return 'to strong-smelling China and its unpoetical inhabitants'.[4] Fifteen years later, Cyprian Bridge comments at length on the horribleness of China – 'habits and customs too filthy to describe', the air 'laden with sickening stenches', the beauty of buildings 'obscured beneath the accumulated foulness and neglect of years' – only to highlight 'how different was the state of things in Japan'.[5]

As a general rule, we can take it that when China is out of political favour perceptions of Japan will be correspondingly rosy. This, of course, can work equally well in reverse. During the Second World War *Time* magazine helpfully printed photographs of two typical Chinese faces and two typical Japanese faces, so that readers would have a better chance of knowing who their friends were. The writer admits that it is far from easy to tell the difference between the two races – 'Even an anthropologist, with calipers and plenty of time to measure heads, noses, shoulders, hips, is sometimes stumped' – but he offers a useful hint: 'Those who know them best often rely on facial expression to tell them apart: the Chinese expression is likely to be more placid, kindly, open; the Japanese more positive, dogmatic, arrogant.'[6] So much for the 'far more agreeable' cast of countenance that Oliphant found among the Japanese. Altogether, the history of alternating western responses to Japan and China would make a case study of our tendency to see what we want to see.

The honeymoon of the mid-nineteenth century was not the first time Japan's image had benefited from western disappointment with other farflung nations. Before Japan, Jesuit experience among the heathen had sometimes been unrewarding. A series of mishits in Africa and Asia made Japanese enthusiasm for the word of God particularly gratifying. They were, said Francis Xavier, 'the best people yet discovered'. Complimentary notes on their cleanliness, politeness and craftsmanship were underpinned by the conviction that the Japanese, practically alone among Asiatics, had shown any aptitude for receiving religious instruction. Since the Jesuits were not there to shop for curios or admire the view, the aesthetic emphasis is never as strong as it becomes in the nineteenth century, but it's by no means absent. Luis Frois, in particular, is often delighted by what he sees. He notes the 'beauty, artistry and neatness' of the monasteries in Kyoto and comments at length on Nobunaga's spectacular castle at Gifu, praising its gardens, where the ponds are lined with pebbles as white as snow, and its lavish rooms, whose 'exquisiteness, perfection and arrangement are quite beyond my powers of description'. In the queen's apartments, there are balconies 'facing the open country with all the music and beauty of birds that you could desire in Japan'.[7] The willingness to give Japan aesthetic credit is here, as in later centuries, partly dependent on its political, or in this case religious, docility. Once the persecutions were underway, this aspect of Japan dropped quickly out of sight.

In the nineteenth century there were occasional hiccups – an assassination here, a commercial wrangle there – but no comparable turning of the tide. Anti-western feeling, especially in the 1860s, created moments of crisis, and western traders developed a somewhat jaundiced view of Japanese business ethics, but these factors did not undermine the general perception of Japan as a nation with a unique aesthetic sensibility apparent in every area of daily life.

As the memory of the Opium Wars receded, this image was sustained less by the contrast between Japan and China than by a growing core of doubt at the heart of the prosperous, industrialised west. The sort of details travellers comment upon – the picturesque rural tranquillity, the polite observation of social hierarchy, the concern with old-fashioned craftsmanship – point to precisely the elements of social life that contemporary England was felt to be in the process of losing. It was not by chance that writers chose to emphasise these aspects of Japan rather than the grim effects of dispossession among the samurai class, deprived of their hereditary rights by Meiji reforms, or the squalor that attended the country's first steps towards industrialisation. At a time when English rural life was deep in crisis, when unionised labour was beginning to threaten traditional relationships between master and employee, when the slums of Britain's cities were at last drawing attention to the price that had been paid for prosperity, the typical Victorian traveller found in Japan an image of exactly what his own country lacked.

8. A Place to Meditate

From early days there were voices willing to proclaim Japan's aesthetic superiority to the west: 'Let not the Europeans any longer flatter themselves with the empty notions of having surpassed all the world beside in stately Palaces, costly Temples, and sumptuous Fabricks; Ancient and modern Rome must now give place: The glory of one Country, Japan alone, has exceeded in beauty and magnificence all the pride of the Vatican at this time, and the Pantheon heretofore . . .'[1] These are evidently the words of an enthusiast, but John Stalker and George Parker, in the preface to their *Treatise of Japaning and Varnishing* (1688), were championing the one aspect of Japanese culture that would have been reasonably familiar to an important section of the British public. By the early seventeenth century the word 'japan' had already become a synonym for the lacquer work fashionable in Jacobean drawing rooms. Most of the owners would have been hard put to distinguish Japan from China, and much of the work called 'japan' was anyway produced in Europe, but in so far as that distant country impinged on western consciousness at all during the long centuries of exclusion, it did so by virtue of its arts and crafts.

As soon as westerners could get back into Japan, they set about buying up everything they could lay their hands on. Within days of Commodore Perry's squadron coming to land, the process had begun. 'The shopping mania which has seized upon our officers is very amusing,' Lieutenant Preble noted in his diary. 'The gallant gentlemen pounce upon anything that in any way represents Japan.'[2] When the British got there a few years later, it was the same story. Having dropped anchor in the bay of Nagasaki, Lord Elgin's party were quick to take advantage of the bazaar on Dejima. Sherard Osborn records their impressions:

> The first feeling was a desire to buy up everything, where all was so pretty. Tables, curiously inlaid with mother-of-pearl – representations of birds and animals, which our papier-mâché manufacturers, or those of France, would give anything to be able to imitate – cabinets, on which golden fish or tortoise stood out in most truthful relief – wonderful little gems in ivory, bone, or wood, fifty times more replete with originality, skill, and wit than anything China ever produced – porcelain so delicate, that you were almost afraid to touch it – in short, a child in a pastrycook's shop never ran from sweet to sweet more perplexed to know which to invest in, than we that morning in Decima bazaar.[3]

A child in a pastrycook's shop aptly sums up the character of western excitement over the ensuing decades. This was the start of an increasing tide of nineteenth-century collectors who scoured the treaty ports for examples of ancient Japanese art, which the obliging locals soon began to mass-produce for their benefit. Even those westerners who were most contemptuous of the Japanese could not resist the urge to buy. In *Japoneries d'automne* Pierre Loti recalls leaving Kyoto with a second rickshaw following behind, filled with his purchases. Before he can reach the station he sees another huge statue which has to be bought, necessitating a third rickshaw. At about the same time Henry Adams remarks in a letter to a friend that bric-à-brac dealers 'consume day after day in opening and displaying stuffs, lacquers, metal-work, books, pictures, crystals and all the curios of Japan. I buy pretty nearly everything that is considered good by Bigelow and the Fenollosas.'[4] By the end of the century Osman Edwards could parody what had become a stock figure:

> Doodle San will leave Japan
> With several tons of cargo;
> Folk will stare, when all his ware
> Is poured into Chicago.[5]

79

The accompanying picture shows a frock-coated traveller with whiskers and moustache handing over large sums of money to purchase the Kamakura Daibutsu. In the background are rickshaws piled high with buddhas and ornamental vases.

This rush to acquire Japanese artefacts was part of the wider aesthetic vogue known as *japonisme*. While Victorian travellers rummaged through the curio shops of Yokohama and Nagasaki, their London acquaintances could browse among the lacquered furniture, porcelain and embroideries offered by Liberty's, which had opened in Regent Street in 1875. (Parisians had been able to pick up items of *japonaiserie* at the shop of M. and Mme. Desoye on the rue de Rivoli since 1862.) Drawing rooms everywhere reflected the prevailing fashion. Japanese fabrics, Japanese fans, Japanese prints and Japanese porcelain all began to make their appearance. In 1890 Almy's Department Store in Salem, Massachusetts, opened a Japanese section which led to further outlets in Boston and Newport. 'There is hardly a drawing room in London or Paris or New York in which there are not objects of Japanese art,' wrote Henry Norman in 1892, 'and yet not until you reach Japan do you discover what the craze for Japanese "curios" really is. The second thought, if not indeed the first, of almost every globe-trotter who comes to the Land of the Morning, is to procure some Japanese artistic antiquities . . .'[6] Gilbert and Sullivan contributed *The Mikado* in 1885, and ten years later Marie Lloyd was singing 'The Geisha' on the stage of the music hall. In the course of half a century Japan had found its way into the popular consciousness in a variety of forms, practically all of them associated with art or culture. As the *Daily Telegraph* put it when *The Mikado* was first performed, 'We are all being more or less Japanned.'

Much of this was ephemeral. In time the craze for things Japanese waned; fans were put away in drawers, screens were folded, ornaments gradually found their way to the attic. But underlying this aesthetic fashion was a more serious recognition of artistic values from which the west could learn. From the early 1860s there were European artists, particularly in Paris, who looked to Japan for release from the dead hand of academic realism. There is scarcely an artistic movement in the second half of the century – Symbolist, Impressionist, Post-Impressionist, Arts and Crafts, Art Nouveau and, above all, the Aesthetic Movement itself – which does not owe something to Japanese influence. Western artists responded both to the economy of Japanese art and to its defiance of the criteria that had dominated nineteenth-century European art.

This contrast between the two traditions had aesthetic reverberations beyond the purely artistic. The decorative emphasis of Japanese art reflected a wider concern with the relationship between aesthetic values and the conditions of everyday life that seemed to be lacking in the west. After his visit to the immaculate home of the grain-dealer in Nagasaki, Kipling moves on to a dealer in curiosities and thence to a tea-house. Lost in admiration for the delicate craftsmanship he sees in each of these places, he is uneasily aware of the contrast between the western journalist in muddy boots and the spotless cleanliness of his surroundings. As he enters the curio-dealer's shop, he has the unusual sensation of finding himself at a disadvantage in his relations with a native: 'I passed in, feeling for the first time that I was a barbarian, and no true *sahib*.' What troubles him in these encounters is a sense of his own grossness in comparison with the refinement of the Japanese. It is the aesthetic perfection of Japanese life that brands him as a barbarian:

> What I wanted to say was, 'Look here, you person. You're much too clean and refined for this life here below, and your house is unfit for a man to live in until he has been taught a lot of things which I have never learned. Consequently I hate you because I feel myself your inferior, and you despise me and my boots because you know me for a savage. Let me go, or I'll pull your house of cedar-wood over your ears.'[7]

The response is jocular, but it carries an awareness that in this area the normal relation of superior to inferior, sahib to native, has been reversed. It also implies a more general perception about English society. When Kipling visits the Kiyomizu potteries in Kyoto, he finds a scene of impeccable neatness and propriety, as befits the work-place of men who are artists. He notes the sprig of cherry blossom to which they can lift their eyes, the gnarled pine nearby and the iris in a little pond:

> Somewhere in dirty England men dream of craftsmen working under conditions which shall help and not stifle the half-formed thought. [...] Would they have their dreams realised, let them see how they make pottery in Japan, each man sitting on a snowy mat with loveliness of line and colour within arm's length of him, while with downcast eyes he – splashes in the conventional diaper of a Satsuma vase as fast as he can! The Barbarians want Satsuma and they shall have it, if it has to be made in Kyoto one piece per twenty minutes.[8]

What starts as a tribute to the exquisiteness of Japanese arrangements ends as an ironic comment on the effects of western influence. Satsuma ware, which properly comes from the Satsuma province of Kyushu, is being mass-produced in Kyoto for the voracious western market. Kipling has raised the possibility that the nations of the west, far from being agents of civilisation, are here agents of corruption. He makes the point explicit a few pages further on when he and the professor emerge from a *cloisonné* factory: ' "'Fessor," I said [...] "let's start a mission and save Japan from herself. I'll run along the streets and knock off the policemen's forage caps, while you go and tear up the railway and pull down the telegraph poles. If they are left to themselves they will make *cloisonnée* [sic] by machinery in another twenty years and build black factories instead of gardens." '[9]

It's clear that saving Japan from herself means saving her from the west. For a man who is seen as an arch-apostle of empire, this is a startling admission. Japan apparently contradicts the fundamental belief that everyone, everywhere, would be better off under European control. Alone among the countries of the east it challenges the ruling assumption of western imperialism, and the grounds on which it does so are aesthetic. Dirty industrial England finds in Japan an image of cleanliness and craftsmanship which undermines the bland conviction of cultural superiority.

But what England is also beginning to find is a mirror image of its own ugliness. The contrast Kipling sees is not just between Japan and England, but between the old Japan of craftsmanship and tradition and the new Japan of factories and mass production which, under the patronage of the west, is now being born.

In different parts of Asia and Africa the west has been arraigned for a whole catalogue of delinquencies from mass murder to racial snobbery, but in its relations with Japan its sins are almost invariably presented as aesthetic. Travellers looked with despair at the streets of the Treaty ports and concluded, like Kipling, that the influence of the west was corrupting the delicacy and refinement of native culture – its art, its dress, its manners. Even the pretty tea-houses, claimed Cyprian Bridge in 1878, were giving way to the requirements of Europeans with their beefy restaurants: 'It is a pitiful tale, this overwhelming of an interesting and even romantic country by a deluge of vulgar common-place.'[10] His gloomy diagnosis that Japan was witnessing 'an irruption of Birmingham into Arcadia' echoes through the closing years of the century. In this fairy world the westerner is a hobnailed clod.

On his first day in Japan Lafcadio Hearn climbs to an ancient temple high in the hills outside Yokohama. When he is about to leave, the old priest, whose smile of welcome had seemed to him 'one of the most exquisite I have ever been greeted with', approaches him with a bowl. Hearn automatically assumes that the man is begging and drops a few coins into the bowl before he realises with shame that it is a bowl of water which the priest is offering for his refreshment. The incident gives us a paradigm of the coarse westerner who imagines himself to be conferring material benefits when in reality the benefits are of another kind and it is the Japanese who confers them. The humiliating lesson cannot be separated from its picturesque setting. Hearn's blunder is a failure to grasp the meaning of the whole aesthetic context – a failure of western sensibility.

It is not difficult to find modern equivalents of Hearn in the temple or Kipling in the curio shop. When Pico Iyer goes to Thanksgiving dinner at the home of Etsuko, a Japanese woman living in Kyoto, he enters a world of artistic refinement that leaves him bemused. Her house is 'a fairy-tale mansion in the Japanese context, its [...] exquisitely appointed living room – a museum in miniature'. In a dining room 'ringed with beautifully arranged blue cups and a gallery of china plates', his hostess serves chrysanthemums in tiny blue bowls and explains how the Japanese have different colours for each wind as well as for every season, telling him, among other things, the different words for moonlight on the water. More than this, she talks 'without strain' about quattrocento churches in Florence, Mozart pieces '(identified by Köchel number)', the early writings of Fosco Maraini, Keats's 'Ode to Autumn', and the latest holdings of the Musée d'Orsay. Iyer is left 'many fathoms out of my depth and amazed to see someone move in this almost Jamesian aura of refinement'.[11]

The image, once again, is that of the educated outsider made to feel like a bumpkin by the superior cultivation of the Japanese. We might be able to string together a few sentences about Mozart's music or the Musée d'Orsay, but Köchel numbers and recent acquisitions take things to a level where the air is getting thinner by the moment. And that's before the conversation turns to the *early* writings of Fosco Maraini. Among these cultural peaks only the super-aesthete can breathe 'without strain'. What's more, this effortless superiority is displayed in the context of western culture; we are beaten on our own ground. Etsuko's command of the western artistic tradition as well as the eastern reflects a shift in cultural power which we shall look at more closely in the next section.

There is nothing in the late twentieth century that quite corresponds to the *japonisme* of the nineteenth, but Japan's aesthetic stock is still high enough to command respect. The Japanese, it is acknowledged, are concerned with matters of aesthetic presentation in a way that we are not – 'You can't beat the Japs for imaginative packaging,' as a *Sunday Times* reporter sensitively put it.[12] These might not be the words Hearn would have chosen, but he was making much the same point a century earlier when he praised the pretty bag for the wooden chopsticks, the coloured wrapper for the toothpicks and the plaited string used by the shopkeeper. Japanese design still has a particular mystique and Japanese goods an aesthetic cachet enjoyed by no other country outside Europe. This is not just a question of designer labels; it's to do with futons and sushi bars and the black and white no-brand goods on sale at Muji's. It is also, crucially, to do with the futuristic Japan whose technology displays a genius for miniaturisation and simplicity of line that goes straight back to the aesthetic priorities of Japanese culture. From the people who gave us the bonsai and the miniature garden come the Walkman, the miniature television and the microchip. In this context the phrase 'small is beautiful' carries its full aesthetic weight. The neatness and ingenuity of Japanese craftsmanship, which was the theme of so many nineteenth-century commentators, has now become the neatness and ingenuity of Japanese technology.

For us, moreover, this craftsmanship is leavened by another element which most Victorians, if they thought about it at all, would have regarded with some suspicion. The nineteenth-century travellers who lamented the corruption of Japanese culture by the coarser values of the west were talking primarily about the obliteration of the picturesque – picturesque clothes, picturesque buildings, picturesque traditions. All were being displaced by a modern ugliness exported from western nations that lacked the refinement of the Japanese. The memory of these blunders was very much a part of the reverential approach to Japanese culture of the post-war years. We were not going to make the same mistake again. Captain Fisby's obtuse colonel descends on the Okinawans with the sort of proselytising zeal that had characterised the worst ambassadors of western culture in the nineteenth century. ('Fisby, why don't you get some of that white mortar and slap it on here?') But by this time Fisby knows where his aesthetic loyalties lie and diverts the colonel to the East China Sea, where he can do battle with imaginary river pirates, well out of harm's way. Fisby has learned that more is at stake than a picturesque scene. The concern with appearance is not just a matter of surfaces; there is a spiritual dimension to the Japanese aesthetic which gradually fosters an understanding of things which neither the army nor his job as a storekeeper had taught him. Sitting in the garden created by First Flower, he begins, cautiously, to accept the idea of meditation.

It is the first step along a road that takes us from the pretty tea-houses described by Oliphant, Satow, Kipling and the rest to the very different sort of tea-house which visitors to the 'Visions of Japan' exhibition were invited to inspect in 1991–2. As the accompanying leaflet made clear, aesthetic consider-ations were heavily overlaid by spiritual ones. The architecture of the tea-house was conditioned by a mixture of *wabi* – 'a lonely, poor and weak state of mind which accepts the imperfections of this life and tries to make a virtue of them' – and *sabi*, 'one of whose meanings is "patina", implying maturity, age and elegant simplicity'. In this austere construction the tea-house window functions so that 'participants in the Tea Ceremony can experi-ence a spiritual space that is cut off from the outside world'. The promise is still of escape from the world, but into a region which bears little resemblance to fairyland.

It's not that this spiritual emphasis is new in Japanese culture, merely that the west's receptiveness is new. The vogue for Zen Buddhism which took off in the 1950s has been largely respon-sible for this. Writing at the end of the war, Benedict could treat Zen as a subject unfamiliar to her readers, addressed for the most part by dismissive western scholars and some more or less incomprehensible Japanese.[13] Fifty years on, as we saw in Chapter 3, Zen has cast its spiritual mantle over everything from popular novels to car manufacture.

This is especially true of the western attitude to Japanese gar-dens. The landscape that First Flower creates around her tea-house is in some respects typical of the scenery that has been part of fairyland Japan from Oliphant to Fodor. With its lotus pond, its hanging lanterns, its arched bridges and tinkling wind bells, it draws on a range of familiar images, but its appeal is not purely picturesque. By luring the over-tense Americans into a more serene and meditative lifestyle, it points in a direction which leads eventually to *Holiday* magazine's 'barefoot pilgrim' and the Zen garden of Ryo-anji.

The modern taste for Japanese gardens reflects an updated – and spiritualised – version of Kipling's contrast between clumsy westerner and refined Japanese. 'A place to meditate – not barbecue' was the rather brutal headline of a recent feature in the *Daily Telegraph*. The accompanying picture showed a Zen garden created in Cheshire by Robert Ketchell 'with a Japanese design, meant to purify the soul with its relaxing, aesthetic nature'. An article explained its attraction:

> Ketchell has completely transformed a typically English garden to reflect the essential elements of *shosha* (refinement), *wabi* (quiet taste), *yugen* (subtleness) and *sabi* (elegant simplicity). Enthusiasts find the relaxing, aesthetic qualities can best be appreciated in solitude and are the perfect antidote to stress.
>
> 'The Japanese garden can be interpreted as a path that leads to a higher state of consciousness. It is supposed to purify the spirit. That is why water is so much part of the design process. It is a pilgrim's progress,' says Sam Youd.[14]

The familiar language of elegance and refinement has been combined with the language of spirituality to produce an antidote to the most typical of modern afflictions – stress.

It's another demonstration of how the vision of aesthetic Japan can be tailored to western requirements. For late Victorians, the rural paradise where childlike inhabitants led a life of laughter devoted to picturesque pursuits in a picturesque landscape was a perfect foil to the grimy adult world of nineteenth-century industrialism. The grace, delicacy and aesthetic concern they found in Japan were the qualities which their own society, with its energetic pursuit of empire and industrial development, had relegated to the feminine margins of national life. Today, for those who look to the tea-house and the Zen garden, the image offers a dream of spiritual peace in the midst of modern urban pressures. Again, it speaks to them of what their society lacks – of restraint in a world of indulgence, tranquillity in a world of turbulence, spirit in a world preoccupied with the material . . . meditation in a world of barbecues.

In an interesting article for the *Independent*, Bryan Appleyard described a well-known tourist excursion in terms that are redolent of the Japan Experience: 'When you visit the Ginkakuji Temple in Kyoto, you are led around a sinuous footpath so that you can see this exquisitely calm and timeless building through trees, from a hillside, across a sand and stone Zen garden. There is not one way to see it, there are many. More profoundly there is not really one object, one truth, there are many.' This is the Japan we revere and from which we seek to learn. Again, its qualities are a foil to our inadequacies:

> Finally, of course, the place works. Everything is clean and maintained, the trains run and crowds of flawlessly uniformed schoolchildren politely bow, smile and make way for you in the street. These are not small things, for they are evidence of a big thing that we may be losing – it may be called civilisation, national will, cultivation or manners. It has aspects, it can be viewed from many angles. But we in the West know that it is one thing and the Japanese have it and we do not.[15]

In presenting this neat and civilised contrast to our increasingly boorish culture, Japan is fulfilling one of its time-honoured roles. But there is a darker strand to Appleyard's article, for he also indicts Japan as a society that frequently fails to meet basic standards of decency and tolerance. This, too, is to be expected. If we acknowledge the superiority of Japan, it is not usually without a conviction of more important kinds of superiority enjoyed by the west. Japan's aesthetic achievements have to be measured against the sturdier qualities of nations that wrap things in brown paper and have little time for the niceties of flower arrangement. It is to this less amiable perspective that we now turn.

9. A Natural Infirmity

Welcomed aboard his Japan Air Lines flight by a 'pretty kimono-ed and obi-ed stewardess', James Bond settles into a comfortable window seat and takes stock of the amenities:

> The sick-bags 'in case of motion disturbance' were embellished with pretty bamboo emblems and, according to the exquisitely bound travel folder, the random scribbles on the luggage rack above his head were 'the traditional and auspicious tortoiseshell motif'. The stewardess bowed and handed him a dainty fan, a small hot towel in a wicker-basket and a sumptuous menu that included a note to the effect that an assortment of cigarettes, perfumes and pearls were available for sale.[1]

Pretty, exquisite, traditional, dainty, small. Within a couple of sentences Bond's first contact with Japan has turned up a comprehensive sample of the terms used to define its aesthetic appeal. So far we're on familiar territory. Lafcadio Hearn, we remember, had found everything Japanese 'delicate, exquisite, admirable' on his first encounter with the country. But James Bond is hardly the Lafcadio Hearn *de nos jours*. People don't emerge from a British public school without a few healthy reservations about words like dainty and exquisite. Such terms belong within a feminine sphere. Otherwise, their implications shift from the feminine to the effeminate. Like the word aesthetic itself, they have a hint of the limp-wristed that takes us back to Gilbert and Sullivan:

A Japanese young man,
A blue and white young man,
Francesca di Rimini, miminy, piminy,
Je-ne-sais-quoi young man![2]

Japan's artistic concerns point to a strain of effeminacy which makes it easy for the western sense of aesthetic inferiority to give way to a sense of masculine superiority.

You Only Live Twice opens with a geisha party at which Bond realises that he has been given a 'pillow geisha' (a sexual partner) rather than one of her more cultivated sisters. He is undismayed: 'to the boorish, brutalised tastes of a *gaijin*, a foreigner, this made more sense than having a *tanka* of thirty-one syllables, which in any case he couldn't understand, equate, in exquisite ideograms, his charms with budding chrysanthemums on the slopes of Mount Fuji'.[3] Boorish and brutalised here become terms of covert self-congratulation on the part of the red-blooded male faced with a culture whose super-refinement has rendered it anaemic. The westerner in muddy boots is at a disadvantage aesthetically, but it's a disadvantage that reflects credit on his masculinity, moral seriousness, sense of responsibility, or whatever.

Kipling may have felt himself a clumsy barbarian in the curio-dealer's shop, but when he turned to Japan's military arrangements he could barely contain his gleeful superiority: 'I peeped into the Quarter-Guard at Osaka fort and withdrew oppressed by laughter. Fans and dainty tea-sets do not go with one's notions of a barrack.' A few lines further on he remarks that 'The Japanese makes a trim little blue-jacket, but he does not understand soldiering.' Or business. Kipling quotes a couple of businessmen discussing the subject in Kyoto: 'The Jap's no use,' says one. 'He isn't man enough to handle a hundred thousand dollars.' Business, like the world of soldiering, is a male preserve from which the Japanese are cut off by their absorption in things aesthetic. The initial opposition Kipling formulated between clumsy westerner and artistic Japanese is being revised. Before long he has redefined it to his satisfaction:

> Verily Japan is a great people. Her masons play with stone, her
> carpenters with wood, her smiths with iron, and her artists with
> life, death, and all the eye can take in. Mercifully she has been
> denied the last touch of firmness in her character which would
> enable her to play with the whole round world. We possess that
> – we, the nation of the glass flower shade, the pink worsted mat,
> the red and green china puppy dog, and the poisonous Brussels
> carpet. It is our compensation . . .'[4]

So it's craftsmanship and aesthetic taste against firmness of
character and imperial power. As in the passage from Fleming,
the note of self-congratulation masquerading as self-criticism is
unmistakable. The grossness of our aesthetic taste stands as a
guarantee of all those sterling qualities that are opposed to the
aesthetic. In effect, these are the qualities that make the western
powers powerful, that distinguish the possessors from the
producers.

Throughout the second half of the nineteenth century this
point was reinforced by the ravenous way in which the west
took possession of Japan's artistic goods. The collection of works
of art is itself an expression of power; collectors tend to come
from among the strong. When the Japanese began to descend
on western art markets in the 1980s and return home with
Impressionist paintings in their luggage, our unease may have
had less to do with the loss of a particular work of art than with
the loss of the cultural power it denoted. (We were left to con-
sole ourselves with the thought that even if the Japanese could
pay for it, they couldn't appreciate it. 'The very real feeling I had
in Japan', wrote Waldemar Januszczak in the *Guardian*, 'was that
most of the new interest in art was directed at its status-giving
potential rather than its contents . . . An awful lot of money is
being made peddling spiritual tit-bits to a materialistic society.'[5]
In a neat reversal, it's the west that here lays claim to spirituality and aesthetic sensibility over against the vulgar materialism
of the all-powerful Japanese.)

Along with the superiority of the collector went the superiority of the spectator; the more powerful culture does the looking
and defining. And the ultimate object of a culture's gaze, the one
that has no function other than to be gazed at, is the work of art.

It is this that gives a characteristic tone to the perpetual references among nineteenth-century travellers to the way the Japanese scene resembles the world depicted on plates, cups, fans, screens, tea-caddies and the like. It is all so picturesque. But the compliment is loaded; a picture exists only for the pleasure of the observer. A work of art can be looked at, understood, framed; it can be collected and possessed. The metaphor of a country and its people as works of art offers a seductive promise to the observer, which in modified form continues in the images of the travel brochure. It is a version of Japan that can still invest the western tourist with a kind of power.

Equally important in the cultural power struggle is the question of size. As adjectives like dainty, delicate and exquisite suggest, the aesthete's world is small in scale. Big westerners clumping into little Japanese homes are at once betrayed by their size, but the perspective can easily change. To be small is to be physically vulnerable. It is to be the child in relation to the adult, the woman in relation to the man – petted, perhaps, but relatively powerless. The stress on Japan's aesthetic stature goes hand in hand with the stress on its lack of physical stature, for the west, as we have seen, allows the aesthetic image to predominate only when Japan is felt to pose no threat. It's no accident that the two periods when this feeling was most prominent were the last half of the nineteenth century and the decades following the Second World War. At both times the military and political ascendancy of the west meant that it really didn't have to *bother* about Japan.

Kipling's image of the imperial British playing with the whole round world transforms the globe into a child's toy, and this is how the Japanese scene tends to be viewed. 'A toy-world' was Henry Adams's phrase. Buildings, people, even the landscape, are rendered faintly absurd by their diminutive scale and picture-book appearance: 'Just now we are established in our doll-house with paper windows and matted floors, the whole front open towards ridiculously Japanese mountains.' From the doll's house in Nikko, Adams sends a photograph of one of the temples to his friend Theodore Dwight: 'You will see that it is evidently a toy, for everything is lacquer, gilding, or green, red and blue paint. I am still in search of something serious in this country, but with little more hope of success.'[6]

If the traditional houses and temples looked like products of toy-town to western visitors, Japan's first steps into the world of technology often fared little better. At Kobe station Pierre Loti finds 'a funny little railway which doesn't look serious, which strikes one, in fact, as laughable, like everything Japanese'. Even the food has the same effect; in Kyoto, he explains, you have to go to the new hotel built for westerners if you want anything to eat, 'since Japanese cuisine can at best serve as an amusement'.[7] The Lilliputian is always slightly laughable. From Gilbert's three little maids to Marie Lloyd's cheeky little Jappie chappie, size is an insistent refrain. 'I know I abuse this adjective "little",' admits Sir Edwin Arnold, after employing it nine times in a single sentence, 'but all in Japan is *chisai, choito,* except the shrimps – which are colossal – and the sea, and the mountains.'[8] Of all the words used about Japan and things Japanese, 'little' recurs most frequently. Or, if you happen to be French, 'petit'. In *Madame Chrysanthème* Loti's narrator interrupts himself, like Arnold, to apologise for using it yet again: 'I'm really overworking the word, I realise that. But how can one avoid it? In describing the features of this country, one's tempted to use it ten times a line. *Petit, mièvre, mignard* – the whole physical and moral character of Japan is contained in these three words.'[9]

The adjectives *mièvre* and *mignard* suggest that it is not just smallness of scale; there is an element of the finicky, the over-nice, the trifling. What Loti makes clear is that 'little' is not a neutral word in the western vocabulary. Small may be beautiful but it's lower down the hierarchy than big and, even when the intention is to compliment, the language of size reflects this hierarchy. It is essentially patronising. The moneyed middle classes in England invariably have at their disposal 'a little man' who can be called in to do the odd jobs for which they themselves are unfitted. The word 'little' confidently assigns him his place in the scale of creation, several rungs below his employers. Exactly the same resonances are brought into play by the relentless emphasis on the smallness of Japanese people and the products of Japanese culture. Our terms of aesthetic praise are in this context inseparable from an element of denigration. However much we may admire the bonsai, there is a sense, deeply rooted in our culture, that it is less worthy of consideration than the full-grown tree. Small equals not quite serious.

Not that we hold this against the Japanese. On the contrary, it can make them rather endearing – like children. When General MacArthur remarked that 'Measured by the standards of modern civilisation, they [the Japanese] would be like a boy of twelve as compared with our development of forty-five years,' he caused enough ill feeling for the projected statue of him in Tokyo Bay to be abandoned, but he was expressing a point of view that goes back to the first American contacts with Japan.[10] The 'innocent and childish delight' with which (according to the official account of the expedition) the Japanese negotiators responded to Commodore Perry's presents was of a piece with the 'almost childish eagerness and delight' shown by the common people of Shimoda who crowded round the visiting Americans to examine their dress and ask 'in their pantomimic way' the names of articles that struck their fancy.[11]

It was a picture that found ready acceptance. 'Everyone, in these days,' wrote de Hübner, 'knows that the Japanese people are gentle, amiable, civil, gay, good-natured, and childish.' Charles Dilke was equally confident: 'All who love children must love the Japanese,' he claimed in 1876. By the end of the century, Douglas Sladen's assertion that 'the Japanese are a nation of children' was as much of a cliché as the opinion referred to by Marie Stopes that the Japanese were a nation of artists. The two were closely related: the prevailing attitude put war, business and industry on the male and adult side, while arts, crafts and leisure were on the female and childish side. Aesthetic Japan – the fairyland that Victorian travellers were so fond of invoking – belonged firmly with the women and children.[12]

To define the Japanese as a race of children is to introduce some of the ambiguity of our response to real children. Together with the innocence that rebukes our tarnished adulthood and makes children the natural inhabitants of paradise, there is an element of irresponsibility, even of amorality, which can be more dubious. Whatever Wordsworthian enthusiasm we may have for them is balanced by a sense of their dangerous independence of civilised codes of behaviour. Taking up a familiar western refrain, a man in Yokohama remarks that the Japanese is naturally dishonest – 'He's like a baby that way' – and Kipling reflects, 'Everywhere the foreigner says the same thing of the neat-handed, polite little people that live among flowers and babies, and smoke tobacco as mild as their own manners. I am sorry; but when you come to think of it, a race without a flaw would be perfect.'[13]

This single flaw is the obverse of those charming attributes of a people who know nothing of business ethics and imperial firmness of character. It is Kipling's more genial version of what Loti had done by linking physical smallness with moral smallness. The daintiness of Japanese aesthetic concerns, always on the brink of triviality, has a moral equivalent in the lightness and irresponsibility that make them think nothing of going back on a contract. 'The want of fixity or commercial honour', Kipling suggests in another letter from Japan, 'may be due to some natural infirmity of the artistic temperament.'[14] For moral substance you need the man with the Brussels carpet.

Crossing the inland sea in 1907, Marie Stopes found herself sailing 'among the fairy islands in a dreamland boat'; her room was 'an aesthetic dream'; Tokyo was 'everywhere a fairy-land of beauty'. But when it came to contracts, her experience was the same as that of the Yokohama merchants. She returned from a walking tour to discover that the house she was to have rented had been sold to someone else: 'The blow that awaited me should not have been unexpected in this land, where no one seems to consider a promise more binding than a compliment is true. [...] I really grieve that it is so utterly impossible to trust the Japanese.'[15]

This perceived untrustworthiness is related to a western sense of Japan's aesthetic accomplishments which has always stressed their cleverness rather than their originality. At Nagasaki in the 1680s, Christopher Fryke admired the lacquer work and noted the proverb current among the Dutch that 'tho' a Dutch Man was Cunning, he might go to School to a Japanese'.[16] It's not difficult to see how the craftsman's cunning becomes the cunning of the plagiarist and the cheat. Comparing Japanese craft-work with 'the tawdry Austrian and Swiss goods which all men abhor', T. W. H. Crosland commented in 1904: 'They are much cleverer truly – fiendishly clever on occasion, indeed – but cleverness is not art, and very clever work can be most unbeautiful.'[17] Craftsmanship that is fiendishly clever raises the possibility of less innocent kinds of fiendishness.

In our models of cultural exchange, the west figures as virile originator, Japan as wily imitator. (Our own productions can sometimes be 'inspired by' Japanese culture, but that's different.) America's first consul in Japan, Townsend Harris, remarked on this aptitude as early as 1857. He had asked the Japanese to fire a salute in honour of Washington's birthday and noted wryly in his journal on 23 February that the two handsome brass howitzers they had sent for the purpose were perfect replicas of the one Commodore Perry had given them: 'every appointment about the gun, down to the smallest particular, was exactly copied: percussion locks, drag ropes, powder or cartridge holder and all'.[18] These imitative skills, regarded indulgently by the confident men of the Victorian age, could take on a different complexion when western nations felt under threat from them. Like manly Esau outwitted by an oriental Jacob, the west has increasingly looked upon Japan as a stealer of birthrights. In 1957, after a press conference at the Dorchester Hotel, the British television reporter Robin Day held up a packet of copied ballbearings to the startled figure of the Japanese foreign minister and demanded an explanation. The episode summed up much of what Japan had come to represent on the industrial scene in the 1950s. (These were the days when Japanese electronic goods sold better if they had a western name . . .)

Twenty-five years later, in June 1982, two representatives of Hitachi walked into an office in California's Silicon Valley, imagining that they were about to acquire secret details of IBM's latest computer, the 3081, for the knockdown price of just over half a million dollars. Instead, they found themselves under arrest; the helpful 'industrial research' consultant who had arranged the deal (and who was laying on something similar for Mitsubishi) was an FBI agent. The 'Japscam' case made headline news. Once again Japan was spotlighted as the villainous commercial pirate who copies but cannot create. In Ridley Scott's film *Black Rain*, set in Osaka, the Japanese police officer boasts to Michael Douglas that the Japanese have won the peace – they are making the machines and building the future. Douglas snaps back the response of embittered America: 'And if there was one of your guys who had an original idea, you'd be so tight you couldn't even pull it outta your ass.'

When all is said, the tributes lavished on the artistic achievements of Japan are hedged around by spoken and unspoken reservations: aesthetic Japan is small in scale, it belongs to the world of the child rather than the adult, it is feminine rather than masculine, contemplative rather than businesslike, imitative rather than original. And beneath these reservations is a deeper misgiving which goes back to the basic opposition between what is natural and what is unnatural. The underlying fear is that aesthetic priorities are fundamentally at odds with human ones.

10. The Inhuman Aesthetic

At the time of the marriage of the Crown Prince of Japan to Owada Masako in June 1993, the *Economist* published an article headlined THE PRINCESS, THE GOD AND THE DEAD FISH. Its theme was the tension between the traditional values of the imperial family and the reformist tendencies of the Oxford- and Harvard-educated career woman:

> The imperial family is doing its best to put its stamp on the future princess. Following her engagement in January, Miss Owada gave up her career in the foreign ministry, acquired a new and frumpy wardrobe, and suffered fifty hours of tuition in Shinto ritual and the traditional poetry that members of the Japanese royal family are supposed to write. Her engagement present was hardly internationalist or fashionable: two dead fish, six casks of saké, some silk for a kimono. After her wedding she will stand naked before a priestess, who will 'purify' her with bran. Her husband, after all, is believed by diehards to be descended from a god.[1]

The article does not leave us in much doubt where the writer's sympathies lie: adoption into the imperial family involves the extinction of just the qualities of vitality and individuality that we are taught to value. With a slight change of angle, it could have been quite different. The Shinto ritual, the traditional poetry, the symbolic presents, the ceremony to 'purify' the bride (note the disdainful inverted commas) could as easily have been slotted into the category of picturesque Japan and presented accordingly. But that is not, by and large, how the western media chose to handle it. In most accounts the princess was treated as an honorary westerner; her association with Oxford and Harvard made her the perfect standard-bearer for the western values of life, liberty and the pursuit of happiness. This was the human (western) side of the equation. On the other side was the dead-fish world of suffocating ritual and archaic eastern religion.

Inset in the *Economist* article was a photograph of the Crown Prince and Miss Owada looking like an illustration for *The Tale of Genji*, rigid as waxworks in their antique robes. 'The royal couple relaxing together' was the sardonic caption. It was a photograph that brought to mind the reaction of all those nineteenth-century writers who had remarked with delight on how like everything was to the pictures on screens and fans. Here too was an image from this picturesque world, but we were no longer asked to applaud. The symmetry of their pose was an inhuman symmetry. Both picture and article intimated that those elements of traditional culture which have historically been one source of 'aesthetic Japan' were life-denying rather than life-enhancing.

This is not a new sentiment. As we have seen, nineteenth-century writers were for ever comparing the Japanese to dolls, waxworks, mechanical toys. But the implications of the image have changed. Since the Second World War, the connection between Japanese aestheticism and a certain inhumanity has acquired a new focus. In *The Lotus and the Robot* (1960) Arthur Koestler has a section entitled 'The Horrors of Flower Arrangement': 'Trees growing straight towards the sky are rarely encountered nowadays in a Japanese park or garden. Their branches must be twisted and tortured into artistic and symbolic shapes. [. . .] In addition to strings and wires, wooden stakes are used to force one branch upward and to pull another down; a row of trees in a park looks like a procession of invalids walking on crutches.'

He goes on to consider one of the many magazines on ikebana:

The first thing one learns from the Beginners' Section in the magazine is that 'in using narcissi for ikebana it is impossible to utilise them in their natural state . . . First remove the flower, then the leaves, one by one from the centre, which will leave the empty white sheath.' When this is done, the stem and leaves are stuck together again in a more pleasing shape. Chrysanthemums are made to display their petals to better advantage by the insertion of a small wire rack into the living flower. If I lived in Japan, I would start an I.S.P.C.F.T. (Imperial Society for the Prevention of Cruelty to Flowers and Trees). But then – I shall come to that later – every Japanese child also has a kind of invisible wire rack inserted into its body and mind.[2]

The artificial is by definition unnatural, but here the word takes on its full pejorative force. The tortured flowers and trees cry out against a cruelty perpetrated in the name of art: aesthetic preoccupations are blinding the Japanese to ordinary human concerns. This can be benign, even endearing – while we're reaching for our umbrellas, the Japanese are searching for a word to describe the rain – but it can also have a more sinister resonance. The rapt aestheticism that is impervious to the pattering rain or the tortured flower can be equally impervious to the tortured human being. (The shift is already hinted at in Koestler's comments on the ikebana magazine.) Worse still, there is a kind of aestheticism that can incorporate the torture in the aesthetic experience. Shortly after Blackthorne's crew have been imprisoned by the Japanese at the start of *Shogun*, Yabu, a sadistic Japanese noble, arranges to have one of them boiled overnight in a cauldron, near the house where he is staying. While the man's screams split the night, Yabu kneels in the garden, watching the moon in the blossom tree and composing poems:

> It took all of Yabu's will to concentrate on the tree and blossoms and sky and night, to feel the gentle touch of the wind, to smell its sea-sweetness, to think of poems, and yet to keep his ears reaching for the agony. His spine felt limp. Only his will made him graven as the rocks. This awareness gave him a level of sensuality beyond articulation. And tonight it was stronger and more violent than it had ever been.[3]

This Japanese figure who can savour the beauty of the night while listening to the screams of the tortured is a specifically post-war addition to the stock of western images. The renewed emphasis on the aesthetic side of Japan following the Second

World War overlaid much of the imagery associated with those years, but it could not erase the memory of what had been experienced. Japan had shown itself capable of cruelties that seemed all the more horrible for their violation of established images. In *The Naked and the Dead* the Japanese-American translator for the American troops understands why the Americans who had been to pre-war Japan had the strongest hatred for the Japanese: 'Before the war they had been so wistful, so charming; the Americans had picked them up like pets, and were feeling the fury now of having a pet bite them . . .'[4]

The contrast between the charming aesthete and the ruthless killer, the worshipper of the chrysanthemum and the wielder of the sword, occasionally surfaced while the war was still going on. E. B. Sledge, who wrote of his experiences on Pelelieu and Okinawa in *With the Old Breed* (1981), described to Studs Terkel some of the atrocities committed in the Pacific war, and added:

> It always struck me as ironic, the Japanese code of behaviour. Flower arranging, music, striving for perfection. And the art of the warrior. Very often we'd get a photograph off a dead Japanese. Here would be this soldier, sitting in a studio, with a screen behind and a table with a little flower on it. Often he'd be holding a rifle, yet there was always that little vase of flowers.[5]

We've been here before. 'Fans and dainty tea-sets do not go with one's notions of a barrack,' Kipling had remarked in 1889. But for Kipling the combination merely highlighted the hopelessly unmilitary bias of the Japanese character. Now that the rifles are used for killing people, the aestheticism has lost its innocence.

It's interesting to look at another writer's reaction to the practices that so disturbed Koestler. To Nikos Kazantzakis, who visited Japan in 1935, the art with which the Japanese gardener trained his shrubs was 'a wonder of patience and love'. He is quoting the monk who has tried to explain to him how a particular pine in the monastery yard acquired its shape – 'With patience and love'. Next morning Kazantzakis sees the gardener in his hotel garden 'caressing and bending the branches of a small plum tree to take the idyllic and impressive shape of a weeping willow. I stood there for a long time and admired the

101

slender, dextrous fingers of the old gardener that tamed nature with such sweetness.'[6]

There is more than a difference of personal observation between Kazantzakis and Koestler, between the perception of love and the perception of cruelty. The Greek writer is looking with eyes untroubled by knowledge of the horrors of the Second World War. It becomes clear how far Koestler's response is conditioned by this knowledge when he goes on, in the chapter called 'Character-Gardening', to argue that the Japanese character is wired and landscaped in much the same way as Japanese plants. This is not an original assertion; Benedict had drawn the same analogy in *The Chrysanthemum and the Sword*. Taking the image of the chrysanthemum whose petals are held in place by a wire rack inserted in the living flower, she refers to the feelings expressed by a samurai woman who, after a rigidly traditional upbringing, was sent to learn English at a mission school in Tokyo where she was given a plant-as-you-please patch of garden: 'Mrs Sugimoto's intoxication when she was given a chance to put aside the wire rack was happy and innocent. The chrysanthemum which had been grown in the little pot and which had submitted to the meticulous disposition of its petals discovered pure joy in being natural.'[7] It is a gentle parable of Japan versus the west, of unnatural artifice versus natural freedom. The aesthetic concerns of Japanese culture are linked with a ruthless system of conditioning that is incompatible with the freedom to develop naturally as a human being.

This is the argument Koestler pursues in *The Lotus and the Robot*. The results of wire-rack conditioning can be seen in the last war:

> The Japanese soldier behaves as if his instinct of self-preservation had been switched off, and his nervous system brought under a kind of remote control which causes the laws of humanity and commonsense to be supplanted by utter ruthlessness towards himself, his comrades, enemies, and prisoners alike. Yet the moment the master-switch is thrown back into normal position, he instantly reverts to his kind and gentle self, without a twinge of remorse.[8]

Koestler is trying to make sense of the apparent contradiction between chrysanthemum and sword, between the kind and gentle Japanese and the utterly ruthless Japanese. The experience of war with Japan had made this the fundamental question. With great accuracy Benedict pinpointed what was to become for the west the central paradox of the culture, subsuming all the others that had been noted from the sixteenth century onwards. However much we choose to stress the aesthetic side of Japanese culture in post-war years, there is a lingering consciousness of its opposite that cannot be suppressed. One way of holding the two sides together is the psychological rationalisation offered by Koestler. Another way is simply to accept it as confirmation of what we have always known – that the Japanese are not like us, that their culture is a mass of bizarre contradictions of which this is the most basic. (Sledge's decent perplexity at the conjunction of rifle and flower reflects this approach.) A third way is to take the two sides, the aesthetic and the violent, and fuse them together.

The sadistic aesthete is one example of this fusion; another is the recurrent figure of the Japanese who meets death with a poem on his lips, like Lustbader's kamikaze pilot who composes a *haiku* when he is about to die. Or the Japanese agent in *You Only Live Twice* who is recovered from the sea, blind and delirious, the lower half of his body terribly burned, unable to do more before his death than babble another *haiku*: 'Desolation! Pink dragon-flies flitting above the graves.'[9]

The idea that the heightened sensibility of the Japanese derives in part from their intimacy with death has wide currency. 'Perhaps that is why we love life so much, Anjin-san,' explains Mariko. 'You see, we have to. Death is part of our air and sea and earth.' Blackthorne discovers the secret for himself when he has just been pulled back from the brink of suicide. Dazed by his brush with death, he sits with Mariko:

> The rain is fine, isn't it?' he said, watching the raindrops breaking and vanishing, astonished by the untoward clarity of his vision.
> 'Yes,' she told him gently, knowing that his senses were on a plane never to be reached by one who had not gone freely out to meet death, and, through an unknowing karma, miraculously come back again.[10]

It's all part of the mysterious Japanese love affair with death, awe-inspiring but odd. There is a powerful sense that at one level Japan's aestheticism is tainted by this association with death. 'To be vitalised by weariness may seem an odd notion to an occidental,' writes Koestler, 'to the Japanese it means what it reads – romantic melancholia as the main source of poetry, the woeful expression of the Nō dancer as a symbol of man's dignity, a *mal de siècle* which dates from the beginning of time.'[11] This is a world away from the cheerful, bric-à-brac version of aesthetic Japan which we find in the nineteenth and early twentieth centuries. Since the war, the note of melancholy in representations of romantic Japan has been deeper and more poignant; the beauty is infected with sadness. How many western love stories set in Japan have a happy ending? The country offers a perfect context for doomed relationships; its beauty speaks of transience, mortality, *lacrimae rerum*. The tragic Japan that Michener presents in *Sayonara* is not distinct from the place of age-old traditions and aesthetic refinement he had described the year before in *Holiday* magazine; it is inseparable from it.

Even the most confident images of Japan's beauty tend to have an elegiac undertow. The kimonoed girls who stand by the water's edge or look shyly towards the camera from under the branches of a cherry tree are still with us, but they have to contend in our imagination both with residual images from the war and with our awareness of a new Japan of hi-tech machinery and modern fashion – a world, glimpsed in films like *Blade Runner* and *Black Rain*, of gleaming surfaces and coloured neon whose aesthetic bent has taken a faintly sinister turn towards the more aggressive, masculine values of the samurai. This is the Japan of William Gibson's *Neuromancer*, the stylish, freaky, dangerous world of cyberpunk. It presents an ominous alternative to the Japan of mountain mists and Zen-blue skies in which Pico Iyer conducts his delicately poised relationship with Sachiko.

But if the cherry-blossom world now looks more vulnerable, this is no more than a shift in emphasis. Paradises are always doomed, and writers about paradise are always elegists.

Victorian travellers who rhapsodised about the old Japan were insistently aware of the new Japan which threatened to engulf it. There has long been a strain of melancholy in the background. Since the war it has grown stronger, and the colours of aesthetic Japan frequently have a more sombre tinge, but the posters and guides and brochures remind us that the images are still in place. Enough of the fairy-tale world has survived virtually untouched from the nineteenth century to furnish planeloads of modern tourists with fantasies not so different from those which inspired the young Ernest Satow.

PART III

Butterflies

11. A Bevy of Damsels

In the spring of 1994 Kay's mail-order company launched a competition called 'Open the Passport to your Dreams'. A series of drawings had to be matched with the names of countries: the Eiffel Tower for France, Big Ben for England, the Statue of Liberty for America, Sydney opera house for Australia, and so on. Every country had its icon. Out of the twelve, only one was represented by a human figure; number 7 was the head of a geisha, identifiable at once by the slanting eyes, the projecting hairpins and the folds of the kimono at her neck. This was Japan as surely as the Taj Mahal was India or the pyramids Egypt.

For many westerners the image of the Japanese woman starts and finishes with the geisha. She is demure, remote, artistic, but she also holds out the promise of sexual pleasure. Her elaborate hair, rich kimono and other-worldly make-up proclaim both her strangeness and, according to popular belief, her availability. In a single exotic figure she unites the principal qualities by which the west has chosen to define the Japanese woman. To see what these are, we can turn to Nakajima Hanayo, known professionally as Hana Chan, an apprentice geisha who made the cover of *The Face* in April 1993.[1] She was pictured in traditional make-up and costume, but her eyes were swivelled towards the camera with a knowing look and she was blowing a pink balloon of bubble-gum. It was a piece of burlesque indirectly picked up by the magazine article. Most of her life Hana Chan spends 'in an ancient Tokyo geisha house, dutifully undertaking her training':

> As a student of the ancient art of geisha, she learns a number of things. The arts of tea ceremony, nōh dancing and ikebana (flower arranging) are supplemented by skills that will help her literally 'be a good companion to men'. In short, Hana is a flirt. In a bustling London photo studio, fully made up in traditional geisha style, she does the best version of the ancient art of blinky eyes you will ever see. [...] The looks are always wide-eyed and imploring. Someone mentions a party, and she gives the geisha look: 'Can I go?' Her eyes are somewhere between Bambi and Beatrice Dalle. All the men present decide she can go.

This explains the geisha costume. What about the bubble-gum? It turns out that when she's not dutifully undertaking her training, Hana Chan has a record contract, a band, 'and most of Tokyo's muso big-wigs queueing to record with her'. She appears as a guest on TV programmes and has given her name to a computer game. 'Hana Chan is a star, and then some. Except she's also just a humble trainee geisha.' It is this paradox – yet another – that qualifies her as a representative of Japan's New Generation. 'There is probably no better example', the writer tells us, 'of the emerging paradoxes and culture clashes of post-bubble Japan, than Hanayo Nakajima.' But though she is billed as a new phenomenon, a symbol of modern Japan, we actually find an image that fits snugly into the conventional categories established in the nineteenth century: Hana Chan is the damsel trained to please men, she is the guardian of the traditional arts, and she is the woman as sexual wanton. To these three aspects of the Japanese woman is added that of cultural icon. Look at the woman and you're looking at Japan, computer games and all. The cover picture shows us everyone's image of Madame Butterfly, with the cheeky addition of bubble-gum for the post-bubble 1990s.

The first, and most conspicuous, of her roles presents the Japanese woman as handmaiden. This was the point of departure for Ernest Satow's youthful vision of Japan as a country where the days were spent under a cloudless sky, lying on a matted floor 'in the company of rosy-lipped black-eyed and attentive damsels'. The origins of this image, as we saw in Chapter 6, go back to Oliphant's account of his mission to Japan a few years earlier. A typical passage describes him stopping at a wayside tea-house in the heat of an August day: 'We find the coolest corner, stretch ourselves full-length on the soft mats, drink tea, eat fruit, smoke infinitesimal pipes, and get ourselves fanned into a comatose state by fair damsels . . .'[2] This is what people had dreamed of doing in the South Seas ever since de Bougainville began promoting them as an earthly paradise in the previous century. Oliphant has simply translated the image to a new location, where it was enthusiastically taken up by contemporary writers. The *Times* correspondent paints a similar picture: 'The traveller, wearied with the noonday heat, need never be at a loss to find rest and refreshment; stretched upon the softest and cleanest matting, imbibing the most delicately flavoured tea, inhaling through a short pipe the fragrant tobacco of Japan, he resigns himself to the ministrations of a bevy of fair damsels, who glide rapidly and noiselessly about, the most zealous and skilful of attendants.'[3]

It's a scene that transforms the average western tourist into an oriental potentate. The role was one that Kipling embraced with delight in the first of his letters:

My very respectable friends at all the clubs and messes, have you ever after a good tiffin lolled on cushions and smoked, with one pretty girl to fill your pipe and four to admire you in an unknown tongue? You do not know what life is. I looked round me at that faultless room, at the dwarf pines and creamy cherry blossom without, at O-Toyo bubbling with laughter because I blew smoke through my nose, and at the ring of *Mikado* maidens over against the golden-brown bearskin rug. Here was colour, form, food, comfort, and beauty enough for half a year's contemplation.[4]

This enviable conjunction of the aesthetic, the exotic and the erotic confirms Japan as a perfect focus for western fantasy.

And in this case it's not a fantasy that changes much. According to Ian McQueen in Lonely Planet's *Japan, a travel survival kit*, 'One of the characteristics of the upbringing of Japanese women is subordination to males, beginning with her brothers. In a relationship she generally looks after her man. (To many western men first exposed to this coddling it seems like paradise arrived . . .)[5] The hero of *Shogun* would have agreed. 'I'll be a God-cursed Spaniard if this isn't the life!' he remarks on being introduced to some of the more traditional forms of coddling:

> Blackthorne lay seraphically on his stomach on thick futons, wrapped partially in a cotton kimono, his head propped on his arms. The girl was running her hands over his back, probing his muscles occasionally, soothing his skin and his spirit, making him almost want to purr with pleasure. Another girl was pouring saké into a tiny porcelain cup. A third waited in reserve, holding a lacquer tray with a heaping bamboo basket of deep-fried fish in Portuguese style, another flask of saké, and some chopsticks.[6]

The western visitor rarely has to go far for these attentions. James Bond is already surrounded by geisha at the start of *You Only Live Twice*. Its opening words are a promise of things to come: 'The Geisha called "Trembling Leaf", on her knees beside James Bond, leant forward from the waist and kissed him chastely on the right cheek.' It's not incidental to this fantasy that the woman should spend much of the time on her knees. Subordination is part of the appeal. Indeed, when Bond makes the mistake of stepping back as he boards a train to allow a woman to go first, he is sharply rebuked by Tiger Tanaka, who is acting as his mentor in matters Japanese: 'Tiger hissed angrily, "First lesson, Bondo-san! Do not make way for women. Push them, trample them down. Women have no priority in this country. You may be polite to very old men, but to no one else. Is that understood?"'[7]

For men brought up in the west, this is heady stuff. The slave-girl fantasies which at home have always been rather shamefaced are legitimate here. More than that, they are practically a cultural requirement. From Oliphant onwards, the 'bevy of damsels' were part of the stock-in-trade of writers on Japan. Only intermittently is this a sexual fantasy; more importantly, it is a fantasy of domination. Before all else, the Japanese woman is submissive; she has no sharp edges on which the male ego can come to harm. When Mr Casaubon marries Dorothea in George Eliot's *Middlemarch*, he imagines he is getting something like 'an elegant-minded canary bird', but Dorothea has a critical intelligence which swiftly demolishes this fantasy. Casaubon finds to his dismay that she cannot be relied on for an unclouded reflection of his own self-esteem. It is from this sort of brutal awakening that the Japanese woman offers a refuge. To ecstatic westerners she seemed the fulfilment of the canary-bird dream, having neither impulses nor intelligence of her own. Delicate creatures like Kipling's O-Toyo and Pinkerton's Butterfly had been brought up to obey.

This is something nineteenth-century writers were anxious to stress. 'The key to the character of the Japanese woman lies in the word obedience,' wrote Henry Norman.[8] His words are an echo of what William Elliot Griffis had said in *The Mikado's Empire* (1876): 'Indeed, the whole sum of excellencies and defects of the Japanese female character arise from one all- including virtue, and the biography of a good woman is written in one word – obedience.'[9] No one took more kindly to this pleasant subservience than George Smith, Bishop of Victoria in Hong Kong. He found the Japanese unsatisfactory in many ways, but when he recalls the tea-house girls his lumbering prose almost develops a twinkle:

> One laughing bright-eyed damsel approached me kneeling with a cup of tea in her hand; another held some sugar, kneeling on the opposite side; while a third from her lowly posture on the ground held to my lips a boiled egg, already broken and peeled, with the spoon containing the inviting morsel duly seasoned with salt. With garrulous vivacity they anticipated every look, and when my wants were supplied they remained kneeling close to my side, and vying in their endeavours to be the first to bring me their native dainties.[10]

The bishop was clearly having the time of his life, and the insistent refrain – 'approached me kneeling ... kneeling on the opposite side . . . lowly posture on the ground . . . remained kneeling close to my side' – points directly to the source of his pleasure. Sir Edwin Arnold showed a similar enthusiasm when praising his daughter's Japanese maid: 'In bringing a message, receiving an order, offering tea or cakes, or doing anything which is not absolutely instantaneous, she always goes down on her little knees, and often upon her little nose, and never permits her master or mistress to enter or quit the house without hastening outside to kneel and bend low upon the doorstep.'[11]

This naïve delight in tokens of servility has a persistent appeal. Some years ago, on a visit to Kyoto, I was urged by a fellow countryman to go at opening time to Takashimaya, the most dignified of Japanese department stores, so that I could enjoy the sensation of an army of assistants bowing to me in order as I moved through the shop, the first customer of the day. 'Like a row of dominoes going down,' he assured me. 'Line after line of them. Magic.' For the western visitor there can still be a tremor of satisfaction in being waited on by kneeling attendants in Japan's more traditional hotels and restaurants. It's not, of course, something people usually admit to, but then there has always been a certain ambivalence about this aspect of Japanese culture. Even while the Victorians recorded with minute appreciation the details of female submissiveness, they shook their heads at the lack of chivalry. 'Japanese women', wrote Basil Hall Chamberlain, 'are most womanly – kind, gentle, faithful, pretty. But the way in which they are treated by the men has hitherto been such as might cause a pang to any generous European heart.'[12]

The position of women allowed scope for moral indignation at the expense of unenlightened Japan while at the same time nourishing the fantasies of female subservience that were an important part of western enjoyment of the place. When Fleming establishes his hero's chivalrous credentials in contrast to the sexist Japanese, he is making a familiar move in the cultural game. Nowadays there's more mileage than ever in this, though we might shrink from talking of chivalry. Writing in the *Independent*, Bryan Appleyard shows a characteristically generous European heart:

Perhaps worst of all, because it is the most pervasive vice, is the sexism. Women are badly paid and oppressed; they are trapped far more profoundly than anything the campaigning sisters back home can imagine. Stories of big company treatment from my interpreters made me want to dismantle a Zen garden and chuck the rocks through the glass curtain walls of Sumitomo or Mitsubishi.[13]

For modern western men, the glow of self-righteousness that comes from observing Japanese sexism is one of the great unsung pleasures of visiting the country. At a time when it's not that easy to feel superior to Japan, this gift of the moral high ground could hardly be more welcome. 'He's old-world Japanese,' Bruce Willis explains to Kim Basinger in *Blind Date*. 'He's got a wife who's more like a slave, and he keeps concubines.'

This is standard fare, but it does little to undermine the basic fantasy. In *Sayonara* the secret of the Japanese woman is located in one all-revealing question. A friend is trying to explain to the hero what makes a Japanese girl so different from the average American: 'With me it's very clear. One thing explains it all. You ever had your back scrubbed by a Japanese girl? Not a bath attendant, mind you. That's simple. But a girl who really loved you?' When the hero fails to get the point, he goes on:

> 'I'm trying to say there are hundreds of ways for men and women to get along together. Some of the ways work in Turkey, some work in China. In America we've constructed our own ways. What I'm saying is that of them all I prefer the Japanese way.' He laughed and saw that I didn't entirely understand, so he banged his beer down and shouted, 'All right! One easy question! Can you imagine Eileen Webster scrubbing your back?'

Now the hero understands. 'It was a crazy question, a truly hellish shot in the dark', but it had gone straight to the nub: he really can't imagine his American girlfriend scrubbing his back.

The same contrast was presented in Pearl Buck's *The Hidden Flower*, published the year before. It too concerns the ill-starred love of an American officer for a Japanese woman:

> He found her attempts to control him as charming as the dictates of a child. She was so sweetly anxious to guide him while she adored and obeyed. [...] She expected no help from him in the little housekeeping duties of the places where they stopped, she waited on him as a matter of course. [...] She showed herself Japanese at heart. An American girl would never have so served him.[15]

He begins to understand why men said it was impossible to love an American woman if one had known 'a woman of the Orient'.[16] Josui's subordination is emphasised by her physical appearance. She is, quite simply, so much smaller than him – almost like a miniature human being. And when his love begins to wane, it is this, as much as anything, that keeps his interest alive: 'Josui was pretty, she had a kitten charm, her little frame, her tiny hands, so neat in their precise movements, her careful absorption in all she did, all was charming once more.'[16]

This is a common theme. The smallness of the women, their diminutive features, their seeming fragility, give an added dimension to the thrill of mastery. It is a version of the benign despotism that can make children such a flattering prop to adult self-esteem. And indeed the Japanese woman, in popular representations of her, rarely escapes the shadow of childhood. Butterfly's childishness is stressed in the opera's libretto, as is Pinkerton's enjoyment of it. When she bursts into 'childish tears', it takes only a word from him for her to be smiling like a child again – 'sorridendo infantilmente'. At about the same time, the narrator of Clive Holland's *My Japanese Wife* (1895), a novel that went through twenty editions in as many years, was introduced to the 'radiant, childish being' who would 'captivate the heart and senses of the "English sir"'.[17]

A similar pattern can be traced half a century later in Richard Mason's *The Wind Cannot Read* (1947). The English officer's affair with his Japanese teacher is conducted partially in a form of teasing baby-talk which reflects the conviction of both that she is still more or less a child. 'Sweet darling Sabby, my child Sabby', he whispers to himself, touched by her naïvety. The point is returned to with cloying frequency, ensuring that we never lose sight of her vulnerability. By the time she dies of the fatal illness which has been in the background from the start, we are as well primed emotionally as for a child's deathbed in Victorian literature. To confirm that the Japanese child-woman has not lost her appeal, we need only turn back to Hana Chan blowing bubblegum on the cover of *The Face*. Another picture shows her with a doll dangling from her hands, the words 'Child's Play'

116

embroidered on its dungarees. (In obvious ways the image of the child-woman as biddable maiden overlaps that of child-woman as sexual prey; we return to it in a later chapter.)

A further advantage of the Japanese woman is that she cannot usually speak the man's language. Apart from cutting out unwelcome backchat, this is one more thing that defines her as a child. Unable to pronounce her 'r's, baffled by long words, she must look to the man for guidance, which is as it should be. Deprived of language, the woman is also easier to assimilate to any number of engaging creatures that are objects of human affection. 'Shy and wild she was at first,' wrote A. B. Mitford of the prettiest of a group of geisha who attended on him at a party in Kyoto, 'but after a while she became quite tame, like a little gazelle that feeds out of your hand, and indeed her eyes had much the look of those of a pet deer.'[18] The Bambi look, perhaps, that is still getting Hana Chan invited to all the parties.

The imagery that identifies the Japanese woman as a child, a butterfly, a bird, a gazelle, or whatever, is often part of a language of compliment, even of idealisation, but it also denies her full human status. Similarly, the numerous images that presented Japanese women as barely distinguishable from the pictures on fans and tea-caddies are poised between the admiring and the dismissive. That Madame Butterfly looks like a figure from a lacquer screen is both a reason for Pinkerton to desire her and a reason why it is so easy to leave her behind. (His fictional example cast a long shadow. In *War Brides of World War Two* Shukert and Scibetta estimate that as many as 100,000 Japanese wives were deserted by US servicemen returning to America.)

Recording his first impressions of Japan, Arnold remarks, 'Here, too, are all the pleasant little people you have known so long upon fans and screens. Take the first that comes along – this tiny Japanese lady, whom you left, as you thought, on the lid of the glove-box at home . . .'[19] The genial tone, patronising but affectionate, is characteristic of the well-disposed westerner in the nineteenth century, but the same imagery lends itself readily to a more disdainful application. To the eye of Loti's narrator,

Chrysanthemum looks 'just like one of the figures on porcelain or silk that fill up our market stalls at the moment', and we are left with the idea of cheap mass-production. 'Evident dolls badly constructed' was one of many similar judgements Henry Adams sent back to America in 1886. In this, as in much of what he says about Japan, he anticipates the image that Loti was to popularise in *Madame Chrysanthème*. 'Is it a woman or a doll?' the narrator asks himself on being introduced to Chrysanthemum. When he turns the scene over in his mind, he reflects ironically that he is about to marry into a family of puppets.[20] Later he's walking in the old part of Nagasaki when he catches sight of a particularly beautiful Japanese girl. She is crossing a bridge in the midday sun against a background of old temples, one hand holding her kimono, the other a red and blue parasol on which is written in white letters 'Clouds, stand still, to watch her pass'. For a moment he is transfixed by the beauty of the picture, but then he reminds himself not to be taken in: 'No doubt she was just a doll like the rest of them, a commonplace doll and nothing more.'[21]

It's a strain of imagery that has lasted well. Hana Chan's upside-down doll functions partly as an inverted image of Hana Chan herself. In *The Japanese* Joe Joseph tells us of the new craze for golf among young women for whom 'keeping within a hundred strokes of par is less important than being seen in the right designer outfit'. These fashion-conscious golfers, whose magazines 'advise less about birdies than about what make-up to wear on the green' and who favour pastel-coloured golf balls to match their clothes, are lineal descendants of Loti's decorative puppets.[22] They are a modern form of what Kazantzakis describes as the Japanese woman of superficial legend: 'A delicate doll with an elaborate coiffure and with high wooden sandals, who knows how to smile, to bow, to put on and take off her kimono'.[23]

Even at its most appreciative, the image of the fair damsel is tinged with contempt. The shy, bowing, giggling girls who minister to the lordly westerner have no emotional or intellectual claim on him, they are merely there to do his bidding. They are butterflies in their lightness and grace but also in their lack of substance. We come across them still in films with a Japanese setting; they are the bystanders who witness the hero's odyssey through Japan's strange cities. He might ask them the way, try to flirt with them, beg them for help – in vain. They do not understand but they are always there – fluttering damsels in the nineteenth-century tea-house or fluttering damsels on the streets of modern Tokyo, part of the eternal scenery of Japan.

12. Butterflies with Hearts

The image of the handmaiden drew much of its popularity from the harem literature of the eighteenth
century. Writers on the Middle East in particular had established a version of the oriental woman that influenced images
of Japan from Oliphant to Fleming and Clavell. For some time
this was the only respectable fantasy within which the Japanese
woman could be situated, but in the 1880s and 1890s a number
of writers, some of whom had married Japanese women, began
to present a new picture. Romantic love between the western
man and the Japanese woman (never the other way round) had
become a socially acceptable possibility, inspiring an alternative
fantasy which balanced and commented on the figure of the
handmaiden. The title of Clive Holland's *My Japanese Wife* is
itself a sign of change. His narrator sets out the revised formula: 'Japanese women are butterflies – *with hearts.*'

The italicised 'with hearts' proclaims a crucial departure from
the usual tea-house damsels, who were, like the ten-year-old
geisha girls Loti came across in Kyoto, *'très charmantes petites
poupées sans âme'* – enchanting little dolls *without a soul*. At the
start of Holland's novel the narrator describes his *mūsmé* as 'a
butterfly from a foreign land': 'My mūsmé! with Dresden-china
tinted cheeks, and tiny ways; playing at life, as it always seemed
to me, with the dainty grace of Japan, that idealised doll's house
land. Mūsmé, who goes with me everywhere, whose *bizarre*

120

clothing attracts notice to her even when the delicately pretty face of a child-woman, with innocent, soft eyes and finely arched brows, is hidden behind the ever-present fan, which she draws from the ample folds of her *obi*.'[1]

The description is thoroughly conventional. With its references to Dresden china, dainty grace, doll's houses and child-women, it is a compendium of the images used by contemporary writers to talk about the little females who were part of the scenery in this alien country. But in this case the woman is not just part of the scenery, she's his wife – and therefore a butterfly with a heart.

As the damsel of the harem fantasy becomes an object of romantic passion, so her submissiveness becomes self-sacrifice and her flirtatiousness gives way to emotional commitment. What this adds up to is the image of the perfect wife, which Griffis had outlined in *The Mikado's Empire*: 'If unvarying obedience, acquiescence, submission, the utter absorption of her personality into that of her husband, constitute the ideal of the perfect woman, then the Japanese married women approach so near that ideal as to be practically perfect . . .'[2] Late in Hearn's life, when he had grown disillusioned with many other features of his adopted country, he summed up this ideal in *Japan, An Attempt at Interpretation*. Dependent on the affection of her husband and his family, the Japanese wife was obliged to win it by gentleness, obedience and kindliness:

> Thus to succeed required angelic goodness and patience; and the Japanese woman realised at least the ideal of a Buddhist angel. A being working only for others, thinking only for others, happy only in making pleasure for others – a being incapable of unkindness, incapable of selfishness, incapable of acting contrary to her own inherited sense of right – and in spite of this softness and gentleness ready, at any moment, to lay down her life, to sacrifice everything at the call of duty: such was the character of the Japanese woman.[3]

The western audience knows about such women from a distance. Tales of patient Griselda stretch back to Boccaccio, but they belong to a past of folklore. In Japan the mould was still unbroken – and to some extent remains so. Western press coverage of Owada Masako's marriage to the Crown Prince in 1993 pictured her as an obedient sacrifice to the needs of state. JAPANESE ROYAL BRIDE IS GIVEN A 'SUICIDE' SWORD was the *Daily Telegraph* headline a week before the wedding: 'The Imperial Palace thoughtfully provided her parents with a budget to pay for the specially commissioned sword, intended as a symbolic reminder that suicide is the only way out should the bride find married life with the future Emperor too rigid and stifling to bear.'[4]

The self-sacrifice required of those who marry commoners is less public but not less complete. After the Second World War Hearn's ideal was reintroduced to western audiences by novels such as *The Hidden Flower* and *Sayonara*, where the selfless Japanese woman is used to make some sharp criticisms of her western counterpart. 'Men with wives back in the States', says Joe Kelly in *Sayonara*, 'talk about Junior's braces and country-club dances and what kind of car their wife bought. But the men with Japanese wives tell you one thing only. What wonderful wives they have.' Later, the hero looks at Kelly's own Japanese wife and realises that he had been wrong to think her ugly: 'Now she seemed to me one of the most perfect women I had ever known, for she had obviously studied her man and had worked out every item of the day's work so that the end result would be a happy husband and a peaceful home.'[5] When the pressures of the outside world can no longer be withstood, she duly commits suicide with her husband.

This has always been a useful measure of commitment. Such is the man's ascendancy that the woman is quite likely to kill herself rather than face life without him. It's a flattering idea, which is conveniently focused in Puccini's opera. Pinkerton enjoys a casual liaison while inspiring a devotion so absolute that it leads to the woman's suicide. The marriage broker assures him that he's getting a garland of fresh flowers, a star from the realms of gold – 'and for nothing: only 100 yen'; but Butterfly is entering on a quite different transaction. She has come, she says, at the summons of love – *'Amiche, io son venuta / al richiamo d'amor'*. Later she explains that she fell in love with him because he was so tall, so strong. Pinkerton is decently remorseful at the end, but Butterfly's love cannot be other than a striking tribute to the attractions of the western male. To buy a woman exhibits power, but to buy her and have her commit suicide for love of you is a refinement of power available only in Japan. The butterfly's heart opens the way to keener fantasies than are offered by her delicate colours and graceful movements.

By now, however, these aesthetic qualities were undergoing a change in status, as the image of painted doll began to shade into that of woman as work of art. Arnold's claim that 'no Japanese painter or carver can make half as pretty and graceful a figure as he, or anybody, may see in a day's walk about Tokio or Kioto' is enlarged by Hearn into a vision of the Japanese woman as supreme expression of her country's aesthetic achievement. Throughout his writings on Japan he returns to the theme, summarising it in his last book: 'For it has well been said that the most wonderful aesthetic products of Japan are not its ivories, nor its bronzes, nor its porcelains, nor its swords, nor any of its marvels in metal or lacquer – but its women.'[6] These are women on a different plane from the 'pretty puppets' of many of Hearn's contemporaries, but they share a sense of the priority of things aesthetic which is still there at the end of the twentieth century. As is clear from her dutiful study of the traditional arts, it has even survived Hana Chan's immersion in the culture of computer games and TV shows.

By reshaping the figure on the painted screen into an image of the ideal, Hearn transformed her from bric-à-brac into art. From this perspective, the 'dainty bits of Dresden' such as Kipling came across at the tea-house in Arashiyama are no longer less than human, they are examples of an artistic perfection that transcends the human. The image of the painted doll does not disappear, but from the late nineteenth century there has been the alternative of the Japanese woman as transcendent work of art.

And like the work of art, she can claim a kind of universality. The heroine of Richard Mason's *The Wind Cannot Read* is more than just an individual woman: 'Like her hands, her face was fashioned with that exquisite delicacy of an oriental figure in ivory; and yet it was impossible for me to regard her as an ornament only, for I seemed to see strange depths of experience in her, as though all the suffering and happiness of womanhood had been hers.'[7]

It is a move from art to essence. To know the individual is to glimpse the universal. A few years later the hero of Michener's *Sayonara* reaches the same understanding through his experience of Hana-ogi:

> I concluded that no man could comprehend women until he had known the women of Japan with their unbelievable combination of unremitting work, endless suffering and boundless warmth – just as I could never have known even the outlines of love had I not lived in a little house where I sometimes drew back the covers of my bed upon the floor to see there the slim golden body of the perpetual woman.

This alchemy that turns yellow bodies to gold heralds the apotheosis of the Japanese woman. She is all women; we find in her the essential female principle:

> As I watched Hana-ogi I knew that in the future, when even the memory of our occupation has grown dim, a quarter of a million American men will love all women more for having tenderly watched some golden-skinned girl fold herself into the shimmering beauty of a kimono. In memory of her feminine grace all women will forever seem more feminine.[8]

Beside this silken femininity the stolid virtues of American womanhood seem gross.

What we have glanced at in the last two chapters is a tradition that depicts the Japanese woman in terms of a number of western fantasies. She is the exotic damsel whose submission confirms the man's sense of mastery; she is the perfect wife whose loyalty outfaces death; she is the work of art whose flawless grace unites with these other qualities to transform her into an ideal of femininity. If, after nearly a hundred years, Madame Butterfly remains the most popular stereotype of the Japanese woman, it is because the opera managed to create a figure who exists at the intersection of these different fantasies. But there are other, less public fantasies to which Madame Butterfly also appeals. It is these more secret longings which are the subject of the next chapter.

13. A Lewd People

I n his book about the cultural differences between Japan and America, Robert J. Collins paints a lip-smacking picture of a society saturated with sex:

> As a Japanese man goes about his day, the lure of sexual satisfaction surrounds him. Magazines, including those published by the stuffy National Railways Company for tired, dusty travelers, devote space to photographs of alluring young things in various states of undress. Sports magazines, reporting baseball scores and sumo results, have some of the most spectacular photographs of flesh. Even adult comic books contain illustrated stories of incredible sexual passion and gratification. [...]
> Coupled with the printed sexual blitz – magazines of this sort are available on the street in vending machines, by the way – there is also the lure of the 'real thing' in countless 'live sex shows' and 'massage' parlors throughout the land. Dinner with a valued client takes on a mellow glow if preceded by a 'total body massage' administered by a lovely young thing wearing bubbles and oil.[1]

In parenthesis, Collins tells us that the Turkish community complained because some of these places were referred to as Turkish baths. 'Did the government ban sexual activities in these establishments? No siree. Instead the government decreed that the establishments be henceforth called "soap lands"!'

This is Japan as sexual Disneyland, home of geisha girls, love hotels and now soap lands. In its modern form, the image dates from the years of the American occupation and the Korean war, but its roots go back much further. Collins has merely given a veneer of late-twentieth-century sexual tolerance to a version of Japan which was familiar to the Victorians. Alongside the travellers who castigated the Japanese for their moral laxity were others, less vocal, who felt the lure of forbidden fruit. Sex, like spices, was one of the reasons for going east. Tennyson's thoughts in 'Locksley Hall' of turning from industrial England to 'yonder shining Orient' were part of a perennial fantasy: 'There the passions cramped no longer shall have scope and breathing space; / I shall take some savage woman, she shall rear my dusky race.'[2] Remote places were always likely to yield exotic women, but Japan was not just another primitive hunting-ground. More subtle than savage in its attractions, it seemed to offer escape from the particular prohibitions which in the west put sex on one side of the line and social decorum, female virtue and childhood on the other. At the far end of the world, where everything was upside-down, polite girls, nice girls and young girls were all within sexual reach.

The subject is one that nineteenth-century writers approached with caution. There's something slightly awkward about the way they keep referring to Japanese women as maids and damsels. In part, they wish to situate the women in a past which can be viewed through a haze of nostalgia, but the arch phrases also betray a certain embarrassment. The status of these girls encountered by western travellers – the tea-house attendants, the geisha, the servants at inns and so on – has a teasing ambiguity. The writer's relationship with them must on the face of it be chaste; his account can suggest at most an element of playful dalliance. At the same time, the roguishness of tone hints at something more; behind the lolling about on native mats with dark-eyed attendants there is the promise of further sensual delights that can never be made quite explicit. The classic image of the oriental damsel is finely balanced between the acceptably sensual and the unacceptably sexual. We sense that the exotic promise is always on the edge of an erotic promise which cannot be articulated.

Today there are plenty of descendants of the tea-house girls to act as a cultural frontline in the game of wooing eager foreigners. Among the various receptionists, tour guides, interpreters and assistants, it is probably the airline hostess, intimate yet submissive, who is the nearest equivalent. In modern representations of the orient she occupies a special place: she is the public face the airline and its country put forward to greet you, but she is also their private promise. The pretty stewardess in kimono who welcomes James Bond aboard his Japan Air Lines flight, then bows and hands him a dainty fan, a small hot towel and a sumptuous menu is herself a menu of the attractions of the country he is going to – which indeed turn out to be primarily feminine.

It tends now to be other Asian airlines that use their stewardesses to make ambiguous promises. Countries that advertise themselves on the charms of their women are generally low on the ladder of international power, and Japan has come a long way since the 1950s. To the extent that the offer of sex reflects cultural submission or economic dependency, she has moved into a different league; but the legacy of the nineteenth century is still very much a part of western perceptions. Its basic premise is clear: sex and the orient go together. Madame Butterfly is a model of delicacy and submissiveness, but what first brings her within Pinkerton's orbit is the fact that she's sexually available. That's the way things are in the lascivious east. After his first meeting with the Japanese girl, Clive Holland's narrator lies awake in bed, thinking about her: 'It is Miss Hyacinth I want, and such a thing should not be impossible – in Japan.'[3] Elsewhere, perhaps – she comes from a respectable family – but not in Japan.

The mysteries of the east, as writers continually hint, are partly sexual mysteries, and the westerners who disembarked on to the streets of Yokohama and Nagasaki were well briefed on what to expect of oriental women. Japan was heir to a stock of images which had reached Europe over previous centuries from places as diverse as the beaches of Tahiti and the baths of Constantinople. Notions of Japanese sensuality had been heated by the fancies of eighteenth-century orientalists; the voluptuous orient conjured up a wash of images drawn from the seraglios and bath-houses of the Middle East. Their influence is apparent not just in the wide-eyed descriptions of Japanese bathing practices and the numerous scenes that present the westerner in Japan as a sultan surrounded by attentive odalisques but in the illustrations that often accompany these Victorian narratives. Captions such as *'en déshabille'*, 'after the bath', and 'after the banquet' provide a recurrent context for tumbling hair, languorous poses and peeping breasts. In the background is the vision of Japanese womanhood exported to the west by the *ukiyo-e* prints of artists like Sukenobu, Kunisada and Utamaro, which were already becoming fashionable by the 1860s. This is Baudelaire's *'langoureuse Asie'*, the orient summed up in Chateaubriand's phrase as *'bains, parfums, danses, délices de l'Asie'*.⁴ Meanwhile, converging on Japan from the opposite side of the world are the fantasies that de Bougainville and others had evoked with their descriptions of life under the palm trees of the South Sea islands.

To these general images of oriental sensuality was added an element specifically Japanese. In 1611 the East India Company had sent its first trading fleet to Japan under the command of John Saris. Three years later Saris was home, with a stock of pornographic books and paintings which he was hoping to smuggle into England. They were discovered and publicly burnt on 10 January 1615. This early evidence of the corrupting influence of Japanese morals was soon confirmed by the career of Richard Cocks, another official of the East India Company who, having travelled out with Saris, had been appointed by him Chief Factor at the trading post in Hirado. He settled into a convivial lifestyle which included a regular supply of Japanese 'wives' and much partying with Dutch and Japanese business associates. However agreeable this may have been, it did little to further the interests of the company, and the senior English merchant in Batavia, a man named Fursland, reported to the East India Office that Cocks and others were 'miserably given over to voluptuousness'. Cocks was saved from disgrace only by his opportune death in March 1624 while on the way back to England to answer for his conduct.⁵

1 Advertisement for the Toyota Supra (p. 33)

2 'The Barefoot Pilgrim' at Ryoanji (p. 72)

JAPAN

FLY QANTAS

AUSTRALIA'S ROUND-THE-WORLD AIRLINE

3 Poster for Qantas Airways (p. 61)

THE FACE

Ba-ba-babes! Saint Etienne's tribute to the girl group

No 55 APRIL 1993 £1.80 • US $4.95
ITALY L7300 · GERMANY 11.90DM · SPAIN 500PTAS · BELG 166BFR

VIRTUAL WAR

Bruce Sterling on the
GI as cyborg-not

NEW ORDER

on life after Factory

CHRIS ISAAK

and the quiff

drugs bores

Roy Of The Rovers RIP

bloody art

Hating Brenda

After the bubble
japan's
NEW GENERATION

Junior geisha Hana Chan
photographed by Schoerner

4 Hana Chan (p. 109)

THE NAME IS MYTHICAL – THE TASTE IS MAGICAL

5 Advertisement for Kirin beer (p. 151)

6 A model in Holland Park's Kyoto Garden
   – the classic pose (p. 69)

Chinese   Japanese

HOW TO TELL YOUR FRIENDS FROM THE JAPS

Of these four faces of young men *(above)* and middle-aged men *(below)* the two on the left are Chinese, the two on the right Japanese. There is no infallible way of telling them apart, because the same racial strains are mixed in both. Even an anthropologist, with calipers and plenty of time to measure heads, noses, shoulders, hips, is sometimes stumped. A few rules of thumb—not always reliable:

▶ Some Chinese are tall (average: 5 ft. 5 in.). Virtually all Japanese are short (average: 5 ft. 2½ in.).

▶ Japanese are likely to be stockier and broader-hipped than short Chinese.

▶ Japanese—except for wrestlers—are seldom fat; they often dry up and grow lean as they age. The Chinese often put on weight, particularly if they are prosperous (in China, with its frequent famines, being fat is esteemed as a sign of being a solid citizen).

▶ Chinese, not as hairy as Japanese, seldom grow an impressive mustache.

▶ Most Chinese avoid horn-rimmed spectacles.

▶ Although both have the typical epicanthic fold of the upper eyelid (which makes them look almond-eyed), Japanese eyes are usually set closer together.

▶ Those who know them best often rely on facial expression to tell them apart: the Chinese expression is likely to be more placid, kindly, open; the Japanese more positive, dogmatic, arrogant.

In Washington, last week, Correspondent Joseph Chiang made things much easier by pinning on his lapel a large badge reading "Chinese Reporter—NOT *Japanese*—Please."

▶ Some aristocratic Japanese have thin, aquiline noses, narrow faces and, except for their eyes, look like Caucasians.

▶ Japanese are hesitant, nervous in conversation, laugh loudly at the wrong time.

▶ Japanese walk stiffly, erect, hard-heeled. Chinese, more relaxed, have an easy gait, sometimes shuffle.

Chinese   Japanese

7 'How to Tell Your Friends from the Japs', *Time* (p. 75)

Two views of Japanese military prowess:

A LESSON IN PATRIOTISM.

JOHN BULL. "*YOUR* ARMY SYSTEM SEEMS TO. WORK SPLENDIDLY. HOW DO YOU MANAGE IT?"
JAPAN. "PERFECTLY SIMPLE. WITH US EVERY MAN IS READY TO SACRIFICE HIMSELF FOR HIS COUNTRY —*AND DOES IT!*"
JOHN BULL. "REMARKABLE SYSTEM! I MUST TRY AND INTRODUCE THAT AT HOME!"

8 'A Lesson in Patriotism', Bernard Partridge, *Punch*
(pp. 37 and 216)

THE MONKEY FOLK

"Always pecking at new things are the bandar-log. This time, if I have any eyesight, they have pecked down trouble for themselves."—*The Jungle Book*.

9 'The Monkey Folk', E.H. Shepard, *Punch* (p. 18)

10 Cover of
*The Camp on
Blood Island,*
HarperCollins
Publishers Ltd
(p. 172)

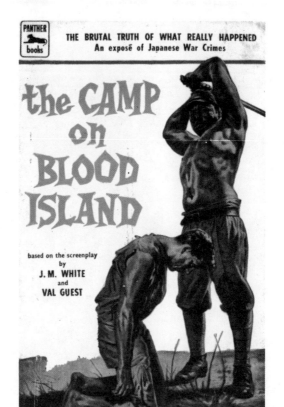

11 'The Yellow Peril' (p. 27)

That two of the East India Company's early representatives should have become embroiled in sexual scandals was not surprising; the Japanese had a reputation for immorality. 'Much addicted to sensual vices and sins' was Valignano's judgement, one of relatively few criticisms in his generally favourable view of their character. The Florentine Francesco Carletti, who visited Japan at the end of the sixteenth century, goes into considerably more detail. The readiness of a girl's parents or brothers to sell her into prostitution for a few pence is just one example of 'an immorality which is so gross and which takes such different forms, as to pass belief'. The Portuguese ships that came to Nagasaki were a particular attraction:

> As soon as ever these Portuguese arrive and disembark, the pimps who control this traffic in women call on them in the houses in which they are quartered for the time of their stay, and enquire whether they would like to purchase, or acquire in any other method they please, a girl, for the period of their sojourn, or to keep her for so many months, or for a night, or for a day, or for an hour, a contract being first made with these brokers, or an agreement entered into with the girl's relations, and the money paid down. [...] To sum up, the country is more plentifully supplied than any other with these sort of means of gratifying the passion for sexual indulgence, just as it abounds in every other sort of vice, in which it surpasses every other place in the world.[6]

Within a few years of Japan's reopening, Bishop George Smith found the same practices in place, but it was now the morals of European company men rather than of Portuguese sailors that were under attack. It was bad enough that the brothels of Yokohama were under government control, but there was worse:

> Not content with these flagitious methods of corrupting the foreign residents, the native officials contributed every facility for the perpetration of domestic vice and impurity. Young men were encouraged to negotiate through the custom-house the terms of payment and the selection of a partner in their dissolute mode of living. It is to be feared that the snare has not been set in vain; and Kanagawa was represented to me by persons generally well informed on local matters, as a deplorable scene of demoralisation and profligate life.[7]

This sets Satow's 'rosy-lipped black-eyed and attentive damsels' in a different light. Indeed, by the time he was posted on to Siam, Satow was himself the father of two half-Japanese children.

If, on the one hand, Japan's reputation transformed conventional descriptions of attendant damsels into a coded promise of sexual gratification, on the other it offered the basis for a suspicion of Japanese customs which found easy corroboration. Among the first westerners to set foot in Japan in the nineteenth century was John Henry Preble, a young officer who arrived with Commodore Perry's squadron in February 1854. His diary of the next four months records a series of shocks to his moral system which all confirmed the indecency of the Japanese. It began before he'd even stepped ashore in Yedo Bay: 'The inhabitants crowded the hill, and beckoned us on shore, and by the most unmistakable signs invited our intercourse with their women. One female went so far as to raise her drapery and expose her person to us. They are either a very lewd and lascivious people, or have catered before this, to the passions of sailors.'[8]

He was not long in doubt. 'Among the presents received by Com. Perry', he writes five days later, 'was a box of obscene paintings of naked men and women, another proof of the lewdness of this exclusive people.' At a meeting in mid-March he notes 'another instance of this people's sensuality': 'Capt. A. remarking to the interpreter that it was a rainy day. Yes, said he, a fine day for lieing with the ladies.' Such casual depravity was a prominent feature of the society: 'The remarkable sensuality of the Japanese is everywhere evidenced by their habit[,] conduct and actions.' Even the places of worship are not safe. Resting at a temple near Hakodate, he notices a pretty unmarried girl among the crowd. A man comes up to her, whispers, then takes her behind a screen five feet away: 'Her companions were not slow, to show us, by the most indecent signs in which the old priest joined, what they had gone for. The women laughing heartily as though it were a first-rate joke and no uncommon occurrence to so pervert their Temples.'

For Preble, as for many early visitors, the focus of these misgivings was the public bath-house, 'where old and young, male and female are mingled promiscuously in a state of unblushing nudity to the gaze of strangers'.[9] There were two standard responses to this. For one sort of traveller it was evidence of prelapsarian innocence. 'In Japan,' wrote the Comte de Beauvoir, 'one lives in full daylight; modesty, or rather immodesty, is unknown there; it is the innocence of the earthly paradise, and the costume of our first parents has nothing which shocks the sensibilities of this people who still live in the golden age.'[10] For the other, and more common, sort of traveller, this lack of shame was a mark of natural depravity. What particularly offended Preble, at both temple and bath-house, was the light-heartedness of it all: 'The only separation of the sexes I noticed, was that the men kept to the right side of this room, and the women to the left. Both would look at us and laugh and point at what every other human being I have ever heard of savage or civilised seeks to conceal. Laugh. It was disgusting.'[11]

Exactly a fortnight earlier another young ensign with Perry's squadron, Edward Yorke McCauley, had paid an even more traumatic visit to the bath-house, where he found a mixed crowd of old and young squatting on the stone floor 'without rag enough to cover a thumb nail': 'They invited us to join in and take a wash – but I was so disgusted with the whole breed, with their lewdness of manner and gesture, that I turned away with a hearty curse upon them for putting evidence conclusive to the unwelcome theory, that "women as a body of beings, can become thoroughly corrupt"'.[12]

A few years later, George Smith found no improvement. He writes indignantly of 'one shameless throng of bathers without signs of modesty or of any apparent sense of moral decorum'.[13] Pitched into the midst of 'one of the most licentious races in the world', the bishop was hard pressed to keep his bearings. It wasn't enough that he left his visiting card with a respectable dame who turned out to be the mama-san of one of Tokyo's brothels, he also managed to buy a set of porcelain cups which proved on closer inspection to be decorated with

131

pornographic designs. Not surprisingly, the bishop had some harsh things to say about Japanese morality.

There were plenty of commentators to endorse his views. 'A more licentious people does not exist,' declared John Tremenheere in 1863. 'The very toys of the children are designed to inoculate the infant mind with vice; shame is unknown, and indecency of language and conduct is all but universal.' This was echoed by Robert Fortune, who offered the opinion that 'no people in the world are more licentious in their behaviour than the Japanese'. By this time Edward Barrington de Fonblanque had added his voice to the chorus. 'The Japanese', he wrote, 'are depraved, sensual, and obscene in every sense.' Indecency was all around, 'painted on their porcelain, embossed on their lacquer, carved in their ivory, and surreptitiously conveyed into their fans'. Everywhere he found evidence of 'that utter absence of modesty and that morbid craving for the obscene which is universal in Japan'. The tone is rather different from that of Robert J. Collins, but the picture of a sex-drenched society is the same. Frank Harris was one of few Victorian visitors who admitted to viewing Japanese sexual attitudes without disapproval, though his summary of them agreed with that of the moralists: 'The sexuality in Japan is perhaps more marked than in any country on earth.' To his delight he found the people even freer than the French: 'Bit by bit I came to understand that there was not a trace of sexual modesty in Japan from one end to the other; most of the women even did not understand what Europeans meant by the concept.'[14]

The immodesty of the women was a particular subject of comment, because it seemed unrelated to the usual categories of sexual delinquency. Baron de Hübner was one of many who expressed surprise that well-conducted Japanese women were willing to laugh openly at indecent displays. Much the same point is made by Fonblanque. What shocked him, as it had Preble, was the tolerance of indecency shown by *ordinary* women:

> Respectable mothers of families, and young girls of otherwise irreproachable conduct, will take an undisguised pleasure in sights

and scenes that would shock an English street-walker; and little innocent-eyed children, toddling by their fond father's side, or nestling in their mother's bosom, may be seen playing with toys so indecent, that one longs to dash them from their tiny hands and trample them under foot.[15]

Fonblanque's reference to the English street-walker is suggestive. The lack of sexual shame which westerners found in these people was of an unfamiliar kind. It was not the shamelessness of the Victorian underworld, where the harlot's immodesty served as a foil to the purity of the angel in the house. Here, it seemed, the immodest woman quite often *was* the angel in the house. This was shocking, but it was also irresistibly attractive. The titillating descriptions of Japanese prostitution got their charge from precisely this combination. The sexual promise is sharpened by the social propriety, and those nineteenth-century travellers who, with a murmur of gentlemanly reticence, lead their readers into the streets of the Yoshiwara are fully aware of it.

The fascination of the Yoshiwara was not that it was an urban area set aside for commercial sex. This was common all over Europe. What distinguished it was the very un-European mixture of commercial sex and social decorum. Western influence, according to Mitford, had somewhat disturbed the atmosphere of the Yoshiwara in the Treaty ports, but in Yedo 'and wherever Japanese customs are untainted, the utmost decorum prevails'. By the standards of most foreigners, even the ports were seemly. 'Nothing quieter, or more decent, could be imagined,' remarked Gilbert Watson of the Yoshiwara in Kobe. 'All is outward propriety and decorum,' wrote another visitor.[16] Here were streets of brothels, run with impeccable propriety and peopled by creatures whose exquisite manners suggested a high degree of refinement. Writers never tired of pointing out how narrow was the line that could separate the respectable daughter from the common prostitute. Griffis approaches the topic with what might almost be mistaken for relish: 'The Japanese maiden, as pure as the purest Christian virgin, will at the command of her father enter the brothel tomorrow, and prostitute herself for life.

Not a murmur escapes her lips as she thus filially obeys. To a life she loathes, and to disease, premature old age, and an early grave, she goes joyfully.'[17]

The image, and all it implied about Japanese culture, was deeply intriguing. The coming together of social propriety and sexual abandon provided the material for a potent fantasy, of which Madame Butterfly – sexual toy, loyal wife and self-sacrificing mother – is a celebrated example. Pornographers long ago realised the erotic appeal of wimpled nuns, uniformed schoolgirls and demure secretaries; the sexual invitation they offer is a thrilling repudiation of their public claim to propriety. In the west, where the madonna and the whore are separate entities, these could only be images of fantasy, but in Japan that seemed not to be the case. The pious daughter who blithely offers herself for sale in the Yoshiwara is both.

And she is so young. This is almost equally important. Loti's geisha in Kyoto were 'scarcely ten years old'. Madame Butterfly is only fifteen, little more than a child. It's an emphasis that lends piquancy to her sexual appeal, adding another tang of the forbidden to this exotic fruit. Like the decorous bearing of the prostitutes in the Yoshiwara, the childlike appearance of the Japanese woman is belied by an undercurrent of sexuality. 'What a child Mūsmé is!' says Holland's narrator. 'And yet there is an indefinable charm inseparable from womanhood about her.'[18] Butterfly's coquetry is 'almost that of a child'. As Pinkerton watches the 'squirrel-like movements' with which she takes off her wedding garment, he muses on her childish appearance: 'To think that this plaything is my wife. My wife! But she displays such grace that I am consumed by the fever of a sudden desire.' This while he smokes a cigarette on the verandah, looking through at her in the bedroom. (The pre-coital cigarette, privilege of the prostitute's client, is a mark of domination as surely as the post-coital one is a mark of self-satisfaction.)

Pinkerton's discriminating commentary on the fifteen-year-old with whom he's about to go to bed reflects another sexual fantasy which the Japanese woman promised to fulfil. The idea of the *ingénue libertine*, the fresh young girl who displays a flattering aptitude for sex under the tutelage of an older man, had been enthusiastically promoted in the eighteenth century, notably in France, and its continuing appeal is attested by numerous aspects of Victorian life, from the brisk trade in child prostitutes to the vogue for photographing naked waifs in poses of coy invitation. It's impossible to read much Victorian literature without recognising a characteristically gloating tone in its treatment of young children, especially young girls. There is often a sinuous thread of sexual anticipation, even of sadism, just below the avuncular surface. Dickens parodies it in the figure of Daniel Quilp, the hideous cigar-smoking dwarf who torments the grandfather in *The Old Curiosity Shop* with his compliments on the charms of Little Nell:

> Such a fresh, blooming, modest little bud, neighbour,' said Quilp, nursing his short leg, and making his eyes twinkle very much; 'such a chubby, rosy, cosy little Nell! [...] She's so,' said Quilp, speaking very slowly, and feigning to be quite absorbed in the subject, 'so small, so compact, so beautifully modelled, so fair, with such blue veins and such a transparent skin, and such little feet, and such winning ways ...'[19]

Dickens conveys vividly the sexual excitement that bubbles through the clichés.

The ambiguity of Victorian responses to children carries over into their images of Japanese women. There is the same uneasy mixture of sentiment and sex. As so often, the attraction of the east is that it offers a context within which the prohibitions of western life can be dissolved; in this case, the child can become the bride, or at least the sexual partner. In *The Real Japan* (1892) Henry Norman summarises the qualities that make the Japanese woman such a versatile source of fantasy:

> If you could take the light from the eyes of a Sister of Mercy at her gracious task, the smile of a maiden looking over the seas for her lover, and the heart of an unspoiled child, and materialise them into a winsome and healthy little body, crowned with a mass of jet-black hair and dressed in bright rustling silks, you would have the typical Japanese woman.[20]

It's an interesting combination of the spiritual and the sexual; the Sister of Mercy and the unspoiled child contend with the suggestions conveyed by the winsome, healthy little body, the jet-black hair and the rustling silks. Her watch for a lover from over the seas provides space for the male reader to insert his fantasy.

The sexual appeal of the child-woman has continued to be a crucial element in western responses to Japanese women. (Pearl Buck's description of Josui – 'her little frame, her tiny hands' – would have brought a glow to Quilp's cigar.) To a western eye, the bobbed hair and sailor suits of adolescent Japanese girls put them firmly in Lolita land. Even adults retain the outlines of childhood; the slighter figure, smaller breasts and less luxuriant pubic hair distance the typical Japanese woman from western ideas of the mature female and align her with the girlish, the immature, the pubescent. And yet 'the indefinable charm inseparable from womanhood' is always in the background. 'Sweet darling Sabby, my child Sabby,' whispers the hero of *The Wind Cannot Read*, but then corrects himself, 'Yet she was not a child, she was a woman, and there was as much woman as there was child in her, a deep age-old womanliness. I wondered how she could be so womanly, so warmly responsive, so passionate, and yet retain that wide-eyed innocence.'[21]

What she offers is the innocent sexuality we lost with the Fall. Like the child, she can lead us back into a world untainted by our fallen, adult existence. Throughout Pico Iyer's *The Lady and the Monk*, Sachiko's childlike ways bewitch the narrator, whose sexual interest is overlaid by a tone of benevolent adult fondness. Towards the end of the book he arranges to meet her in Korea:

> It was, as I had expected, a pleasure unalloyed to see her setting foot abroad, so electric with elation, and so high that, as she readily admitted, 'My stomach little hurt. Too much excited. Cannot control. Cannot sleep!' Eager to be charmed, ready for delight, she felt herself swept up in such a surge of freedom that, her first day out of Japan, she literally began skipping across her hotel room like a hopscotch-playing schoolgirl.[22]

When he takes her to a bar in the red-light district of Seoul, her naïve fascination wins over the bar-girl who comes to serve them, 'and soon the two of them were sitting side by side, chatting away in an unlikely English and telling one another, through shining eyes, their hopes for one another's future'. Around them the sexual business of the bar goes on, 'but all the world was lost to Sachiko and her friend as, earnestly, they exchanged their hearts'.[23] She has created a little circle of innocence in this sinful setting. It is the same childish simplicity that makes her scamper barefoot through the streets of Sydney and that simultaneously excites the narrator's sexual attention and proclaims her own sexual innocence.

With the innocence of the child goes a certain vulnerability which can add another sensual charge. There's a hint of it in *The Wind Cannot Read* when the hero looks at Sabby's hands: 'They were very small, pretty, fluttering hands, and afterwards in the ghari, when I enclosed one in my own, I was half afraid that I should crush it because it was so fragile. I thought it was like having the tiny body of a bird in my palm, its soft feathers covering a quivering little skeleton.'[24] Here the pleasure of sexual contact is pushing towards the edge of sadism. To be kind when one could be cruel is a sweet delight.

As with more conventional paedophile fantasies, the appeal of the child-woman is partly a question of sex, partly of power. It takes us back to the images of dominance discussed in Chapter 11. The scene described by Kipling and the bishop, in which kneeling damsels attend the western master, has an obvious sequel behind closed doors, even though neither of these distinguished men may have experienced it. The sexual relationship is one of power – of westerner over oriental, of male over female, of adult over child.

By the end of the century the sexuality of the Japanese woman is defined by two contrasting strands of imagery, both of which contribute to the figure of Madame Butterfly: she is the libertine of orientalist mythology and the vulnerable child-woman at the mercy of the adult male. Her ability to reconcile contradictory fantasies is part of her continuing appeal. (Hana Chan's eyes, we recall, are 'somewhere between Bambi and Beatrice Dalle', Disney's innocent faun and the explosively sexual heroine of

Betty Blue.) The best-selling *Japan Handbook* has this advice for its readers:

> A Japanese woman expects you to be the aggressor, and in the old-fashioned sense to 'make' her. Obviously, this by no means includes force, but it does include directness. You lead and she responds. There's a bit of Scarlett O'Hara in the Japanese woman. She wants Rhett Butler to sweep her off her feet and manfully carry her to the bedroom. This in a way exonerates her from responsibility because, after all, she couldn't refuse. Western travelers also remark at how bold Japanese women can be. If you're being too thick headed, she might take the lead. Japanese women enjoy sex and unlike westerners who didn't seem to discover the clitoris until the mid 1970s, they knew that it existed at least a thousand yrs. ago. They are orgasmic, warm and affectionate.[25]

So you can take your pick. Side by side with the old-world heroine who expects the man to take the lead is the clitorally educated freelance with a thousand years of sexual experience to call upon. If the romance of *Gone with the Wind* doesn't appeal, you can get Masters and Johnson as part of the same package. Here in one breathtaking paragraph, is a measure of the range of fantasies the Japanese woman is expected to fulfil.

The sexual expertise associated with the world of the geisha has long fuelled suspicions that the Japanese woman possesses arts beyond the knowledge of her clumsier western sisters. In the first volume of his memoirs Frank Harris promises details of the instruction he received in the art of love from the 'adepts' of the east – 'unimaginable refinements, for they have studied the body as deeply as the soul'.[26] When he gets around to this, four volumes later, we find that technical sophistication is linked to another virtue of the Japanese woman – self-sacrifice. On one of his first nights in Japan, Harris is invited to a festive evening where the entertainment is provided by a special corps of geisha, attended by *mousmées* who sit with the guests while the geisha dance: 'The little mousmée who came to me was the prettiest of the whole lot and I suppose I showed her that I admired her. At any rate, the dance was not half over when her hand began to stray, and from light touches she soon went on to bolder demonstrations of desire. At length I said to her, "Later", one of the few Japanese words I knew. She pouted and then laughed with enjoyment, nodding her head.'[27]

When they are alone together she begins to show 'a mixture of affection and passion impossible to describe', proving that she has 'learned all the tricks of the love trade'. Her body, he concludes, was 'a perfect instrument of love'. But in true Butterfly fashion she combines this expertise with a heart of gold. Next morning Harris gives his friend ten pounds to pass on to her: 'To my wonder and his the money was refused and the mousmée told me with a brave glance that she would always be willing to welcome me without money and without price.'[28] As with Madame Butterfly, the westerner gets it both ways: he pays for sex and gets love as well. Later, the girl completes the picture by offering herself as his servant. He accepts, and she educates him in the accomplishments of Japanese women – 'There was nothing in the way of sex she did not know' – while supplying him with a series of girls to sample, personally selected. 'When I think of the devotion of that mousmée,' Harris reflects with satisfaction, 'I am always astonished. She loved me, yet never showed any sex jealousy.'[29]

Going abroad, going east in particular, has always involved a shedding of sexual restraints. 'In the ports of the Orient,' remarks Kazantzakis, 'the bounds of virtue are different, and vice has other and far wider privileges.'[30] But in Japan the western visitor found more than this: not just the freedom to sin, but the freedom from sin. Prelapsarian images of unblushing nudity were accompanied by a wider sense that Japan had escaped the awareness of sin and shame which were a consequence of the Fall. The dismay of the moralists emphasised the scope of its sexual invitation, and its image as a place where sex is purged of sin continues to excite us. What intrigues westerners about the love-hotel is its sheer brazenness. There's not a capital in Europe that doesn't cater for our sexual fantasies; the visitor who knows where to go can find a sympathetic welcome in even the most sedate of cities. But this is a hidden or separate world, not, as we're led to believe it is in Japan, part of the mainstream of everyday social life. In *Japan-Think*,

Ameri-Think (1992) Robert Collins retells the story of the Fall, and goes on:

> What *is* crystal clear, however, is that the Japanese have never heard *one word* of this remarkable story – yet they somehow managed to get by for centuries and centuries in blind, unholy ignorance. (I know, it *is* mind-boggling.) They *don't even know* that there's an inherent element of shame connected with sex, nakedness, and all those other awful things . . .[31]

The heavy jocularity merely puts a new gloss on an old point: unlike us, the Japanese don't mind about sex. One strand of Blackthorne's education in things Japanese is learning not to squirm with embarrassment whenever sex is mentioned. His outrage when the beautiful interpreter serenely offers him a boy for the night after he has turned down the proposal of a girl gradually gives way to a more tolerant view. Later he meets the local courtesan who gives him a guided tour of the kinds of sexual apparatus she has at her disposal – Pleasure Pearls, Secret Skin, Weary Armaments, bells, seeds, salves, potions of every kind and a generous provision of dildoes. All part of the culture, Anjin-san.

James Bond undergoes a similar, though less comprehensive, introduction to the Japanese way of sex when Tiger Tanaka arranges for him to have a massage. As soon as the girl begins to unbutton his trousers, Bond calls a halt and gets Tanaka back to explain what's going on:

> 'You really must learn to obey orders without asking questions, Bondo-san. That is the essence of our relationship during the next few days. You see that box? When she has undressed you, she will put you in the box which has a charcoal fire under it. You will sweat. After perhaps ten minutes she will help you out of the box and wash you from head to foot. She will even tenderly clean out your ears with a special ivory instrument. [...] She will then give you a massage on that couch and, according to your indications, she will make this massage as delightful, as prolonged as you wish. You will then go to sleep. When you are awakened with eggs and bacon and coffee you will kiss the girl good morning and shave, or the other way round, and that will be that.'[32]

That will be that – no strings, no hang-ups. The Japanese experience of sex offers a merciful escape from complications; and when the complications change, so does the experience. Like other fantasies, its precise outlines reflect the constraints and insecurities of the moment. Where it once responded to the prohibitions of the Victorians, it can now adapt itself to the new sexual sins defined by western feminism. In an age when submissive females are in short supply and dominant males are looked on with general disfavour, the moral of the *Japan Handbook* is clear: if you want to play Rhett Butler, go to Japan not Georgia.

A recent item on BBC's *Newsnight* looked at the body-con phenomenon in modern Tokyo: office girls dress up in revealing outfits after work and head for selected clubs where they can indulge in exhibitionist dancing on stage. It's symptomatic of a new liberation in Japan, but hardly what we understand by liberation in the west. While western feminists are fighting to prevent the woman from being turned into a sex object, body-con revels in it; the whole point is to become an object of the male gaze – the west's new forbidden fruit.

As the debates grind on in Europe and America about various forms of sexual oppression, the minefield gets no easier to chart. It is, as always, a region where occasions of sin are manifold, even if the nature of the sins has changed. For western men nervous of the thorns of feminism, petrified of getting caught in an act of sexism, weary of agonising about Relationships, the image of the Japanese woman still offers a truant fantasy of what is not available in the west.

14. Cultural Penetration

In choosing a geisha to represent Japan, the devisers of the mail-order competition were taking a well-worn path. 'Japan', wrote Nikos Kazantzakis, 'has been the geisha of nations; she has kept smiling over the distant waters, full of pleasure and mystery.' The image of the Japanese woman is the image of Japan itself. Long before Kazantzakis, Pierre Loti had used a similar conceit, more intimately explored, to suggest the welcome afforded by Japan. At the start of *Madame Chrysanthème* he describes his ship entering the bay of Nagasaki. It passes into a shady channel between two ranges of hills – 'as though Japan was opening herself before us, in an enchanted cleft, to allow us to penetrate right to her heart'.[1] The image is unmistakably sexual, and it anticipates the way Loti himself will try to 'penetrate' Japan.

By the late nineteenth century most countries in Asia from which the west had anything to gain were under the domination of European powers, and it was in this context that oriental women were enjoyed by westerners. They were one of the fringe benefits of colonial rule; possession of the woman was an adjunct to possession of the country – of no particular significance. But Japan, once again, was an exception. It had skilfully avoided a military incursion by the west and had no intention of being possessed by anyone. In the absence of military conquest, the imagery of sexual conquest acquires a special

142

resonance. To possess the woman is as close as one can get to possessing Japan; an embodiment of the culture, she offers the chance to purchase it, to dominate it, to penetrate its mysteries and its secret knowledge.

From this perspective the images we have been looking at in the past three chapters have a different complexion. They are cultural fantasies as well as sexual ones. To recline with your pipe while attended by a bevy of submissive damsels is to enjoy a surrogate form of colonial domination. For the westerner unsustained by political or administrative authority, the Japanese woman provides a reassuring sense of superiority. The timid geisha with the eyes and manner of a wild hart, the tea-house girl on her knees, the maid bending low upon your doorstep – these are more than women whose services you have bought; they are images of Japan, and their submissiveness is the submissiveness of Japan. By the same token, their sexual availability reflects a Japan that is ripe for commercial exploitation. The country has been brought into the market place, and its women offer proof of the potential reach of commerce. There is nothing, no one, that cannot be bought. 'It is Miss Hyacinth I want, and such a thing should not be impossible – in Japan.'

Each of the classic images of the Japanese woman has an analogue in western views of Japan. If the submissive damsel is a Japan that can be dominated, and the sexually available mousmé a Japan that can be bought, the woman as work of art is a Japan to be admired, and the perfect wife a Japan to be idealised and envied. The indignation expressed by western writers about the lowly status of Japanese women has, as we've seen, more than a tinge of complacency, not just because it flatters westerners' notions of their own chivalry but because the relationship between man and woman is seen as analogous to that between male and female cultures. To refer to 'the neat-handed, polite little people that live among flowers and babies' is to offer a feminised version of Japanese culture which reflects a belief that it is subordinate to the masculine cultures of Europe and America. The relations of female to male are also those of child to adult and servant to master, and ultimately those of Japan to the west.

It is clear that part of the mastery exercised by Pinkerton over Butterfly is the mastery of America over Japan. Butterfly insists that she is an American citizen, and before she goes behind the screen to commit suicide she hands her child an American flag. (The significance of this becomes even more apparent if we imagine what it would have meant for her to give him a Japanese flag.) Pinkerton's treatment has not undermined her allegiance to America; it is there that the child's future lies. The woman of Japan has given herself to an American body and soul, and the fruit of their union will belong to America.

Madame Butterfly and her kind continued to delight western audiences well into the twentieth century; titles like *The Geisha, A Flower of Yeddo, The Lady of the Weeping-Willow Tree, A Japanese Marriage* were common currency.[2] But as Japan's international role changed and it came to be seen, with increasing concern, as a world power, the figure of the Japanese woman was less often emphasised. The defeat of Russia in 1905 was an immediate challenge to the image of feminine Japan. While the war was still going on, T. W. H. Crosland railed against our 'habit of thinking of the Japanese as a dainty, innocuous, kind-hearted, artistic lovable people, who lead a butterfly life in a butterfly country, and may be safely left to do whatever childish thing occurs to them, encouraged of course with our own ineffable pats on the back and indulgent smiles'.[3] Writing in the following year, Baron Falkenegg addressed the question explicitly in a passage quoted by Jean-Pierre Lehmann:

> To express it in a word, the Japanese consider themselves to be a thoroughly masculine people, whereas most Western nations, especially those above all, on whom, in any conflict with the Mongoloid races, everything will depend, have, without exception, become 'feminine'; that is, the Japanese have absolutely manly aspirations, and allow themselves to be influenced only by strong, masculine thoughts; the people of Europe are mostly dependent on feminine and womanly influences; they are imitators and degenerates.[4]

Imitative and effeminate, the western nations have taken over the two central attributes of subordination. Japan has, in effect, switched places with them. 'Mars', Falkenegg says, 'is in the ascendancy, Venus and her erotic companions must be silent.' Venus was far from silent; not only did *Madame Butterfly* and its derivatives retain their popularity, but, as Endymion Wilkinson has pointed out, the one enduring bestseller of the inter-war years on a Japanese theme was Arthur Waley's translation of *The Tale of Genji*. Nonetheless, although the popularity of *Genji* suggests a continuing public appetite for the Japan of cherry blossom and rustling silk, there were few visitors during this period who did not also comment on what William Plomer called Japan's 'split personality': 'She loved peace but she also loved war.'[5] What Plomer saw in the 1920s was far more pronounced by the time Kazantzakis went there in the 1930s: 'The old Japan of beauty – with its kimonos, its lanterns, its fans – disappears, vanishes. The new Japan of force, with its factories and cannons, wakes up and grows wild.'[6] Within a few more years, the transformation from smiling damsel to louring ogre was complete.

(The pattern is in some ways alarmingly similar to what we have witnessed over the past twenty years, as the feminine post-war Japan is redefined in the popular imagination as an invasive male culture, threatening the lush pastures of Europe and America. In an image that sums up its change in sexual role, Fred Hiatt's novel, *The Secret Sun*, describes the underground laboratory where the Japanese are supposed to be producing miniaturised atomic devices as 'the center of their rape of the west'.)

After the Second World War, westerners – Americans in particular, since it was they who had come most fiercely into conflict with the Japanese – had to relearn things about Japan that the war had suppressed. For many, James Michener's novel *Sayonara* was a significant part of this process. Published in 1953–4, it stayed on the bestseller lists for five months and provided a powerful antidote to the images spawned by war. The Japanese soldier is more or less forgotten. In Michener's version of Japan the woman is once again at the centre. The book's hero, Lloyd Gruver, is an ace American pilot in the Korean war who at the start of the novel shares all the usual post-war prejudices about Japan. 'Dirty streets, little paper houses, squat men and fat round women' are the images he thinks of when told that he is to be sent there from Korea. He is engaged to a 'fine, good-looking American girl' and can see nothing in Japan to attract him: 'How can our men – good average guys – how can they marry these yellow girls?'[7] These are the notions which are about to be revolutionised by his encounter with The Japanese Woman. The rest of the story tells of his bitter-sweet affair with the beautiful Hana-ogi and of the tragic marriage between an enlisted man, Joe Kelly, and another Japanese woman, Katsumi.

The two relationships combine to present an image of Japan as a seductive feminine culture temptingly opposed to the hard male world of America. Gruver's re-education begins when he goes to the village of Takarazuka and sees the dancers returning in the evening under the cherry blossoms to the dormitory where they live in nunlike seclusion. Beautiful but aloof, they represent something that eludes the western observer. Gruver is captivated by the poetic swaying of their skirts and the 'lithe, hidden movements of their beautiful bodies', but they pass into the darkness where his eye cannot follow them. The solitary girl who comes after them leaves him feeling as if he had been 'brushed across the eyes by some terrible essence of beauty'.[8]

It is the beauty not just of a woman but of a whole alien culture, as he comes to understand when he falls in love with Hana-ogi. The appreciation of the woman and of her culture go together: 'I discovered not only Hana-ogi's enormous love but I also discovered her land, the tragic, doomed land of Japan.' Through her dancing he 'fell under the spell of Japanese art'. Later, when they are living together, he becomes aware of the change in himself: 'I cannot recall a moment when there were not flowers in our alcove and I – who had never known a violet from a daisy – came to love them.'[9] This is a world America has left out of count, the world Captain Fisby was discovering at about the same time as he sat in First Flower's tea-house, looking out at the lotus pond and listening to the breeze in the pines.

The Japanese woman is again the key to the culture, as she

had been in the nineteenth century. She redeems a country tainted by the war and explains a culture that the west has been taught to despise. The recurrent pattern is of a hero who dislikes or dismisses Japan being drawn into sympathy with its ways by his love for a Japanese woman. In the process, differences of race and culture dissolve: 'All the problems we used to laugh about as being so strange – so unlike America – I saw explained this afternoon. The Japanese were no different from us.' The understanding of Japan, the assimilation of the alien, is the gift of its women. As Gruver and Hana-ogi look for a place to make love, he realises what has happened: 'There was now no thought of Japanese or American. We were timeless human beings without nation or speech or different color. [...] You find a girl as lovely as Hana-ogi – and she is not Japanese and you are not American.'[10]

Clearly influenced by Michener, *Tamiko* was an English contribution to the genre by Ronald Kirkbride. A popular novel published in 1959, it is another story of a Japan-hater transformed by the love of a good woman – an ideal woman. The paperback cover shows in the foreground a naked woman with slanting eyes holding a towel seductively to her breast. (This is presumably why the British Library kept the innocuous book in its restricted section for over thirty years.) She is standing under a cherry tree in blossom. In the background is a placid lake with a temple torii in the middle of it, and behind it Mount Fuji. These are the usual features of Japan as picturesque dreamland, but the woman in the foreground unites them and provides access to them. She is Japan and they are aspects of her.

Like Lloyd Gruver, the book's hero is hostile to everything Japanese, and particularly to Japanese women. In a scene that recalls *Sayonara*, he goes to the American embassy and sees the GIs lining up with their brides, 'ugly round- faced Japanese girls with their gold teeth and greasy bobbed hair'. He knows how it happens, 'for they were good bed companions', but it still seems a shameful waste: 'These boys had homes in the States, families to return to, clean-cut American girls with good backgrounds waiting for them, and they were throwing themselves away on these tarts who ran after them simply because they had money in their pockets.'[11]

In a re-run of the familiar story, he soon encounters a beautiful Japanese girl, Tamiko, and, despite the opposition of her brother and the contempt of the rich American girl with whom he's having an affair, falls in love with her. She, as always, provides the key to understanding the strangeness of Japan: 'He realised then why over a million foreigners had married Japanese girls, realised that in Tamiko lay the true spirit of Japan, the reflection of generations of Japanese women who had been brought up to live, to toil, to love, to suffer and never to show pain or disappointment.'[12] What sparks this realisation is Tamiko's departure. Knowing that he is determined to go to America, she quietly slips away one morning, accepting without drama or recrimination her traditional role as deserted lover.

In the end, things work out for them, but this is perhaps less exceptional than it seems. The author has avoided breaking too many taboos. In the first place, the hero is not altogether a westerner (he is half-Chinese), and in the second place, his visa for the United States is refused at the last moment on medical grounds. So it's not quite a surrender of west to east, and Madame Butterfly is not after all leaving for America.

On the whole, writers were willing to celebrate relationships between Japanese women and western men but reluctant to allow them to become permanent or to be carried back to the west. Japanese wives may have been heading west by the plane-load in the 1950s, but their fictional counterparts were rarely allowed to make the same journey. If they ventured on an affair with a westerner, they were lucky to escape with their lives. The popular stereotype of the doomed relationship between east and west has its own iron laws. The woman's devotion usually has to be sealed by death, or by an act of self-sacrifice that is only one step away from death. What she endures is a measure of her value. The heroine of *The Wind Cannot Read* suffers from an unspecified though fatal disease, but for most of the novel she keeps the pain of her illness and the knowledge of her imminent death a secret from her English lover. In their last scene together she and the hero indulge a fantasy of life in a Gloucestershire village, dreaming of a future they both know will never come. From a western perspective, the Japanese woman shares her culture's intimacy with death, and this is what gives the relationships their intensity. Images of cosy retirement in the Cotswolds have no place here.

Marriage is often desired but rarely achieved, partly because racial differences are hard for the popular novel to swallow, but also because the war was still too close. The Japanese woman spoke for the new post-war Japan whose priorities were presented as feminine and aesthetic rather than masculine and warlike. As such, she was an object of general approval in the west, and the balance of sympathy was usually tilted further by giving her a war record of suffering; but to link oneself permanently with her was nonetheless perceived, at a level deeper than that of social approval or disapproval, as a betrayal which had to be punished – more in sorrow than in anger by this stage, but punished all the same. Grief for the man; exile or death for the woman. In this, too, she did duty for the whole culture; Japan was now a friend, but the excesses of the recent past were not forgotten and, by many, not entirely forgiven. Surrogate forms of reprisal had their attraction.

Romance between east and west puts fundamental issues at stake. To discover that 'she is not Japanese and you are not American' may be fine for a lover but it's not so good for a soldier, or even a citizen. The progress of the relationship undermines the racial and cultural certainties with which the hero starts; he will never be quite so clean-cut again. Increasing sympathy with things Japanese involves a withdrawal of allegiance from America. The official document which notifies Joe Kelly that he is to be sent home puts the case plainly: 'American military personnel married to Japanese wives will be rotated home immediately lest their allegiance to the United States be eroded.'[13] It is the dilemma at the centre of *Antony and Cleopatra.* Japan is Egypt to America's Rome; it sets a female world of art and love over against a male world of power and duty.

Gruver finally turns his back on Japan and accepts promotion to lieutenant-colonel and the prospect of Eileen, the 'good sport', as his future wife. In saying sayonara to Hana-ogi, he is saying it to all the seductions of the exotic: 'To the alley and the canal and the little houses and the pachinko parlour and to the flutes at night – sayonara. And you, Japan, you crowded islands, you tragic land – sayonara, you enemy, you friend.'[14] Japan is both enemy and friend because the cultural subtleties its friendship invites us to share are a challenge to the values of our own culture. The Japanese woman who teaches the all-American boy about art and flowers and love unfits him both for life among soldiers and for life back home, where the subjects of interest are 'Junior's braces and country-club dances and what kind of car their wife bought'. Or she does if she hangs around. As long as she dies or renounces him or accepts desertion, we are allowed to see the hero as a man matured and strengthened by his experience. While it may be acceptable to take on board the perspectives of the east, it is unacceptable to shift allegiance to them, except in trivial matters. The west reclaims its own.

Anyone who managed to sit through *Seven Nights in Japan* (1976), in which Michael York plays the young Prince of Wales having an affair with a Japanese tour guide, will have recognised the same formula in flared trousers and English accents. At the end, the prince's limousine goes one way and the guide's coach the other, but it was a near thing. When they were together in the inevitable Japanese house beside the lake, he was ready to abandon all – duty, crown and country – for the sake of his Japanese love.

This is a recurrent fear about the oriental woman. Like Circe, she can lure the hero from his task, undermining by her sexual magic the values on which his life is based. Dido did it to Aeneas, Cleopatra to Antony; the naïve westerner who steps ashore armed only with the prejudices of his race always runs a risk. It's no coincidence that the classic image of the vamp, as seen, for example, in the figure of Theda Bara with her helmet of dark hair and half-shut eyes, has a distinctly oriental cast. Looking for the first time at the daughter of Fu Manchu, whom he imagines to be the wife of his friend Petrie, Sterling experiences 'vile impulses' that take him by surprise, a 'sudden lawless desire for the wife of my best friend – a desire so wild that it threatened to swamp everything – friendship, tradition, honour!'[15] The most basic obligations go down like skittles before the lure of the oriental woman, whose sexuality erodes the ordinary western decencies. Behind Bishop Smith's attack on prostitution in Yokohama is the same idea of upright Englishmen ensnared by oriental sexuality.

When the Japanese woman and all she represents had practically dropped out of sight in the west during the Second World War, this one image survived: Tokyo Rose, whose insinuating voice broadcast propaganda to the west, was for many the sole representative of Japanese womanhood. Beautiful and treacherous, she was a perfect counterpart to the malevolent Japanese male.[16]

The image of a dangerous, devious sexuality which tempts men to betray their true loyalties still has a certain amount of life, and we shall perhaps see more of it as Japan's international power grows. The recent advertising campaign for Kirin beer consisted simply of a picture of a Japanese woman, in half-profile, with full lips, slanting eyes and long straight hair falling across a bare shoulder stamped with the Kirin blazing dragon. Farther down her shoulder, in the corner of the picture, was a bottle of beer and the campaign slogan, 'The Name Is Mythical – The Taste Is Magical'. The promise is of an alien sensuality that offers something unexplored by the west; it is an erotic invitation to change sides. But it is also a version of the Japanese woman which is aggressively unpretty; there is nothing here of the simpering maiden in kimono. The sensuality is commanding rather than coy, and the woman, unsmiling and tattooed, makes no appeal to any fantasy of sexual or cultural power; she is there to dominate rather than to be dominated. She reflects, as it were, the Japan that can say no.

This is the new powerful Japan with which the ninja blockbusters of Eric Lustbader are concerned. In the opening chapter of *The Ninja* we are told how the hero has learned that in Japan 'women were like flowers one had to unfold like origami, with infinite care and deliberateness finding that, when fully opened, they were filled with exquisite tenderness and devious violence.'[17] Another marriage of contraries from this paradoxical country. What it means becomes clearer in the next volume. The Miko (sorceress) of the title is a woman named Akiko. The daughter of a geisha, she excites her first martial-arts teacher by her physical immaturity: 'Her hair, just beginning to come, grew only along the centre strip of her pubic mound, leaving the sides as smooth and bare as a small child's gully. This only increased his ardour since he had before him both woman and girl.' But Akiko is not just a sexual cliché, she is a serial murderess, introduced at the start of the novel decapitating another of her teachers in the middle of the tea ceremony. Later she reappears in the tranquil setting of a Zen garden. Slipping off her kimono, she steps naked onto the raked pebbles of the garden: 'Between two of the jutting black rocks she spread herself, draped on the flat ground, curled and serpentine, half in light, half in shadow, and became one with all that surrounded her.'[18]

The mixture of art, sexuality and serpentine malevolence makes up a classic image of the oriental vamp, and indeed, later in the novel, the hero reacts much as Stirling does to the daughter of Fu Manchu. Momentarily bewitched by her, forgetting that she is the wife of his friend, forgetting his own fiancée, he loses all restraint: 'He could not help himself. His body yearned for Akiko as if she were food, drink, oxygen to fill his lungs. He could no more disentangle himself from her than he could still his own pulse.'[19] If Tokyo Rose was a counterpart of the wartime Japanese male, this siren with magic powers is a counterpart of the business warrior of the late twentieth century.

But neither this figure nor the girl in kimono standing beside the waterfall is the characteristic Japanese heroine of our time. For that we must turn back to the dominant western image of contemporary Japan. Back, for example, to Channel 4's *Travelog*. As the television reporter emerges from the Osaka underground and looks about him at the display of neon, he sees what reporters always see: a society pulled in different directions by the traditional and the modern. 'Over three-quarters of all

Japanese live crowded into these fantastic, futuristic city-scapes,' he tells us, 'and these vivid hi-tech visions now compete with the ancient, elegant images as symbols of the nation.'[20] On one side temples, tatami mats and tea ceremonies, on the other skyscrapers, neon lights and video games. Ancient, traditional Japan is of the east; modern, technological Japan is of the west. And as we might expect, it's the Japanese woman who offers the most appealing image of this cultural union. For the west, the heroine of post-war Japan is the woman with a foot in both camps, the westernised oriental.

Giggling geisha and accommodating masseuses are attractive enough in their way, but they aren't the stuff of which heroines in a James Bond novel are made. From the start, Kissy Suzuki is distinguished from them: 'One girl, rather taller than the rest, seemed to pay no attention to the men on the jetty or to the police launch riding beside it. She was the centre of a crowd of laughing girls as she waded with a rather long, perhaps studied, stride over the shiny black pebbles and up the beach. She flung back a remark at her companions and they giggled, putting their hands up to their mouths.' Japanese girls aren't supposed to 'fling back' remarks. Her stature, her long stride, the contrast with her giggling companions distance her from conventional Japanese femininity. The impression is strengthened when she forestalls the bow with which Bond intends to greet her: 'She laughed gaily. She didn't titter or giggle, she actually laughed. She said, "You don't have to bow to me and I shall never bow to you." She held out her hand. "How do you do. My name is Kissy Suzuki."'

This manly frankness is followed by a playful exchange that leaves us in no doubt of her credentials: 'Bond was delighted. Thank God for a straightforward girl at last! No more bowing and hissing!'[21] She might almost be a product of the home counties. And that, of course, is the point – what distinguishes Kissy Suzuki from her companions is that she's less Japanese and more western. We discover that she lived for a time in Hollywood. Her stay was not a success, but it has left the redeeming mark of the west upon her – no more bowing and hissing.

Kyoko, the girl in Fred Hiatt's *The Secret Sun*, is another example. Though beautiful and Japanese, she is not a typical Japanese beauty: 'Her eyes were rounder, her nose more Semitic, her lips a bit fuller, and she was relatively tall, with wide shoulders, full breasts, a narrow waist, and the walk and poise of an athlete.' The suspicion that she is being deliberately westernised is confirmed when the hero looks at her in Ueno station and reflects that 'she might have been a university student from Berkeley'.[22] The fusion of California girl and Tokyo girl has influenced western responses to a range of Japanese women, from the body-con dancers to the bride of the Crown Prince. For the western media, Owada Masako was a perfect contemporary heroine – like Hana Chan, whose growing popularity, we are told, is due to 'her concurrent acceptance and interpretation of the zaniest in western pop culture, the new directions of contemporary Tokyo, *and* the traditional values of the old Japan'.

The most lovingly realised treatment both of this version of Japan and of the whole concept of the Japanese woman as image of the culture is Pico Iyer's *The Lady and the Monk*. Kyoto, says the paperback blurb, is a place of temples, monks and ancient ritual,

> But even living in a monastery, Iyer finds distractions and unsettling contradictions. The monks wear Nike shoes, ride motorcycles and spend their evenings watching TV game shows, while out on the streets, the traditional Japan of lily-ponds and lanterns clashes uneasily with the high-tech commercialism of modern city life.
>
> Then he meets Sachiko. Locked into an arranged marriage with a corporate executive on a twelve-hour day, dreaming of America and in love with Western rock stars, she is in her way the essence of modern Japan. Through her, Iyer's affair with the idea of her country blossoms delicately into a romance of a special and very different kind.

There is nothing new about the bewildering mixture of ancient and modern; people were describing Japan in those terms a hundred years ago. But the new Japan of the late nineteenth century was seen as a stumbling imitation of what had been imported from the west, whereas today the new Japan seems to offer the west an image of the future: the glamour of its technology balances the glamour of its past. The Japanese woman has always been a focus for a certain kind of nostalgia. If women in kimono appear more often in guidebooks and brochures than in reality, it is because they enshrine an image of the dress, the manners, the accomplishments of the past, and Iyer's description of Sachiko pays this image its due. But the true excitement of the relationship, and of Japan, springs from the coexistence of these elements with the raw, vulgar modernity of the Walkman culture.

Like the Sister of Mercy in rustling silks, or the prostitute who is also a pious daughter, or the mousmé who is both innocent child and sexual adept, the Japanese woman is again presented as a combination of contradictory qualities. This is the heart of the western fantasy: beyond the nineteenth-century desire to resolve the antithesis between madonna and whore is the popular belief that in the east we can find escape from a way of thinking that divides the world into opposing categories. We are less likely now to talk in terms of madonnas and whores, but the pattern persists, translated into the tension between traditional and modern, the claims of the past and the claims of the future. The girl from *Gone with the Wind* belongs to the old world, the orgasmic girl who takes the sexual lead to the new; the girl in traditional geisha costume who studies nōh dancing and ikebana belongs to the old world, the girl who blows bubble-gum and stars in a computer game to the new. In the west they would be different people with different kinds of social and moral allegiance. In Japan, it seems, the conflict can be resolved into oriental harmony.

This is the focus of Iyer's book. The jacket design shows a Japanese woman whose clothes, hair and posture suggest an eighteenth-century woodcut, but she has sunglasses and Walkman earphones, and a jet plane roars into the picture overhead. It is this strange conjunction which is the real source of romance. Though the story is concerned with Sachiko's difficulties in adjusting to the pressures of the new Japan, it presents her as an intriguing and unwestern blend of the traditional and the modern. She and Hana Chan are sisters under the skin, images of the combination of technological adventure and cultural conservatism which now constitutes Japan's main attraction for the west. With some justification *Time* magazine referred to Iyer's book as 'a *Madame Butterfly* for the 90s'.[23]

PART IV

Samurai

15. A Streak of Violence

'I think there is no country in the world', wrote Kazantzakis in 1935, 'that reminds me more than Japan of what ancient Greece might have been in its most shining moments. [...] This is one of the faces of Japan – the face of beauty. But it has another face, austere, hard, determined.'[1] By the 1940s the features of this other face had grown more familiar and more brutal. There is a scene in *The Wind Cannot Read* in which the hero looks idly through some books at a kiosk in Bombay:

> Then I saw one called *Two Faces of Japan*, on which the cruel male face stood out in front of a faint drawing of a kneeling woman. The woman was pretty. I looked inside the book, and there were a great many more pictures of pretty, laughing Japanese girls. Facing each there was a picture of steel-helmeted Japanese youths, or a threatening display of bayonets, or a Japanese atrocity in China.[2]

He puts the book back and takes another from the shelf. Entitled *The Three Bamboos*, it is dedicated 'To the gentle, self-effacing, and long-suffering mothers of the cruellest, most arrogant and treacherous sons who walk this earth – to the women of Japan – who will, as always, reap the richest harvest of suffering as their reward'.[3] On one side, the kneeling woman, on the other, the steel-helmeted youth; on one side, the gentle mother, on the other, the cruel and treacherous son.

159

Mason offers a convenient summary of what happens when we turn from the female stereotype to the male.

'Name a Japanese and you name an executioner,' wrote Bernardino de Avila Girón, a Spanish trader who reached the country towards the end of the sixteenth century. He gives us one of our first portraits of the two-sworded man who became, even in the west, the epitome of the warrior:

> They use scimitars, called *katana*, which have a blade about six spans long and a hilt of one span, or longer if need be; and if the blade is longer, so must also be the hilt in due proportion. They wield this weapon with both hands, raising it above the head and waiting for a suitable opportunity before inflicting a wound with a downward stroke of the cutting edge. They usually carry in their sashes a small *katana*, the length of the blade being about one span and two, four or six fingers. They call this a *wakizashi* and they use it for stabbing. When they go out, they gird themselves with both weapons and strut around as arrogantly as if they were the only people in the world.[4]

By the time Avila was writing, the west was already beginning to structure its perceptions of Japan on an opposition between the world of the women ('as pious as their menfolk are cruel', says Avila) and the world of the warrior. Alongside praise of Japanese women and admiration for the politeness, cleanliness and intelligence of Japanese people in general, there are recurrent references to the cruel ways and disregard for life associated with the figure of the samurai.

John Saris describes his uncomfortable entry into the town of Suruga past the bodies of crucified malefactors. He was less troubled by the recognisable corpses than by the left-over bits of others on which samurai had tested their swords. This was a practice much commented on by westerners. In the 1590s Francesco Carletti witnessed the fate of one criminal whose wretched body was 'chopped into mincemeat, being left there as food for the dogs and the birds'. The casualness of the business demonstrated a cast of mind which seemed to him totally different from that of people in the west: 'And this brings to an end their sport of proving their swords, which among us would be reckoned an impiety fit to make one's hair stand on end, to use a common expression. But with them the whole thing is carried out as a pastime, without turning a hair...'[5]

Killing is as natural to them as breathing. The samurai who can't take a Sunday stroll without slicing off someone's head has become part of our mythology. In Chapter One of *Shogun* Blackthorne meets his first Japanese, a young samurai named Omi. The interview goes satisfactorily until Omi brings it to an end, at which point one of the bystanders fails to bow:

> With blinding speed the killing sword made a hissing silver arc and the man's head toppled off his shoulders and a fountain of blood sprayed the earth. The body rippled a few times and was still. Involuntarily, the priest had backed off a pace. No one else in the street had moved a muscle. Their heads remained low and motionless. Blackthorne was rigid, in shock.
>
> Omi put his foot carelessly on the corpse. '*Ikinasai!*' he said, motioning them away.

Left in the empty street, Omi begins to laugh uproariously: 'When his laughter exhausted, he grasped his sword with both hands and began to hack the body methodically into small pieces.'[6]

Across the centuries between Carletti and Clavell, the figure of the ruthless samurai has sometimes been prominent, sometimes not, but he has always been there in the background to give menacing reality to the unease inspired by a people who seem moved by impulses so unlike our own. Even the Victorians, in spite of their generally picturesque version of Japan, were never allowed to put the possibility of violence quite out of mind. 'The Japanese are a proud and warlike race,' wrote Alexander Knox in 1852. 'They are careless of danger and indifferent to life.'[7] There were enough incidents in the ensuing years to keep this warning fresh. Elements of the samurai class were strongly opposed to the reopening of Japan, and the sense of danger in the early years was ever-present. Satow bought a revolver on his arrival: 'The trade to Japan in these weapons must have been very great in these days, as everyone wore a pistol whenever he ventured beyond the limits of the foreign settlement, and constantly slept with one under his pillow.'[8]

This is confirmed by Mitford, who says that he 'never wrote a note without having a revolver on the table, and never went to bed without a Spencer rifle and bayonet at my hand'.[9]

In the first two decades of renewed contact, episodes such as the attack on the British minister, Sir Harry Parkes, in Kyoto, and the murder of an English merchant named Richardson while he was riding near Yokohama added to the nervousness of westerners, who frequently encountered the sort of figures Avila had written about two and a half centuries earlier. Fonblanque remarks on how samurai in Edo 'swaggered and sometimes reeled by us with a defiant and insolent air', and ten years later, according to Baron de Hübner, one of the typical sights of the city was still 'samurai, with their two sabres passed horizontally into their waistbands, and their arms resting fiercely on their haunches, like men who feel and know that every one will get out of their way to give them a free passage'. These are the 'swaggering, blustering bullies' on whom Rutherford Alcock had commented, arrogant but also frightening because they seemed as willing to die as to kill.[10]

After the Meiji restoration (1868) we begin to hear less of them; their caste was effectively abolished by the reforms of the 1870s. In 1877 a last-ditch attempt was made by former samurai of the Satsuma province to halt the process of change, but their defeat by the government's new conscript army marked the end of any serious challenge to Meiji reforms. As the political temperature cooled, the picturesque Japan of tea-houses and geisha became the standard western image. Those few writers who wanted to draw attention to more hostile aspects of Japan could do so only in terms of metaphors of unmasking: what was threatening was out of sight, beneath the surface. 'Under the obsequious friendliness of this people,' wrote Loti, 'there is an old fund of hatred towards us who come from Europe.'[11] A few years later Kipling made a similar observation, though without Loti's tinge of paranoia: 'The Japanese, in common with the rest of the East, have a strain of blood-thirstiness in their compositions. It is very carefully veiled now, but some of Hokusai's pictures show it, and show that not long ago the people revelled in its outward expression.'[12]

In other words, Japan is an oriental nation, and what she has in common with other orientals is natural savagery. It is 'in their compositions', part of their make-up. Rana Kabbani has observed that there are two central elements in Europe's depiction of the Other: 'The first is the insistent claim that the East was a place of lascivious sensuality, and the second that it was a realm characterised by inherent violence.'[13] In the case of Japan, the samurai was an obvious focus for the second of these, just as the geisha was for the first. Writing about the attack on Sir Harry Parkes, de Hübner comments, 'This fanaticism, which is essentially political and not religious, seems to come out of the very bowels of the nation.' This belief has stayed with us, confirming our sense that the violence of the west is of a different kind. Whereas we resort to arms as a rational response to circumstance, the Japanese do it as an expression of their natural savagery. 'Violence is the eternal undertone of Japanese life,' claims Simon Harcourt-Smith in his wartime study of events in Asia. 'Beneath the elaborate structure of bows and nervous giggles there simmers a Mount Fuji of dark frenzy. Little sense of humour or humanity restrains it; [...] with the Japanese, viol-ence is not, as it is for us, a lamentable interruption of life's ordinary rhythm; for them it is a harmonic of that rhythm itself.' When James Bond speaks knowledgeably of 'the streak of viol-ence that seems to run all through the history of Japan', the reader is unlikely to ask how many countries do not have a streak of violence running through their history.[14]

For a fictional secret agent to rehearse these clichés is one thing, for an American president to do the same is more worry-ing, particularly when he has just got hold of the atomic bomb. An entry in Truman's wartime diary notes with regret that it will be necessary to use the bomb on the Japanese because they are 'savages, ruthless, merciless, and fanatic'.[15]

At the end of the twentieth century we're still using the same terms of reference – Japan's innate aggression and the west's rational response to it – as a way of interpreting the

163

complexities of modern international relations. Peregrine Hodson quotes a friend's explanation of Japan's economic advance:

> You know how it is. You get the other guy before he gets you. You go for the kill. They learn it at school, practising kendo. Maybe it's genetic: all those rice merchants in the eighteenth century, marrying into the Samurai families – what do you get? Warrior merchants. That's what we're up against. It's them or us.[16]

It's in their genes, part of their heredity, part of their culture. This sort of determinism is traditional orientalist doctrine. Eighty years earlier Homer Lea made much the same point in *The Valor of Ignorance* (1909), which was reissued to great acclaim during the Second World War. The way of the samurai, he argued, is at the core of the Japanese character, preserved and inculcated by the country's social institutions: 'In all phases of national life Japan is pregnant with the spirit of militarism.' This was the spectre that prompted Lothrop Stoddard's warnings, published when America was working itself up to pass the Immigration Acts that would prohibit Japanese entry. 'The longing to hack a path to greatness by the samurai sword', he wrote in *The Rising Tide of Color* (1920), 'lurks ever in the back of Japanese minds.'[17]

If war is the expression of Japan's true nature, then indeed it follows that all the agreeable trappings of civilisation, all the politeness and friendliness, are no more than a mask. In *The Wind Cannot Read* Mason's narrator sees a poster that has been displayed throughout India: 'It was the face of a Japanese – a smiling and not unpleasant face. But this face was only a mask. Beneath it, teeth bared but not smiling, eyes narrowed and cruel, was the real face of yellow flesh; and beside it the caption: "Beware the mask of friendship – it may hide Japanese treachery."'[18]

By the end of the Second World War Loti's image of a Japan that conceals its aggression under a cloak of friendliness was an accepted way of representing Japanese hostility. Avila's 'Name a Japanese and you name an executioner' is matched three and a half centuries later by the old Japan hand in *You Only Live Twice* who tells Bond, 'Scratch a Japanese and you'll find a *samurai*'. The only change is that there's now a veneer between the Japanese and the executioner. This image has wide currency, even in more serious attempts to come to terms with Japanese culture. Benedict's genuine respect for the Japanese does not prevent her from reproducing it. The Japanese character, she suggests, is built up by a process of lacquering; and when she elaborates, it becomes clear that what the lacquering covers is the same underlying aggression:

> The contradictions in Japanese male behaviour which are so conspicuous to Westerners are made possible by the discontinuity of their upbringing, which leaves in their consciousness, even after all the 'lacquering' they undergo, the deep imprint of a time when they were like little gods in their little world, when they were free to gratify even aggressions, and when all satisfactions seemed possible.[19]

The popularity of this image results from the bewildering Japanese onslaught in the Second World War. Above all, the west needed to explain to itself how it had got things so wrong, how the neat-handed, polite little people that live among flowers and babies had turned into a race of fanatical murderers bent on conquering the world. The simple point that the west had constructed its own image of Japan and then steadfastly refused to look at any evidence that contradicted it was obviously unpalatable. Instead, we fell back on the numerous images of a cloak that had been thrown off, a mask that had been set aside, a veneer that had been stripped away, a lacquer surface that had cracked open.

This explanation had the effect of attributing our costly mistake not to failure of perception on our part but to the exercise of oriental cunning on theirs. They had been doubly deceitful, because the mask of friendliness was formed by that 'veneer' of westernisation which Japan had acquired since the mid-nineteenth century. It wasn't just that they had pretended to be something they weren't, they had pretended to be like *us*. Since the 1870s they had been adopting our democratic institutions and our industrial goals, making use of our technological advances, wearing, quite literally, western clothes; then suddenly they had shed these clothes like an old snake skin and shown themselves still to be primitive oriental savages.

Clothes are an important metaphor. The idea that the *real* Japan is never far below the westernised (i.e., civilised) exterior is presented in the image of the Japanese whose western clothes are no more than a flimsy covering over the dangerous reality. 'It is curious to think', remarks Kipling, 'that any one of the dapper little men with top-hats and reticules who have a Constitution of their own, may, in time of mental stress, strip to the waist, shake their hair over their brows, and, after prayer, rip themselves open.'[20] The appearance of western normality cannot be trusted. 'Underneath the stiff collars and striped pants in the government departments,' Bond is warned, 'there's still plenty of the old *samurai* tucked away.' The westerner who mistakes the outer show for the inner reality is heading for trouble – 'Just because people play baseball and wear bowler hats doesn't mean they're quote civilised unquote.'[21]

The single act that did more than any other to establish the image of Japanese duplicity was the attack on Pearl Harbor in December 1941. When Japan had used the same tactic in a surprise attack on the Russian fleet at Port Arthur in 1904, it had been hailed in the west as a brilliant military manoeuvre. 'There is nothing but admiration here for the decision and skill of the Japanese in their first attack on the Russian fleet,' wrote the New York correspondent of *The Times*, who went on to quote a couple of American newspapers. According to the *Evening Post*, 'the Japanese have begun the war with remarkable dash and enterprise. They have known where to strike and how to strike quickly.' Even more enthusiastic was the *Globe*: 'With a celerity and directness that raise still higher the Japanese reputation for gallantry, Japan has struck the first blow.'[22]

The response in 1941 was rather different. 'Amazement as much as fury was provoked in the Anglo-Saxon world by this blow,' wrote Harcourt-Smith. 'A public hardened to international wrong-doing could yet be dazed by this murderous perfidy.'[23] This was an accurate reflection of popular attitudes. 'Japan tears off the mask and turns the once Pacific ocean into a sea of blood,' declared the Pathé newsreel; 'American soldiers and sailors are struck down by the treacherous orientals before their country is at war.' John Dower tells us that in the wake of the attack 'the single word favoured above all others by Americans as best characterising the Japanese people was "treacherous".'[24]

Over the years Pearl Harbor has become an enduring reference point for Japanese untrustworthiness. The fiftieth anniversary was marked by rhetoric which suggested that in parts of America feelings have scarcely changed. 'If a next-door neighbour had raped and murdered our mother fifty years ago,' commented the historian of the Pearl Harbor Survivors' Association, 'would we be inviting him over now for brunch?'[25] In recent years the innate sneakiness of the oriental has been kept in the public mind by well-orchestrated complaints about underhand business practices and, at another level, by the teenage cult of the ninja, whose legendary stealth is an aspect of his Japanese heritage. In various forms, the suspicion persists that Japan's post-war friendliness is no more than a cloak for its evil designs.

Among the most sustained representations of this view is the thriller by Fred Hiatt, former Tokyo correspondent of the *Washington Post*. The hero of *The Secret Sun* is also an American correspondent in Tokyo. Faced with the inevitable anniversary article on Hiroshima, he decides to investigate his assistant's vague recollection that Japan had tried to develop a nuclear bomb during the war. What he discovers is that not only did the Japanese try to make a bomb but they continued the research afterwards in a remote underground complex. As well as developing nuclear weapons, they have successfully miniaturised them. ('But as you know, we are masters at miniaturisation,' one of the scientists tells the hero.) Worse, some of these miniature nuclear devices have been implanted in the computers, televisions, cars and VCRs which Japan exports to the west. America, meanwhile, has responded to the Japanese economic invasion by formulating a bill that allows for the expropriation of Japanese factories in the USA. If the president signs it, the Japanese will detonate one of their devices, destroying most of Detroit. The plot is foiled, but at the end of the novel we are left with the possibility that one or two of these devices may nonetheless have found their way to the west.

This is an updated version of the beast behind the mask. The dust-jacket's assertion that the hero and his assistant 'soon find themselves in a dark world of fanatical pride and ruthless patriotism hidden behind the smiles and bows and polite circumlocutions' rounds up the usual suspects with brisk economy: on the surface, smiles, bows and politeness; underneath, fanaticism and ruthlessness. The clichés are all in place. What they add up to is the prospect of another Pearl Harbor. While the Americans are lulled by protestations of friendship, the Japanese ready themselves to strike: 'And all the while their goons were at work, and the establishment was plotting its takeover of the world – well, maybe not the world, but whatever choice, juicy parts of it Japan felt like biting off – and smiling, smiling, smiling, our precious friendship with the American people...'[26]

The ending reverts to a classic horror-story formula. As with the undiscovered pods transported to a new town at the end of *The Invasion of the Body Snatchers* or the defeated vampire who has transmitted his vampirism before death to another human, the source of evil remains to threaten us. Within the harmless crates that bring our videos and televisions could be the seeds of our destruction. The innocent commercial face that Japan now turns towards the west may hide something even more deadly than the bombs which fell on Pearl Harbor.

The dust-jacket tells us that the novel 'reveals as much about Japan's present as it does about its past'. Its present? Its past? What is the book revealing? Such a question would not normally be necessary, but in the case of Japan the boundaries of fantasy are hard to define. At the start of *Japan Versus Europe* (1980), Endymion Wilkinson refers to a survey in 1978 of five countries in the European Community which revealed that half those questioned thought Japan possessed or intended to possess the atomic bomb. It's a statistic that makes one wonder about the reception of a book like *The Secret Sun*. Perhaps, after all, the Japanese have been making an atomic bomb. How can we tell? Who knows what goes on behind the smiles?

It's the old problem of the inscrutable oriental, which westerners encountered almost as soon as they got to Japan. 'Among the Japanese,' wrote Francisco Cabral, the Jesuit mission superior between 1570 and 1581, 'it is considered a matter of honour and wisdom not to disclose the inner self, to prevent anyone's reading therein. They are trained to this from childhood; they are educated to be inscrutable and false.'[27] The long period of exclusion only strengthened the west's sense of Japan as an enigma. At the beginning of the nineteenth century the Swiss historian Johannes von Mueller summed up the situation in three words: 'Japan remains locked.' His comment is quoted by Kurt Singer, who adds that since then this terse formula 'has only acquired a more disquieting significance. [...] The state of virtual closure has, in a deeper sense, not ended.'[28] What used to be a physical barrier is now a cultural one. On this point, at least, the view of Japanologists has always coincided with the popular image: the Japanese and their country are peculiarly impenetrable. This is what makes their smile so disconcerting. What in the west we like to think of as an expression of feeling is here a concealment of it. At the start of *You Only Live Twice* Tiger Tanaka challenges Bond to a game of Scissors, Paper, Stone: 'The big, creased brown face that Bond had come to know so well in the past month split expansively. The wide smile closed the almond eyes to slits – slits that glittered. Bond knew that smile. It wasn't a smile. It was a mask with a golden hole in it.'[29].

Towards the end of a programme in the BBC's *Assignment* series, a veteran of Pearl Harbor was asked what he thought of Japanese rearmament. It seemed to him, understandably enough, a dangerous business. He shook his head warily, 'You don't know what those ancient warlords are thinking.'

16. The Sadist

In general, we do not assume that torturers exemplify the characteristics of their race or nation. The Europeans who once broke malefactors upon the wheel or pulled out their entrails while they were still alive are thought of as products of their time rather than of their race. A personal taste for cruelty is normally attributed to the psychology of the individual rather than of the nation. But stereotypes are formed by making the individual stand for the general. If we've met only one Martian, his characteristics will be those of all Martians. The individual case is significant in proportion to the scarcity of other information. That a torturer is European tells you nothing about Europe; that he is Japanese tells you much about Japan.

And there are plenty of Japanese torturers. The image of the sadistic Jap, derived from a fusion of the savage and the sneaky, is mainly a twentieth-century creation, but not entirely. Francesco Carletti's account of the samurai hacking a dead body to pieces for 'sport' implies the important distinction between cruelty in the line of duty and cruelty for pleasure. Among us it would be a horror, 'but with them the whole thing is carried out as a pastime, without turning a hair'. The persecution of Christians from the end of the sixteenth century gave additional authority to the image of the cruel Japanese. Detailed descriptions make it clear that these were men who enjoyed their work.

By the time westerners forced their way back into Japan in the 1850s, the perspective had changed. The sadistic samurai makes little showing in the nineteenth-century. Sadism involves the exercise of power, and until well into the twentieth century popular images of the Japanese denied them power over anything more threatening than a paint-brush. Violent incidents like the hacking to death of Richardson tended to be seen as acts of fanaticism rather than sadism.

Just occasionally a hint of something else breaks the surface. In Kyoto de Hübner attended a banquet at which the principal dish was a large fish cut into slices while it was still alive. The idea was then, by applying a drop of vinegar to the eyes, to induce a convulsion in the fish that would pull the slices apart. De Hübner found it a 'cruel and disgusting spectacle', as did Christopher Dresser, who referred to it some years later as 'a refinement of barbaric cruelty... which contrasts strangely with the geniality and loving nature of the Japanese'.[1] Such comments were passing observations rather than a serious challenge to the image of the Japanese as a gentle and peace-loving people. Even when Japan became identified as a more aggressive nation in the wake of the Russo-Japanese war, there was generally a positive emphasis on its prowess rather than a negative one on its cruelty.

It is only when we come into conflict with the Japanese ourselves that we look for straws in the wind, and instances of domestic cruelty take on new significance. In a radio broadcast for the BBC a few weeks after Pearl Harbor, Tom Harrisson, founder of Mass Observation, talked of a Japanese he had encountered on an island in the Pacific before the war. Apart from demonstrating how the Japanese had captured Port Arthur, the man's chief occupation was hurting his cats:

> He gave them very little to eat, and his main pleasure in life was to put out a nice plate of food by the door and then hide behind the door with a big rasp-file in his hand. If any cat tried to get at the food, he would smack down on it with the file, but being careful to avoid hitting it on the head and so killing it. His cats were scarred from end to end where he had scored hits. They were wise to his idea of sport but they had to eat. They used to positively

hurl themselves to the food and away again. And this made it all
the more exciting for him, to see if he could slosh them before they
got away. Sometimes I wake up in the night dreaming about that
disgusting little Jap, with whom I was marooned in the hurricane
season.[2]

The Japanese who delights in torturing cats is a sign of things
to come. Early in 1942, he can be taken as a fair sample of his
race.

Few people under forty will have heard of *The Camp on Blood
Island*. It has sunk almost without trace, unacknowledged even
in the catalogue of the British Library. And yet in 1958, the year
of its publication, it went through nine printings, and is one of
the best-sellers mentioned by Ken Worpole in *Dockers and
Detectives* (1983), his study of popular reading. 'It is likely', he
says, 'that in the 1950s the most widely read books in Britain
were books that dealt with the experience of male combatants
in the Second World War.' He suggests that a score of paper-
backs on the subject constituted 'the staple reading diet of the
adult male British reading public, and, possibly, of a significant
proportion of the female reading public'.[3] Of the nineteen titles
he lists, four are concerned directly with Japan: *The Bridge on the
River Kwai, The Naked Island, The Knights of Bushido* and *The Camp
on Blood Island*. All deal with the experience of prisoners of war.
The Knights of Bushido is Lord Russell of Liverpool's compila-
tion of Japanese atrocities; *The Naked Island*, which has recently
been reissued, recounts Braddon's experiences after he was
made a prisoner in Malaya; and *The Bridge on the River Kwai*,
deservedly the most famous of the four, has the construction of
the Siam–Burma railway as its setting. Only *The Camp on Blood
Island* is unavailable, long out of print, long forgotten.

It was based on a film whose original screenplay by Val Guest
and J. M. White is in the British Film Archive. The story is set
in a prison camp in the Malayan jungle. It opens with Captain
Sakamura overseeing the execution of a young British officer
who has just dug his own grave. Sakamura is waiting to give
the signal. 'He permits himself a slight, sadistic smile of
triumph' – the moment has come. 'With a brutal swing he brings

the sword flashing down', and the rattle of a machine-gun dis-patches the young Briton. When Lambert, the senior British offi-cer, complains about the execution, Colonel Yamamitsu, commandant of both the men's and women's camps, spits in his face, then strides up and down the room, 'a tirade of Japanese coming from his ugly, uncultured mouth'. It emerges that the war has ended, but Yamamitsu doesn't know it. Lambert is try-ing to prevent him from finding out, because Yamamitsu has pledged to kill every man, woman and child in both camps if Japan loses. The British have no doubt he will keep his word, since he 'knows he's got nothing left to lose by perpetrating every form of sadism and murder'. Eventually, the prisoners rise against the Japanese and at heavy cost take over the camp.

The most striking aspect of the story to anyone reading it now is the relentless emphasis on the sadism of the Japanese. This is underlined by a succession of images, from the giggling guard who shoots the doctor in front of his wife to Yamamitsu who, in an act that conjures up the ghost of Captain Bligh, flogs a cap-tured American flier with a cat-o'-nine-tails. Sakamura is more refined than Yamamitsu but also more sadistic. He illustrates the barbarity of traditional Japanese 'civilisation'. After beating up the elderly colonial administrator who is a prisoner in the camp, he tells him with a laugh, 'Ancient Japanese sport – ju-jitsu . . . ' When more prisoners have been executed, he brings their identity discs to Lambert: 'Six prisoners die honourably. Heads cut off. This is Japanese chivalry.'

Apart from some minor changes to the plot, the novel pre-sents much the same picture as the film. Its cover shows a burly Japanese soldier, naked to the waist, sword raised high in both hands, about to behead a ragged prisoner who kneels in front of him. The paragraph on the first page which gives us the con-text of the story is a fair sample:

> Late in 1942 the little yellow men had escorted hundreds of men, women and children on to the island. Then they had beaten them and raped them while the prisoners, of all nations, had built their own camps. The men built one at the southern end of the island. The women theirs at the northern end. During the building the

nameless island had been named Blood Island. But to the Japanese it was the Island of Paradise. As well as the lush tropical foliage there was human entertainment. The guards never tired of savaging the inmates of the male compound, while those held in the female camp provided them with unlimited practice in fornicating. No Japanese could ask for more. Except, of course, a special execution, on a day that was too hot and too humid ...[4]

This is a book published more than twelve years after the end of the war. Altogether it went through eleven printings between January 1958 and September 1959; a new edition was published in October 1959 and reprinted four times over the next three years.

The ironic exposure of Japanese chivalry is emphasised in the title of another of the books on Worpole's list, Russell's *The Knights of Bushido*. This grim volume, published in the same year as *The Camp on Blood Island*, is an illustrated record of Japanese war crimes. Quite what purpose it was intended to serve, so long after the end of the war, is unclear. In a short preface the author writes of his 'regret that it has been necessary to include so much that is unpleasant', but assures us that 'for every revolting incident which has been described, a hundred have been omitted'. Through the following pages atrocity is piled upon atrocity, from the Rape of Nanking to the closing days of the war. The author rarely flinches: 'Despite their horror,' he tells us, before embarking on another account of mangled bodies and mutilated genitals, 'the details are given here to illustrate the devilish sadism to which the Japanese troops sometimes gave way.' What we are told renders what is left untold even more horrifying: 'Many of the coolies of both sexes and of all ages were also subjected to obscene brutalities, which cannot be described here, to gratify the perverted sadism of their captors.'[5]

Towards the end of this record of inhumanity, a chapter entitled 'Cannibalism, Vivisection and Mutilation' turns to 'a particularly disgusting aspect of Japanese savagery'. The extent to which cannibalism was practised is open to debate, but its usefulness in branding someone as beyond the pale is unquestionable.[6] In *The Naked Island* Braddon notes the moral strength of the British in contrast with the Japanese, who 'frequently resorted to cannibalism' in New Guinea.[7] There is, however, a difference between the cannibalism to which men are driven by hunger and the cannibalism which is a refinement of cruelty. Lord Russell makes it clear that Japanese cannibalism was by no means always a matter of necessity. 'Indeed, it was sometimes made into something of a festive occasion in the officers' mess. As has already been described, even admirals and generals took part in these festivities, and the flesh of murdered prisoners, or soup made from such flesh, was served to the other ranks.'[8]

Reading Russell's account, one is left in no doubt that a practice which would turn any civilised stomach could be regarded by high-ranking Japanese with chilling unconcern: 'Admiral Mori on his way back from the first party given by 307 Battalion, at which human flesh was served and eaten, discussed the matter with Major Matoba, and asked him whether he would be so kind as to bring along a little liver next time an enemy pilot was executed by 308 Battalion, which was under Matoba's command.'[9] The tone of bland social exchange marks the difference between their concept of normality and ours.

Such images have not disappeared. In *Rising Sun* the antipathy felt towards the Japanese by Detective Graham is partly explained by the fact that his uncle died at their hands during the war, probably one of a number of American soldiers who were killed in medical experiments. 'There were stories about the Japanese feeding their livers to subordinates as a joke, things like that,' Connor adds by way of explanation.[10] After this reminder, his pious declaration that these things are best forgotten rings a little hollow.

But in the context of Japanese sadism, cannibalism is a byway. The high road leads from figures like Captain Sakamura to the modern Japanese with whom Joe Joseph regales us. His chapter on education takes the reader into a world with more than a passing resemblance to the camp on Blood Island. There is the case of the girl in central Japan who tried to protest to her mother about a teacher who regularly beat and humiliated her. 'One day the mother and daughter were summoned to the school and the teacher took the girl into an adjoining room for a beating. The mother listened to the daughter's screams but would not enter the room.' The idea was to persuade the child that resistance was futile. Then there were the seven teachers who 'took two of their pupils off to a remote beach in southern Japan and buried them up to their necks for twenty minutes as a punishment'. Or the teacher who killed a pupil by trapping her head 'between the 500lb metal gate and a concrete gatepost'. He had slammed the gate shut on her 'to teach her a lesson for being a few seconds late for school'. Another story tells us of the headmaster of a private reform school who detained a couple of teenagers inside an airtight railway freight container: 'With temperatures outside topping 90°F, and temperatures inside the makeshift prison cell at least thirty degrees higher than that, the children died of heatstroke and acute dehydration. The fourteen-year-old boy and the sixteen-year-old girl, both handcuffed, had been locked up in the steel box for forty-four hours because they had been caught smoking.'[11] Much like the punishment meted out to Alec Guinness in *Bridge on the River Kwai*. Same old Japanese. Underneath the stiff collars and striped pants . . .

It's an easy tactic. The National Front newspaper used to run a column on the back page, Nightmare File, which consisted of a series of short items, culled, presumably, from local newspapers up and down the country, detailing bizarre delinquencies on the part of Africans and Asians: a Pakistani brandishing a three-foot snake had attacked two young women in Oldham, an Indian butcher in Stafford had been keeping human flesh on top of the fridge, a Buddhist monk was accused of raping a woman at knifepoint in Gravesend, a West Indian in Stepney had been masturbating in a parked car with a razor in his hand, and so on. The intention was to create an image of lunatic violence so alien to our concepts of normal behaviour that it would seem outrageous for these people to have a place in civilised society. The trick can work for anyone: it's a matter of stringing together atrocity stories, cutting away any explanatory context and leaving the one linking thread that holds them together. They were all done by blacks, by Jews, by Christians . . . by Japanese. No doubt there are many things wrong with Japanese education, but falling back on the sadistic prison-camp commandant turned schoolteacher is not the way to understand them.

It's worth staying with Joseph's book for a moment. Published in 1993 by Penguin, and written by a former Tokyo correspondent of *The Times*, *The Japanese* attracted generous critical attention. It is a measure of how far we remain in thrall to stereotypes that its tired clichés could pass muster as a study of modern Japan, one which takes us, in the words of the dust-jacket, 'on a rollercoaster ride through the life and times of a previously unfathomable people to show us the Japanese as we have never seen them before'. Except in a thousand other books, films, magazine articles and newspaper stories that set out 'to crack the mysteries of Japan'.

The game shows come in for their usual share of attention, particularly one called *Super People of the World*. According to Joseph, it's reckoned by its producers to be the most popular in Japan. 'In a typical scene from one of the shows, an Indian had his long, twisted fingernails cut for the first time in twenty-five years, for an undisclosed fee. As the last fingernail was clipped, he broke down and wept.' Just the sort of thing the Japanese love.

And they're unkind to animals as well: 'Some Japanese have their dogs' vocal chords cut or make their dogs wear anti-barking shock collars so that the animals do not disturb their neighbours.'[12] It might be interesting to know how many Japanese do this. Some Britons get their pleasure from watching dogs tear each other to pieces in organised fights; the rest of us don't.

Behind all our examples of Japanese inhumanity there is the shadow of Captain Sakamura, or someone like him. The war may not be mentioned, but it provides the reservoir of images on which we draw; and when occasion offers, its memories are resurrected with zest. HIROHITO'S THUGS CAUGHT BABIES ON THEIR BAYONETS is not a propaganda line from 1942 but a *Sun* headline from September 1988, at the time of the emperor's last illness. Quoting a 'top historian', the reporter detailed some of the atrocities committed by Japanese troops in Nanking: '. . . prisoners were "trussed up and used as live dummies for bayonet practice. Others were bound together, doused in petrol and burnt alive or slung on stakes and roasted; still others were buried up to their necks in sand and left to rot or have their skulls squashed by tanks." '[13]

The excuse for rehearsing these atrocities over fifty years later was to set the historical record straight about the emperor's part in the war; but in reality it was a question of touching base. In these days when the car in front is a Toyota, this sort of item keeps Japan in focus. After all, it's still the place where they bury schoolchildren up to their necks in sand, squash their skulls and give electric shocks to their dogs.

Westerners who collect evidence of Japanese sadism sometimes seem unnecessarily diligent. The possibility that the sadism might be partly our own is raised not simply by the graphic detail in which atrocity stories are relayed but by the way we respond to those aspects of Japanese culture that are thought to illustrate their sadism. The game show *Endurance* has had far wider currency in Britain than it ever did in Japan. In part this is explained by the glow of cultural superiority it gives us, but might it not also owe something to our enjoyment of precisely what we laugh at the Japanese for enjoying – the spectacle of a handful of apparent lunatics undergoing a series of sadistic tests of endurance?

Another instance is the British response to manga. One of our most fashionable imports from Japan at the moment, it seems to typify the strain of psychopathic violence which is 'the eternal undertone of Japanese life'. An article on the subject in the *Big Issue* exemplified the ambiguity of western responses.[14] 'Blood, guts and sex at breakneck pace', it began, 'are par for the course in Japan's latest cultural export – manga.' Meanwhile, anime, the feature-length animated version, 'presents viewers with the obsessions of post-war Japanese man – demons, robots and violent sex amid scenes of apocalypse':

> To western eyes, manga and anime certainly look violent, porno-graphic and misogynist. *Legend of the Overfiend* – which manga fans insist is an extreme example – includes a demon with a hun-dred penises raping a schoolgirl, and its sequel, *Legend of the Demon Womb*, features sexual acts with machines and monsters with oversized genitalia. It's a far cry from *Spiderman* and *The Beano*.
>
> In the West, comics are still regarded as kids' stuff or subvers-ive trash. But in Japan the reverse is true and manga, which trans-lates as 'irresponsible pictures', can be traced back to scrolls from the Middle Ages. The Japanese tradition of pictorial narrative remains strong to this day. Thousands of comics are read by every-one, from young children to professionals, and the number of female readers is almost as high as male. Manga is an integral part of Japanese culture . . .

In the west this sort of thing is marginal; in Japan it's part of the fabric of the culture. The argument has a familiar ring which might take us back to Harcourt-Smith's *Japanese Frenzy*, written in the grimmest days of the Second World War. For the Japanese, 'violence is not, as it is for us, a lamentable interruption of life's ordinary rhythm; for them it is a harmonic of that rhythm itself.'

Only in the final column of the article does attention shift to 'an element of the genre which is often overlooked – the magi-cal, lyrical animations, comedies and fantasies, which have no hint of a dark side'. Overlooked is right. That's the last we hear of it. The next sentence takes us back to the interesting stuff: 'Although such a small percentage focus on sexual abuse, it is films like *Legend of the Overfiend* that attract the most attention and become regarded as typical of manga and anime. The bot-tom line is that sex and violence sell. The latest hot release is . . .'

It's not hard to see why sexual violence comes to be regarded as typical of manga, since the article telling us that this accounts for only a small percentage of the total is itself almost entirely concerned with it. The Overfiend may be an extreme example, but he's the one chosen to illustrate the article; a striking pic-ture shows us the monster lying back while his penile tentacles entwine the body of a naked woman held aloft above him.

The main question here is not about how accurately this version of manga reflects Japanese culture, but about the way in which western responses are angled so that our complicity in the sexual violence largely disappears. It is the west that has selected this side of manga, but the emphasis is on what it reveals about Japan. The lurid illustration is seen as an example of what the Japanese like, not of what we like. A craze for these images may be 'sweeping the West', but this casts no shadow on our own culture, which remains anchored in the reassuring world of *Beano* and *Spiderman*, on the opposite side of the cultural fence from these products of the Japanese tradition.

One thing that western interest in manga brings to the fore is the sexual element in Japan's trail of violence. The Japanese male is not much associated with sex, since that would trespass on the westerner's fantasised rights over the Japanese woman, but when he does show any sexual inclinations they are usually perverse. A casual reference in the *Big Issue* article to 'the Japanese male's obsession with schoolgirls' knickers' is characteristic of the assumption that there is something more or less unsavoury about the sexuality of Japanese men. ('After the break we're off to Japan, where men drool over models of schoolgirls,' announces a breezy voice on late-night television.)[15] The narrator's girlfriend in *A Circle Round the Sun* draws the obvious conclusion from the popularity of manga: 'If Japanese men buy that sort of thing to look at on the train,' she asks, 'what's their attitude towards sex?'[16] In *Rising Sun* the American mistress of one of the Japanese characters begins to answer this, but falters into silence at the sheer difficulty of finding words for it: '"A lot of them, they are so polite, so correct, but when they get turned on, they have this ... this way ..."' She broke off, shaking her head. "They're strange people."'[17]

We're left to speculate what they get up to, but anyone who has seen a picture of the Overfiend will be able to guess at some suitably weird possibilities. 'These guys are known world-class perversion freaks,' as Detective Graham puts it in the film version of *Rising Sun*. Later, he and another cop look through the window of a luxurious room where the pampered son of a Japanese industrialist is reclining with two naked western women. In a scene that mimes Japan's cultural domination, he slowly picks a piece of sushi off the stomach of one of them, then licks saké from the nipples of the other. 'Plundering our natural resources,' mutters one of the cops. The humour has an edge of bitterness.

Sex and the oriental male have never added up to anything very romantic in western eyes. About a hundred years before *Rising Sun* another wave of anti-Japanese feeling, documented by Roger Daniels in *The Politics of Prejudice* (1966), had begun to gather force in America, and that too had called up the old stereotype of the lascivious oriental. In a speech in San Francisco in 1892 the leader of the California Workingmen's Party spoke of Japanese 'being brought here in count- less numbers', while the American tax-payer footed the bill for allowing 'fully developed men who know no morals but vice to sit beside our ... daughters [and] to debauch [and] to demoralise them'. Only a matter of time before they're licking saké off western nipples.

The same point was made a few years later by a leading anti- Japanese campaigner, Grove Johnson:

> I am responsible to the mothers and fathers of Sacramento County who have their little daughters sitting side by side with matured Japs, with their base minds, their lascivious thoughts, multiplied by their race and strengthened by their mode of life ... I have seen Japanese twenty-five years old sitting in the seats next to the pure maids of California. ... I shudder... to think of such a condition.[18]

It's not what they've actually done, it's what's going on in their minds, their thoughts – behind the mask. So polite, so correct, but when they get turned on... Once the mask is off, we are looking into the abyss.

The *Oxford English Dictionary*, even in its updated form, gives no definition of rape that quite corresponds to its use in what has become known to the west as the Rape of Nanking, the episode in which Japanese troops indulged in a frenzy of murder, pillage, rape and arson after entering the city in mid-December 1937. The meanings of plunder and devastation are clearly part of it, but so also is the meaning of sexual violation. As a symbol of the worst that Japan is capable of, the phrase combines the savage and the sexual in a way which reflects the atrocities committed there but which also crystallises a particular western perception about the nature of Japanese aggression. The bayonet of the Japanese soldier is a sexual implement as well as a military one; it is used for the pleasure it gives.

'What do we do with woman when we finished with her?' asks one of the soldiers in *The Camp on Blood Island:*

> Sakamura thought for a moment then said, 'You use her for bayonet practice.'
> 'Bayonet practice!' Nagasiki was delighted. He had never bayoneted anything, let alone a woman.[19]

The novel is free to treat the sexual element of Japanese sadism in more detail than the film. One of the guards in the women's camp has noticed Kate Keiller, the doctor's wife: 'He saw clearly the outline of her buttocks, and the sway of her hips and his eyes glinted. He had just arrived at the camp from Japan and he had never known a white woman.'[20] The glint in his eyes anticipates more than just a sexual encounter: 'The hut was set apart from the others, so nobody would hear her screams. And he would make her scream all right. ...'[21] As the most attractive of the women prisoners, Kate Keiller comes in for a lot of this. Sakamura too has his eye on her, though he wonders whether he may not have to kill her instead: 'If she had to die, he would behead her himself. The thought of cutting off such a pretty head sent a faint shiver of pleasure through his scrawny body.'[22] But what he really wants to do is save her for his enjoyment and execute another prisoner, a Chinese woman: 'He had already planned how she would die; he planned it with the consummate care of a chef preparing a banquet. She would be the centre piece in a dish of bloody perversion.'[23]

Like so many of the images attached to Japan, the sadistic Jap is a useful focus for feelings we wish to define as the opposite of our own. They are not, of course, which is why we're so fascinated by them. Sex and violence – violent sex and sexy violence, to use the phrase of one commentator on manga – are what sell, and they sell because we like them. When they come from Japan, we are doubly blessed. The association confirms our prejudices and excuses our indulgence; we can condemn while we enjoy.

17. Bushido

Comments from early European visitors about the cruelty and ruthlessness of Japanese men are matched by tributes to their bravery, their concern for honour and their fearlessness of death. Both Jesuits and traders repeatedly acknowledge these qualities – alongside the treacherous oriental with bared teeth and narrowed eyes stands the noble warrior.

The Victorians had little time for him. At first, the sword-wielding samurai was a source of unpredictable danger, an embodiment of fanaticism rather than chivalry; later, he faded to a picturesque memory of old Japan. Mitford's account of the *seppuku* of Taki Zenzaburo, who had given the order to open fire on the foreign settlement in Kobe, provides a rare glimpse of the samurai ideal.[1] Though the scene is alien, even barbaric, Mitford's language deliberately assimilates Taki to the ethos of the British gentleman. He was 'a stalwart man . . . with a noble air'; he mounted the raised floor 'slowly and with great dignity'; throughout the sickeningly painful operation 'he never moved a muscle of his face'; his remains are those of 'a brave and chivalrous man'. The *kaishaku*, who completes the ritual by beheading the condemned man, is not, Mitford insists, an executioner. 'The office is that of a gentleman', and their relationship is comparable to that between principal and second in a duel. Details such as this establish an area of common ground from which the reader can respond sympathetically to Taki's conduct.

No doubt it was for this reason that the account was quoted at length by Nitobe Inazo in the book which became the basis of western conceptions of the samurai. *Bushido: The Soul of Japan* was a phenomenal success. Published in 1899, it was into its tenth edition by 1905. Theodore Roosevelt distributed copies to his friends, and writers on Japan quickly turned it into a canonical text. Using parallels and analogies that drew in everyone from Plato to Tom Brown, Nitobe created an ideal Japanese warrior perfectly adapted for western consumption. Nitobe did not invent the institution of Bushido (as Basil Hall Chamberlain later argued), but he defined it for western audiences, transforming it into something that could be recognised and appreciated by people who had never set foot in Japan. The way of the warrior became synonymous with all the virtues – politeness, benevolence, loyalty, honour – that the author wished to claim for Japanese society at its best.

It is perhaps a mark of his skill that within a year or two Admiral Togo was fêted on the cover of the *Illustrated London News*. Indeed, the reporting of the war with Russia owed much to Nitobe's influence. The Japanese reputation for gallantry which the *Globe* thought enhanced by the attack on Port Arthur was an achievement of public relations as well as of military action. Successive editions of Nitobe's book promoted the image of the noble warrior with an effectiveness that made the experience of World War II even more of a shock. Those westerners who weren't thinking in terms of short-sighted midgets with buck teeth had a residual notion of Japanese chivalry that turned out to be equally wide of the mark. 'The code of Bushido isn't just a myth, you know,' argues the ineffectual old administrator in *The Camp on Blood Island*, to which Lambert replies: 'How does the code of Bushido measure up with camps like this?'

The Second World War could have been the end of the noble samurai. Chivalry had been notably absent from Japanese conduct and the apocalyptic fate of Hiroshima seemed to have turned the sword-bearing warrior into an anachronism. 'The atom bombs had one good result,' wrote D. J. Enright in *The World of Dew* (1955); 'they made the myth of the samurai, strutting about with his two feeble swords, look remarkably silly.'[2]

This sounds reasonable enough, but the samurai with his *katana* has refused to die. The significance of the sword is worth pausing over. On the one hand, it can serve to sharpen the edge of brutality in warfare. The bullet, in imagination at least, is clean by comparison with the sword. The beheading of the second batch of prisoners in *The Camp on Blood Island* is an escalation in the level of horror. To use the sword is to get close to the blood, to feed on the intimacy it brings to the act of killing. As Kurt Singer put it, 'In every type of man in whom the primitive "killer" is waiting there must be a preference for methods of fighting that allow him to see and feel the enemy dying under his hands.'[3] From a western perspective, this does much to explain Japanese fondness for the sword. Even in films and novels with a modern setting, the true Japanese will usually favour a sword, and western audiences have grown accustomed to seeing Japanese men in dark suits cutting down their enemies with a *katana*. It's part of their heritage, the line that runs from *Shogun* to the boardrooms of *The Miko*.

Ridley Scott's *Black Rain* gives the image a new spin by putting the villain on a motorbike. Having lured the American policeman through an Osaka shopping arcade, down a neon-lit escalator and into a deserted underground car-park, he beheads him in a climactic charge, his sword striking sparks from the stone floor as he rides towards the victim. It's a mixture of hi-tech setting and traditional violence which emphasises the sinister potential of the ultra-modern cityscape. There are no words from the Japanese killer. It is in the nature of things that he performs without emotion actions that would, in the words of Carletti, make one's hair stand on end. The use of the sword reveals both a primitive satisfaction in the act of killing and an inhuman detachment from the emotions that would normally accompany it.

On the other hand, there is a mythology of the swordsman which casts him in a quite different light, as the noble individual who acts with full knowledge and responsibility, exposing himself to retaliation in a way that the anonymous figure behind the gun does not. When the Spanish Jesuit Cosme de Torres arrived in Japan with Francis Xavier in 1549, he found that firearms were held in general contempt: 'They do not have any kind of guns because they declare that they are for cowards alone.'[4] Today, when killing has become a more mechanised business, the sword challenges the supremacy of the machine and reaffirms the role of the individual warrior. Lustbader's ninja books are gratifying partly because they embody this fantasy: with 'primitive' weapons, the lone individual, by his skill and resourcefulness, triumphs over everything modern technology can set against him. 'Even today,' reflects Nicholas Linnear, 'no arsenal in the world could claim such a magnificent weapon as the Japanese *katana*.'[5] This, of course, is part of a wider cultural debate about technology (identified with the west) versus traditional skills (identified with the east). When Indiana Jones casually shoots the sword-swirling Arab in *Raiders of the Lost Ark*, he puts the American side of the argument. But by that time the Vietnam war had done its bit to shake American confidence in the power of superior technology, and in doing so had provided fertile ground for the cult of martial arts and the mysteries of the ninja.

Enright's claim that the atom bomb has made the samurai look foolish is not borne out by experience; in practice, it has done the opposite. Far from becoming a figure of the past, the lone samurai has become a hero of our time. It started in 1954 with Kurosawa Akira's *The Seven Samurai*. Released in America as *The Magnificent Seven*, the film acquired its present title only in 1960 when John Sturges revised the story for a western version in which the samurai became American gunfighters. Predictably, what has appealed to post-war Europe and America is not the samurai as loyal retainer but the masterless ronin who goes wherever fate takes him and fights for private reasons of money, honour or revenge.

In 1961 Kurosawa's *Yojimbo* took the westernisation of the samurai a stage further by inspiring the run of spaghetti westerns starring Clint Eastwood which began with *A Fistful of Dollars*. Sergio Leone, the director, did more than just borrow the plot; Eastwood's wandering gunfighter is modelled on Mifune Toshiro's wandering samurai. In particular, he kills with the total impassivity that is recognised in the west as the hallmark of the samurai. The Japanese swordsman executes a few swift strokes which leave his enemies slaughtered around him, then carefully resheathes his sword without a muscle in his face having moved; Eastwood flips back his poncho, dispatches half a dozen villains in a burst of gunfire, then takes a puff at the cigar which is still in his mouth. With the lack of expression goes a tendency, especially in the later westerns, to choreograph the acts of violence. The stylised sequence that results – a killers' ballet – again owes much to western images of Japanese swordsmanship and the martial arts.

Impenetrable and imperturbable, the hero of these encounters has a Zen calm. His only obligation is to himself and to the perfection of his art. His isolation, like that of Alain Delon's professional hitman in *Le Samourai*, is a sign of his supremacy.[6] It is no surprise to find that Kevin Costner in *The Bodyguard* keeps a samurai sword on his wall; it marks him out as a warrior (rather than a hired thug) and as a man dedicated to perfecting his skills. It signals also a certain asceticism; a fighter with a Japanese sword on his wall is unlikely to drink, smoke or even smile very much. While the rest of us are having breakfast, he will be engaged in a solitary exercise routine or sitting cross-legged on the floor, with calm face, concentrating his energies for the next battle. There is something inhuman about the perfect warrior, and in this he is linked to the other hero-killers of our time, the Robocops and Terminators and Universal Soldiers. Nonetheless, he *is* human, and that's what makes him different. Where killing is for the most part done by remote control, the samurai has reacquired his title to nobility.

Together with supreme skill, he brings two other qualities that have made him an attractive figure for the west. His impassivity is not just a symptom of his carelessness of life, it is a mark of his spiritual and moral security. The skills of the warrior are underpinned by a code of ethics which is harsh but reassuring. In a world where most people are torn by conflicting claims and beset by moral uncertainty, the warrior walks a straight line. When Steve McQueen tries to discourage the young would-be gunfighter in *The Magnificent Seven* with a list of the sacrifices involved – 'Home: none. Wife: none. Kids: none. Prospects: zero', Yul Brynner supplies the other half of the equation – 'Places you're tied down to: none. People with a hold on you: none. Men you step aside for: none.' There is a nostalgia for this simple arithmetic and the straightforward code of honour that goes with it which grows stronger as confidence in the laws of society wanes.

The closed world of the Japanese gangster is often portrayed as having a moral structure which society lacks. 'One hundred years ago they were called samurai,' claims the cover of Leonard Schroder's *The Yakuza* (1975). Pollack's film, on which the book was based, shows Robert Mitchum not just as a warrior but as a man who has learned to accept the warrior's obligations. By cutting a joint from his finger at the end of the film, he earns the respect of his Japanese enemy-friend. It is this, rather than his effectiveness as a killer, that finally establishes his credentials.

More recently, *American Yakuza* (1993) contrasted the values of a Japanese gangster clan with both the forces of social order, represented by the FBI, and the traditional criminal group, represented by the Mafia. 'Loyalty – you know, they understand that word,' says the hero, Nick Davis, to his FBI colleague. United by this loyalty, the yakuza offer Davis the family he had never known. Towards the end of the film most of the yakuza are murdered by the Mafia with the complicity of the FBI. 'The Japanese', says the Mafia boss, in a speech that points up the corruption of western values, 'have always been a strong and cunning people, but tonight we've proved that American drive and know-how is still number one.' That's before the one surviving Japanese and the American hero return to take their revenge – the American with his gun, the Japanese with his sword.

The dedication of the samurai and the straightness of his

moral path give him a purity reflected in his spiritual poise. Raymond Hicks, the central figure of Robert Stone's *Dog Soldiers* (1973), is another warrior who uses the samurai as a point of reference. Hicks is a drug-dealer, a killer, and half an inch short of being a psychopath, but he is also the Lone Ranger, fighting single-handed against the forces of evil. In an America that has been warped by the massive insanity of the Vietnam war, he relies on what he has learned from 'his close and respectful study of Japanese culture' while living in Japan:

> He had brought a Japanese woman home with him, and he had come, during his years as a professional marine, to think of himself as a kind of samurai. Although he had never approached satori, he was a student of Zen and he had once had a master, a German who could read the texts and was said to be a roshi. Even dealing, he endeavoured to maintain a spiritual life.[7]

To become a warrior one must study more than the skills of combat. Zen is shorthand for a spiritual dimension the west too often neglects. There is a recurring narrative in which the impatient westerner is led to understand that the practical side of his enterprise is only part of it; success or failure will depend on his spiritual outlook. He must learn reverence for the ways of the east. The success of the Karate Kid films has been built on repeating this formula over and over again. The impulsive American youth has to practise his karate, but more importantly he has to develop the right state of mind. In *Karate Kid III*, while the villains prepare for the climactic tournament by smashing blocks of wood and hitting each other, the hero and his Japanese master are alone on the shore, the ocean spray rising behind them, as they go through a series of elegant, balletic movements, silhouetted against the sky. They are not even facing each other; this is all about *personal* equilibrium.

In contrast to the headstrong boy, his master, old Mr Miyage, is unruffled by anything that happens. His only passion is for his bonsai trees. In linking the supreme warrior with one of the traditional arts of Japan, the film again follows an established pattern. (The *katana* itself, though it can be an instrument of brutality, can also, like the sword which Sato gave to Yeats, be 'a changeless work of art'.) The flowers that puzzled E. B. Sledge in the photographs of Japanese soldiers (see p.101) reflect an association between the samurai and the aesthete which in its tainted form produces a figure like Yabu, the sadistic aesthete in *Shogun*, but which also emphasises a disinterested poetry in the way of the warrior. 'To the Japanese,' wrote Singer, 'the true character of the samurai is expressed in the cherry-blossoms; which suddenly open under the morning sun and as suddenly fall to the ground when shaken by the winds of spring.'[8] The same connection was the subject of Alfred Noyes's 'A Knight of Old Japan'. Initially the young, untried samurai disdains thoughts of the cherry blossom, but in the next stanza we see him returned from the battle: 'A mail-clad warrior watched each delicate flower / Close in that cloud of beauty against the West.'

The conviction that the true Japanese warrior was as much concerned with poetry as with battle is again derived mainly from Nitobe, whose *Bushido* deliberately grafted the ethic of the warrior onto the contemporary image of aesthetic Japan. The first words of the book set the tone: 'Chivalry is a flower no less indigenous to the soil of Japan than its emblem, the cherry blossom.' And, sure enough, embossed on the cover of my 1905 edition from Putnam's is a sprig of cherry blossom against a red sun.

All this may well have had little to do with reality. In a lecture to the British Association for Japanese Studies Marie Conte-Helm quotes F. T. Jane's book, *The Imperial Japanese Navy* (1904):

> Art books tell us of Japanese art instinct, of their feeling for decorative art, and so forth. Japanese artists may possess, or have possessed, this feeling, but it is conspicuous for its absence in Japanese naval officers, who are as 'Philistine' as British officers – if possible, more so. The decorative art that their nation is supposed to live for they cordially despise.[9]

We're a long way here from the poetic paladins of *Bushido*. Nonetheless, Nitobe's vision of the ideal samurai proved to have remarkable staying power. Mr Miyage's bonsai are another tribute to it.

The only surprising thing about the Karate Kid films, apart from their popularity, is the genial view they present of Japanese influence on the young American hero. Released between 1984 and 1989, they have a notably pacific tone; the oriental wisdom Miyage dispenses in a flow of sage axioms is all about restraint, tranquillity and spiritual peace. In other words, he represents very much the Japan of twenty or thirty years earlier, when Alan Watts was passing on Zen to the masses and Gary Snyder was setting off to study in the temples of Kyoto.

Since then, the dominant image of Japan in American culture has changed, calling into question the pacifist message sent out each year by the anniversaries of Hiroshima and Nagasaki. For just on half a century the memory of the atom bombs has guaranteed Japan's status as a country of peace. There, in the middle of Hiroshima, at what was the epicentre of the blast, are the Peace Memorial Park, the Peace Memorial Hall, the Peace Memorial Museum and the World Peace Memorial Cathedral. The Japanese sage who speaks of the need for restraint, for contemplation, for the mastery of aggression, speaks with the authority of these monuments. His serenity has been hard earned, and the Japanese Constitution has enshrined the nation's desire for continuing peace in Article 9, which states that 'the Japanese people forever renounce war'.

Against this background, the image of the bonsai-loving samurai whose strength was as much spiritual as martial could flourish; but recently there have been unmistakable moves to reposition Japan. The hero of *The Secret Sun* reflects sourly on the moral capital the Japanese have gained from the atom bomb: 'Japanese texts on World War II tended to focus on the victims of Hiroshima and Nagasaki, casting the Americans as monsters and jumping quickly over minor incidents like Pearl Harbor. If Japan had been trying to get the bomb too, it would shine a different light on their moral innocence, he thought.'

The appeal of this idea is that it seems to make the bombing of Hiroshima morally neutral. Later, he imagines a possible newspaper lead: 'If the Japanese generals had had their way, the world might be commemorating the horror of Seattle today instead of marking the anniversary of the inferno of Hiroshima.'[10] In the event, it turns out that under all the smiling talk of peace they really were trying to get the bomb. So much for cherry blossom and bonsai.

In March 1994 the BBC showed a documentary on Japanese rearmament. ('*Assignment* asks if Japan's growing thirst for power and influence can be contained.') The title, 'Keeping the Cork in the Bottle', provided the viewer with a guiding metaphor of oriental genii waiting to burst upon the world. However balanced the programme tried to be after that, there was no escaping the gravitational pull of the old stereotypes. 'Bushido – the way of the samurai warrior – demands that the body is hardened by exercising in harsh, adverse conditions,' explained the reporter, as we saw a handful of swimmers in the snow-chilled waters of mid-winter. 'Today Bushido inspires a devotion to punishing ordeals like this.' It all ties in – the fanatical swimmers (close kin to the *Endurance* freaks), the code of the samurai, the threat of another war. As it happens, people do much the same on England's Brighton beach in the middle of winter, but that's not usually put down to Bushido. We have our own more generous stereotypes; the English, as everyone knows, are a nation of eccentric individualists.

There is little doubt that we have been carried back towards a more aggressive, threatening version of Japan, and with it a more negative version of the samurai, but this is not on the whole inspired by fears of Japan's military potential. If Mr Miyage, with his bonsai and his wispy spirituality, looks rather dated, it's because there have been changes of another kind. Signs of them were there by the end of the 1950s, when Robin Day held up the copied ball-bearings to Japan's foreign minister, but it was not until a decade later that the west really began to take stock of what was happening. A new breed of samurai had come on the scene.

18. Samurai in Suits

The fear that Japan's threat to the west might be economic rather than military has been around for at least a hundred years. In April 1895 Hearn visited the national exhibition in Kyoto. Though it was mainly concerned with industrial items, he found it 'nearly all delightful . . . because of the wondrous application of art to all varieties of production'. But not everyone viewed it in this light: 'Foreign merchants and keener observers than I find in it other and sinister meaning – the most formidable menace to Occidental trade and industry ever made by the Orient.'[1] He quotes a report from *The Times*, which talks, in tones that have since become familiar, of 'the Japanese invasion of Lancashire'. Later in the same book Hearn gives a shrewd analysis of how the Japanese are reclaiming their country from foreigners by keen competition. Everything the westerner needs, from soap and shoes to wine and cigars, can be provided more cheaply by local Japanese importers and manufacturers. Gradually, the foreign suppliers who have set up shop in the Treaty ports are being forced out of business.

More than this, the Japanese are taking over those services which in other parts of the east were an exclusively western preserve – even a foreign doctor now finds it hard to make a living. It's the same problem that we noted in the first chapter: the Japanese have never been willing to accept their status as orientals, with all the limits on their behaviour which that definition imposes. When Kipling visits Osaka, he is frankly unsettled to find the inhabitants preoccupied with the cherry blossom: 'The men and women were obviously admiring the view. It is an astounding thing to see an Oriental so engaged; it is as though he had stolen something from a *sahib*.'[2]

This sense that the Japanese have a way of trespassing on ground properly reserved for the white man permeates discussion of Japan's economic encroachments in the west. On the Pacific coast of America they soon began to compete with local suppliers, and by the end of the nineteenth century demands were growing for their exclusion. In an article for the *Annals of the American Academy of Political and Social Science* Chester H. Powell, editor of the *Fresno Republican*, reflected on their unsatisfactoriness in comparison with the Chinese: '. . . we find the Chinese fitting much better than the Japanese into the status which the white American prefers them both to occupy – that of biped domestic animals in the white man's service'. He allows that they are a delightfully polite and genial people', but they have no sense of their place. Unlike the Chinese, who readily accept the ghettos in which they are expected to live, 'the Japanese do not confine themselves to "Japtown", nor permit the white man to determine the limits of their residence. They buy up town and country property, and wherever they settle the white man moves out.' The problem is summed up in the same volume by a San Francisco journalist, Sidney G. P. Coryn: 'The Chinaman is entirely content to do those kinds of labor that the white man shrinks from; the Japanese wishes to meet the white man on his own ground, and to oust him from it.'[3]

Whenever Japan is perceived as an economic threat, we hear the same note. The California fruit grower who referred to the 'saucy, debonair Jap, who would like to do all his work in a white starched shirt with cuffs and white collar accompaniments' was merely expressing the general annoyance with an oriental nation that seemed dangerously inclined to give itself airs.[4] White collars one day, business suits the next. Give them half a chance and they'll be trying to buy the Rockefeller Center.

The fears voiced in Europe and America around the turn of the century were echoed in the late 1920s and early 1930s when economic depression increased western vulnerability, but, in spite of occasional awareness of her more aggressive military posture, Japan made little popular impact during these years. Only in the past quarter of a century has the image of her as economic invader caught the headlines. Invader rather than competitor: the imagery has a distinctly military character.

Just as the Japanese had concealed their designs in the years leading up to Pearl Harbor, so they retreated behind the same smiling mask after their defeat. In 1964 Fleming restated the classic image in *You Only Live Twice*, a book which already reflects British nervousness about the shifting balance of power. Bond's mission is to get hold of a new decoding device which the Japanese have developed under the guidance of the CIA. ('They've got the right mentality for finicky problems in letters and numbers.') Unfortunately, the Japanese don't think much of the British these days – they've given away their empire, bungled Suez and handed over their intelligence service to traitors. It's up to Bond to show Tiger Tanaka that the British are still worth something, and so persuade him to give them access to Japanese technology. The sense of Britain as suppliant to its defeated enemy makes Bond unusually sensitive, and when Tanaka paints a picture of Britain as a pitiful ruin, he reacts angrily: 'Balls to you, Tiger! And balls again! Just because you're a pack of militant potential murderers here, longing to get rid of your American masters and play at being *samurai* again, snarling behind your subservient smiles, you only judge people by your own jungle standards.'[5]

Back to the wartime stereotype: the inherent violence, the smiling mask, the jungle savage lurking behind it. Whatever their appearance, the Japanese are samurai in waiting. This was an image seized on by economic commentators. Much as the Kyoto exhibition had caused tremors of unease in 1895, the International Exhibition at Osaka flashed warnings across the world in 1970. *Time* magazine's cover story made the point in menacing detail:

The salesman is a more pallid – but also more successful – descendant of two other Japanese prototypes. One was the swashbuckling *wako*, or warrior-trader, who began plundering Asia as early as the fourteenth century. The second was the soldier bureaucrat who went to war a generation ago to develop a 'Greater East Asia Co-Prosperity Sphere', stretching from Manchuria to Burma. [. . .] Today the Japanese have come closer to establishing an informal Co-Prosperity Sphere than ever before. The difference is that the latter-day *wako* carries a *soboran* (abacus) instead of a sword and wears blue serge instead of the khaki of General Hideki Tojo's Imperial Army.[6]

Accompanying the article was a map, 'Japan's Reach', which shaded in the new 'Co-Prosperity Sphere'.

From this time on, when Japanese business practices are discussed, the figure of the samurai is never far away, whether one's reading Ezra Vogel or Eric Lustbader. Linnear gives his partner the sort of advice we've become accustomed to: 'The Japanese know that you never come to a negotiation showing your true nature. To deal effectively with you, they must find this out. It's called To Move the Shade. It's from the warrior Miyamoto Musashi's guide to strategy. He wrote it in 1645 but all good Japanese businessmen apply his principles to their business practices.'[7] It's a game of masks at which the Japanese are adept. Though they seem to accept the way things are, they still smart from their defeat in the Second World War and are looking to reassert themselves through their new source of power – modern technology. For years they have hidden the snarl behind the subservient smile, and now they are ready to bite.

This is the model for presenting the new antagonism to Japan. Nangi, the Japanese businessman in *The Miko*, had piloted the launch plane for one of the early kamikaze attacks. (Tanaka, we recall, had also trained as a kamikaze pilot.) At his first meeting with the Americans who want to merge with his company, he turns on them ('his eyes were glittering, as hard as obsidian') and reminds them of the past, revealing his need to compensate for the humiliation of the war: 'He rose up even straighter, an adder about to strike. "Times have indeed changed, as you yourself pointed out. We are no longer your vanquished foe, subject to the blind acceptance of your demands." '⁸

In the following volume Nangi is on the receiving end of similar sentiments from one of the members of Nami. (Nami is supposed to be a small group of powerful men with a controlling influence over Japan's social and economic policy – in other words, just the sort of organisation that nourishes western fears.) The days of being an underdog are over:

> 'You must understand, Nangi-san, that for a decade Nami has chafed beneath the harness the Americans – and, indeed, the world – have placed around our necks. Over and over we have been reminded that we are a defeated, an impoverished country. [. . .] Now the tables are turned, Nangi-san. Now it is we who are invading America, buying up real estate, record companies, banks, electronic businesses.'⁹

In *The Secret Sun* the plan to ship miniaturised atomic devices to the outside world has been inspired by the same resentments. 'These are angry people we are dealing with,' the hero is told, 'angry about losing the war, angry about being pushed around by big brother ever since.'¹⁰ The tendency to harbour long-standing grudges under a smiling exterior is an oriental characteristic that applies with special force to the Japanese; it is an aspect of their fanaticism. In spite of their aggressive modernity, they are also obsessed by the past, and their economic surge over the past thirty years has to be understood in these terms. What they could not do militarily, they are doing economically.

This is the core of western suspicions about Japan. At the end of *The Naked Island* Braddon speaks of the continuing conflict between east and west. The military defeat of Japan marks a pause in hostilities, but the real war, 'of Asia against the white man', still has ninety-five years to go. It's an idea that most educated westerners would dismiss as racist nonsense, and yet there is a strong element of it in recent attitudes to Japan's economic success. (Braddon himself has devoted a whole book to the subject.) The war with Germany ended in 1945, but in the case of Japan there is a recurring sense of unfinished business.

The economic struggle is another phase of the same war. In May 1971, in an article accompanying its cover headline, 'How to Cope with Japan's Business Invasion', *Time* quoted a member of the Nixon cabinet: 'The Japanese are still fighting the war, only now instead of a shooting war it is an economic war. Their immediate intention is to try to dominate the Pacific and then perhaps the world.'[11]

This set the tone for much of what was said about Japan's economic success over the next twenty years, and by the end of the 1980s it seemed to many people to have been justified by events. A couple of influential articles for the *Atlantic* by James Fallows in 1989 made the case that unless Japan could be contained, American ideals and interests would be in jeopardy.[12] Two years later his analysis was given massive popular endorsement by Michael Crichton's *Rising Sun*, a novel which pulls together several of the strands which form the image of the business samurai. Its thesis is bluntly stated by Senator Morton, who tells the hero, John Connor, 'We are at war with Japan'. It wasn't really necessary to tell Connor this; he himself had made the same point a hundred pages earlier – 'We are definitely at war with Japan' – confirming what Detective Graham had said two pages before that: 'This country is in a war and some people understand it, and some other people are siding with the enemy. Just like in World War II, some people were paid by Germany to promote Nazi propaganda.' And in case the point slides by us, the book's epigraph, billed as a 'Japanese motto', repeats it: 'Business is war'.[13]

The story (about the investigation of a murder in Nakamoto Tower – Los Angeles, not Tokyo) is less important than the setting, which presents us with an America largely owned and run by the Japanese. They've bought up the real estate and control the computer and TV market; they can bring pressure to bear on the newspapers and the universities; most of the big stores would go out of business without them; America is even dependent on them militarily. Nakamoto Tower is a state within a state. When Graham hears the elevator announcements in Japanese, he is outraged: 'If an elevator's going to talk, it should be English. This is still America.' Just. As he realises later, the Japanese own the US government as well – 'They're turning this country into another Japan.'[14]

It's a horrifying vision, but this new threat is not really so new. Eighty years earlier Sidney Coryn had looked around San Francisco and seen similar evidence:

> Japanese shoe repairing shops, for instance, are to be found dotted all over the city. Japanese laundries are nearly as numerous. There are hundreds of Japanese janitors, and Japanese house cleaners, while the invasion of other branches of activity is steady and persistent. Divisions of the city are becoming known as Japanese quarters, and Japanese stores in a chronic state of 'selling off' are to be found everywhere. All these things mean the dispossession of white men.[15]

Moreover, there is a suspicion that the cobblers are controlled by a Mr Big in Tokyo, who requires each of them to employ a Japanese apprentice who will in turn set up a shop and employ a Japanese apprentice who will in turn etc. As always, there is nothing random about these invasions; they are part of a grand strategy for domination, directed by some remote intelligence back in Tokyo, the Nami of the time.

The imagery of infiltration, invasion and conspiracy is exactly reproduced in *Rising Sun*; the only change is one of scale. Every way the investigators turn, they meet an impenetrable wall of Japanese influence. Luckily, Connor has lived in Japan and knows how to deal with its people; he charts his way through this strange society like a cowboy who can speak Apache. And like the old Red Indians, the Japanese are a sneaky enemy – bribery, fraud, blackmail and improper influence are standard methods of doing business. The opening scene in the film, after the credits, shows us the boardroom of Nakamoto Tower, where the Japanese are making a take-over bid for an American computer-chip company which will give them control of advanced military equipment. Unknown to the Americans, however, the room has been bugged, so that everything they say is relayed to the Japanese. This is much what one would expect from the people who brought us the Hitachi scandal in

1982 and the Toshiba scandal in 1987,[16] not to mention what happened in 1941. When Senator Morton declares that 'we are at war with Japan', Connor replies, 'And remember Pearl Harbor.'[17]

If it's a war, then it's one the west has been losing. From Impressionist paintings to Columbia Pictures, from Aquascutum to Intercontinental Hotels, the evidence of dispossession is all around. Even Turnberry golf course has been bought by them. And there are the increasingly visible Japanese themselves, whose omnipresent cameras now record our heritage with the acquisitive eye of a prospective purchaser. 'Do the Japanese celebrate Christmas?' asks the high-powered lawyer in Norman Jewison's *Other People's Money*. 'No,' her assistant replies, 'but I hear they're buying it.' In their admirably informative *Nippon: New Superpower*, William Horsley and Roger Buckley quote the Pontiac advertisement which came out in the wake of the deal that gave Mitsubishi a controlling interest in the Rockefeller Center: 'It's December, and the whole family's going to see the big Christmas Tree at Hirohito Center . . . Go on, keep buying Japanese cars.'[18]

How much further will we allow it to go? As the hero of *The Secret Sun* strolls through Ginza, the Americans he sees are representatives of a defeated nation: 'Occasionally he passed a bedraggled, beaten-down couple of American tourists in crushproof travelling raincoats, clutching each other as they disbelievingly converted yen price tags to dollars in their minds, looking for something, anything, that they could afford to bring home as a souvenir or present for the kids . . .'[19] Like ragged visitors from the third world, they press their faces against the shop windows and wonder at the prosperity of the new master race. 'Basically,' says the reporter in *Rising Sun*, '[the Japanese] treat us as an underdeveloped country.'[20] Even on their own turf Americans can be forced into second place. When *L. A. Law* deals with the case of an American who has been refused the kidney transplant she needs – 'a dying woman, two years on the waiting-list, suddenly pushed aside for a rich alien who can pay twice as much' – the rich alien is, inevitably, Japanese.

According to the preferred western version, it is Japan that has been unable to forget the thwarted ambitions of the Second World War and now seeks to realise them by other means, but there is at least as much evidence to suggest that it is Britain and America that find it difficult to forget the glory days of the last war. When it ended, Britain still had an empire and America had money to spend. In Hiatt's description of bedraggled couples on the Ginza there is palpable nostalgia for a time when the American tourist had the same kind of spending power as the Japanese tourist has now. To have been relegated to the status of an underdeveloped country is a reversal of the natural order of things which cries out for redress. The persistent imagery of warfare acts partly as a rallying cry but it also reformulates the situation in terms which favour our chances of ultimate victory. The war may begin with Pearl Harbor, but it ends with Hiroshima.

In this economic sequel to World War II, the forms of combat have, of course, changed. The most potent weapon in the new offensive is money. One of the fears about Japan in Peregrine Hodson's *A Circle Round the Sun* is voiced by a woman who lived there during the 1930s and sees a similar spiritual malaise overtaking the country now – 'something wrong with the national psyche'. It is a diagnosis confirmed by the man Hodson meets in a noodle shop: ' "Money is a sickness," he said, "people get it, then they die. Japan is sick." '[21] Where the Japan of the 1930s was driven towards conflict by fanatical militarism, the Japan of the present is being driven in the same direction by an equally fanatical obsession with money.

Crichton's vision of a foreign power which has bought massive influence over American life is paralleled by Joe Joseph's account of how Japanese money has reached its tentacles into the fabric of British life, from the university teachers and musicians who 'depend on Japanese boardrooms for their salaries' to the seaside landladies who are being told to provide green teabags and sachets of *miso* soup. 'When you play a round of golf at Turnberry or stay at an Intercontinental hotel or buy a few cases of some of France's ritzier clarets, you give your custom to Tokyo.' Cooks, architects, schoolteachers, museum curators have all felt the pressure of the yen: 'Today, a big chunk of Japan's cultural influence comes from the pages of a cheque book, with Britain begging for more.' And this is just the start:

> Britain provides an instructive example of Japan's influence on the world, even in those countries where its influence is barely acknowledged as obvious or intrusive, and certainly not as irksome enough for the locals to get upset or angry about. What has happened in Britain is either already being mirrored in other countries, or will be replicated as Japan's reach spreads.

It is basic to Joseph's analysis that forms of investment which in the case of, say, America would be seen as largely benign – the endowment of university chairs, the building of factories, the subsidising of orchestras – are assumed to be part of some overall strategy of domination. Today Britain, tomorrow the world.[22]

And in the front line are our golf courses. One of the lighter aspects of the whole business is the extent to which golf has become a focus for western resentments. The Japanese businessmen of *Rising Sun* conduct many of their sinister activities on the golf course, even trying to bribe the hero with membership of their club. Golf is one of the weapons of the business samurai, and the golf course is an open-air operations room.

In the late 1970s Hitachi wanted to open a TV factory in the north-east of England. A campaign that eventually killed the project was mounted by the television industry and the unions. It culminated in a programme on Granada TV that opened with a picture of a Japanese industrialist swinging a golf club, which faded into a samurai warrior wielding a sword.[23] The idea was reminiscent of a Pathé newsreel in December 1941 which declared in sombre tones, 'For many years Japan has had designs on the Kra isthmus', then cut from scenes of modern warfare to a figure in full samurai armour slashing at the map with his sword. Swords, guns, golf clubs – the weapons change, the enemy doesn't.

There is a special outrage at this oriental appropriation of the game which in England and America has been the preserve of the respectable middle class. Fortunately, the Japanese aren't very good at it; in fact, most of the time they don't get as far as playing it at all. The image of them flailing away at the driving range with a fanatical intensity that is hopelessly at odds with their lack of aptitude is one that offers comfort to the western sensibility. The venom we reserve for these specimens is expressed, predictably, by Joseph:

> As many as fifteen million Japanese – more than one in ten of the population – claim to be golfers, even though the closest most of them get to swinging a club is visiting their local driving range. These are honeycombs of cubicles in which golfers thrash practice balls to nowhere. They are built inside a vast wire or net cage, often on an office roof. Many are open all night to cater to the crowds who go to practise, practise, practise, even though many will grow wings and fly before they get on to a real golf-course.[24]

Little better than caged insects when you come down to it. They can buy our courses but they can't play the game. It's much the same as all the paintings they buy without being able to appreciate them.

If golf seems to play a surprisingly large part in modern images of the Japanese, it's because it acts as a focus for so many of our stereotypes. In Martin Cruz Smith's thriller *Red Square* the hero's investigation takes him to a golf range set up by Borya, one of the new breed of Russian entrepreneurs. The Japanese are there already, in a group of course: 'On the tees a tier overhead, the Japanese hit a unified salvo, followed by excited shouts of "Banzai!" Borya smiled and pointed his club up. "They fly from Tokyo to Hawaii for a weekend of golf. I have to throw them out at night." '[25] It's an insignificant passage, intended merely to add colour, but it casually reinforces a whole package of stereotypes – the fanatical samurai, the conformist group, the conspicuous spender, the comic alien. These images are so generally recognised and accepted that they can be presented, without context or explanation, as part of our cultural currency. In the end, our idea of Japan may have less to do with specific attempts to describe or analyse it than with the steady drip of incidental references like this, which take a particular view of the country and its culture for granted.

Borya's smile is standard issue in the west. We react to the Japanese with a derision that has been well honed. A recent study of British newspapers found that items about Japan very often focused on what were seen to be the comic aspects of the society and its people.[26] From the Victorians a certain humorous condescension was to be expected; on the part of late-twentieth-century Britain – crumbling, grubby and increasingly seen by visitors as a third-world country – it is less easy to understand. Perhaps the brutal Japanese guard whom Braddon and his fellow prisoners christened the Ice-Cream Man (see p. 22) could give us a clue. The clown may be a harmless figure of fun, but he may also be a threatening figure who has been turned into an object of laughter by way of defence. In the old Mystery Plays Satan was usually a clown, and there's more than a trace of this long tradition of jesting with the devil in recent images of Japan.

The newly rich Japanese who come to our country to look and buy are not the first; it's happened before, on a smaller scale. After the war it was the Americans, then the Arabs, now it's the turn of the Japanese. In each case Britain has managed to preserve its dignity, courting the new plutocrats with due servility while laughing up its sleeve at their excesses. From this point of view the Japanese are an easy mark, because there is a large store of images to call upon. The line of comic Japanese stretches back through *The Mikado* to the quaint officials with whom Oliphant found himself dealing in 1858.

In some respects little has changed. Speaking English is still something we do better than the Japanese, so their lamentable pronunciation diverts us in much the same way as it did the Victorians. But the laughter has a different pitch; what was an expression of security for the Victorians is now more often a symptom of the need for reassurance. Our comic parodies – the bowing and bespectacled businessman, the fanatical golfer, the over-zealous factory worker, the mass-produced tourist – are designed to cut the Japanese down to size. The satirist is attracted by their obsession with work, their perfectionism, their earnestness, their conformism. The factors that put us at

205

an economic disadvantage and pose the most fundamental questions about our own individualist society are precisely those which become the targets of our mirth.

Derision, then, does not preclude anxiety; it can be an expression of it. The fanaticism with which the Japanese seem to approach their sports may be laughable, but it also reflects the extent to which the samurai ethic has infected areas of everyday life. Baseball has gone the same way as golf. The Japanese, says Joseph, have 'reinvented it in their own image, investing it with the code of martial arts, the spirit of the samurai and the dawn-to-midnight work ethic of the corporation salaryman'. Most of what he says about baseball in modern Japan goes back many decades to a coach and journalist named Tobita Suishu, whose 'idea of training was other people's idea of a penal colony. He is particularly famous for his view that, "If the players do not try so hard as to vomit blood in practice, then they cannot hope to win games. One must suffer to be good." ' Tobita, it seems, 'liked to compare baseball to Bushido', and one of his disciples 'became famous for blurring the familiar distinction between training camp and an abattoir by forcing his players to sharpen their concentration by walking barefoot along the cutting edge of a samurai longsword'. Can we wonder that these people came up with the idea of kamikaze pilots?[27]

Never mind that these horror stories have been dredged up from the 1920s and 1930s; they correspond too well to our prejudices to be wasted, so they are rehashed as a statement about modern Japanese baseball. (And just to be sure that no cliché about the Japanese is left unturned, we are told that it's 'a sport that in a perfect world would probably be played by robots'.) Along with the conviction that the Japanese have no sense of humour goes the belief that they really have no concept of sport. (Look at sumo: for the average Briton its main contribution has been the inflatable sumo suit – itself a brilliant stroke of cultural parody – and a few comic advertisements.) By a convenient fiction we ignore the single-minded fanaticism which has overtaken almost every professional sport in the west and flatter ourselves with an imagined contrast between joyless oriental maniacs and leisurely western sportsmen.

Japan's economic success has sharpened western sensitivity to its faults. It's not surprising that the modern winners should also be seen as the modern sinners: 'Japan: ageist, racist, sexist and drunk,' writes Bryan Appleyard in a moment of disenchantment.[28] The various -isms of which Japan is guilty define it as a thoroughgoing contemporary villain. In *A Circle Round the Sun* the narrator's girlfriend catalogues the familiar charges: 'What about the rainforests? All the trees disappearing because the Japanese use throwaway wooden chopsticks. All the dolphins. All the whales. All the child prostitutes in Thailand and the Philippines. Japanese money. Japanese world.'[29]

Japanese money. Japanese world. The link is unbreakable. The Japanese are now in a position to shape the world to their inclinations. And as killers of whales and destroyers of forests, they have taken their place at the head of the world's eco-villains. In the 1980s and early 1990s, these images of brutality combined with the threatening reach of Japan's economy to reawaken all the old antagonisms. As the effects of the recession on Japan become more apparent, western perceptions will no doubt change again, but for the moment the samurai is firmly back in the spotlight.

19. Back to the Yellow Peril?

The more remote a country is, the broader and more indiscriminate are the stereotypes we form of it. 'Let us make no mistake,' wrote Harcourt-Smith in 1942, 'our enemies are not only the Japanese militarists but the Japanese people as well.' The distinctions that would have been made in the case of Germany are explicitly rejected: 'Let us remember that here is no decent reasonable populace, exploited by a pack of militaristic gangsters, but seventy-five million madmen, all prepared to commit any crime at the behest of the State.'[1] The seventy-five million madmen comprise the whole population of Japan – mad men, mad women and mad children.

People did not shrink from the implications of this analysis. John Dower quotes the weekly report of the British ambassador in Washington for New Year's Day 1944, which refers to the 'universal "exterminationist" anti-Japanese feeling here'. Dower goes on to give a flavour of what this meant:

> Elliott Roosevelt, the president's son and confidant, told Henry Wallace in 1945 that the United States should continue bombing Japan 'until we have destroyed about half the Japanese civilian population'. While the president's son was expressing such personal views in private, the chairman of the War Manpower Commission, Paul V. McNutt, told a public audience in April 1945 that he favored 'the extermination of the Japanese *in toto*'. When asked if he meant the Japanese military or the people as a whole, he confirmed he meant the latter, 'for I know the Japanese people'.[2]

McNutt later explained that he was expressing a personal view rather than official policy, but talk of genocide in relation to Japan was sufficiently respectable for Dower to present a long and depressing record of examples.

The image that welds together soldier and civilian, man and woman, guilty and innocent, is that of the Yellow Peril. Without it, such talk would not be possible. As we have seen, the image originated soon after the Sino-Japanese war and has enjoyed intermittent peaks of popularity ever since. It was the guiding image behind Coryn's vision of San Francisco overrun by a tide of Japanese cobblers, cleaners and laundry operators, just as eighty years later it is the guiding image behind Crichton's vision of America strangled by Japanese financial influence. The attitudes and identities of individual Japanese are submerged in the general racial threat.

It would be a mistake to imagine that this is simply the province of tabloid journalism and popular fiction. A year before the publication of *Rising Sun*, at about the time that *The Coming War with Japan* by George Friedman and Meredith Lebard was hitting the Tokyo bookstores and within a week or two of Edith Cresson's reference to Japan's 'absolute desire to conquer the world',[3] news filtered through of a report on Japan which caused even more dismay. According to *The Sunday Times*, 'A CIA-sponsored report, leaked last week, described the Japanese as "creatures of an ageless, amoral, manipulative and controlling culture", who are intent on "world economic dominance". The report said Japan is a racist and non-democratic country whose population believes might is right and feels superior to other people.'[4]

There is a certain irony in the charge of racism. The language of the report is itself so redolent of wartime antagonisms that one is almost surprised not to find the colour of the Japanese added to the list of their other iniquities. Impossible, of course, in our enlightened times, but the yellowness of the Yellow Peril is never far below the surface. The threat posed by Japan is never purely military or purely economic; it is also, always, racial. The conventions of public utterance mean that this rarely becomes explicit, but continual recourse to wartime imagery ensures that it is not forgotten. The yellowness of the enemy, as opposed to our own whiteness, is a defining characteristic; we remember that under the smiling mask in Mason's poster was 'the real face of yellow flesh'. When *Time* magazine struggled to formulate the American response to Pearl Harbor, it came up with the following: 'Over the US and its history there was a great unanswered question: What would the people, the 132,000,000, say in the face of the mightiest event of their time? What they said – tens of thousands of them – was: "Why, the yellow bastards!" '[5]

It's not irrelevant to linger over these wartime responses. Memories of the war still have such significance because most people in the west have given very little thought to Japan in any other context. Our relationship with Germany and Italy is long enough and varied enough, at least in Britain, for the Second World War to take its place as another episode in history, whereas with Japan it looms disproportionately large. Contacts with the two European countries are too numerous for wartime stereotypes to retain their grip, but this is not true of Japan to anything like the same extent. On the contrary, the stereotypes can be redeployed with remarkable ease, as the imagery of economic invaders and whale-killers attests. The resurgence of American hostility in the early 1970s showed how undiscriminating these stereotypes still were. David Ushio, who was national executive director of the Japanese-American Citizens' League, commented on their effect:

> Intentionally or not, anti-Japanese bias is being sown in the class-room, and America's children are being taught that a whole race of people are cruel, barbaric, and hold disrespect for the law. In their zeal to save the whales, impressionable youngsters are beginning to turn their energy toward the only visible symbol of Japan, their innocent little Japanese American classmates.[6]

The process of defining 'a whole race of people' by a single image has obvious attractions: in war it simplifies the business of killing them, in peace it removes the need to think about them. Stereotypes offer an illusion of understanding by presenting us with a reality that is known rather than unknown. They short-circuit the painstaking explorations and discriminations by which we can try to learn something of the world; instead of being a first step towards understanding, they become a complacent alternative to it. The schoolchildren of whom Ushio speaks do not use personal knowledge of their Japanese classmates to dismantle the stereotype; they allow the stereotype to override personal knowledge and redefine their classmates.

This pattern of response is not peculiar to children. The man in charge of the Western Defence Command after Pearl Harbor was General John L. DeWitt. A fervent advocate of internment, he saw the Japanese-Americans on the Pacific coast as 'over 112,000 potential enemies' still at large. The fact that not one act of sabotage had been attempted might have given another man pause, but General DeWitt knew too well the cunning of the Japanese. 'The very fact that no sabotage has taken place to date', he argued with devastating logic, 'is a disturbing and confirming indication that such action will be taken.'[7]

Given the history of our relations with Japan, it is not a frivolous exercise to ask how much the past 150 years have taught us about the country which now affects our lives in such a variety of ways. That the west has so often responded to Japanese success over the past two decades by resurrecting the samurai and turning back to the imagery of the Second World War is not a cheerful omen. Instead of merely shuffling our pack of stereotypes whenever the political climate changes, we need to start challenging them. If we don't, the same stereotype will sooner or later produce the same reaction. In response to Connor's warning that he should 'remember Pearl Harbor', Senator Morton replies, 'You know, I have colleagues who say sooner or later we're going to have to drop another bomb. They think it'll come to that.'[8] Even in fiction, it's an ugly conjecture.

As long as we are satisfied with a handful of clichés, we shall continue to read about dog-collars that give electric shocks and baseball players who have to walk on samurai swords, and believe that we are learning something about Japan. To identify the stereotypes and to be aware of our dependence on them is a start, but the only prospect of real change lies in the gradual humanising effect of individual contact. Among the American troops sent to occupy Nagasaki in September 1945 was a marine, Victor Tolley, whose memories of the time were recorded in Studs Terkel's *The Good War*. Wandering through the town one day, he got lost and tried to ask a Japanese child the way back to his base, but the child's attention was caught by a bracelet he wore containing pictures of his wife and two small daughters:

> He saw it and pointed. I opened it up and he saw the pictures. His face beamed. He started to jump up and down. He pointed upstairs where he lived. He said, 'Sister, sister.' He motioned that she was pregnant.
>
> This little kid ran upstairs and brought his father down. A very nice Japanese gentleman. He could speak English. He bowed and said, 'We would be honoured if you would come upstairs and have some tea with us.' I went upstairs in this strange Japanese house. I noticed on the mantel a picture of a young Japanese soldier. I asked him, 'Is this your son?' He said, 'That is my daughter's husband. We don't know if he's alive. We haven't heard.'
>
> The minute he said that, it dawned on me that they suffered the same as we did. They lost sons and daughters and relatives, and they hurt too.
>
> Terkel: *Until that moment ... ?*
>
> I had nothing but contempt for the Japanese. I used to hear all the horror stories. We were trained to kill them. They're our enemy. Look what they did in Pearl Harbor. They asked for it and now we're gonna give it to 'em. That's how I felt until I met this young boy and his family. His sister came out. She bowed. She was very pregnant. I'll never forget that moment.[9]

It is the moment, rare enough in the troubled history of our dealings with Japan, when the stereotype disintegrates and the human being emerges.

Notes

Throughout the book, Japanese names have been given with the family name first.

1. A Question of Category

1 See C. R. Boxer, *The Christian Century in Japan, 1549–1650*, University of California Press, 1951, p. 75.
2 Michael Cooper, S. J., *They Came to Japan, An Anthology of European Reports on Japan, 1543–1640*, Thames and Hudson, 1965, p. 229.
3 See R. Storry, *A History of Modern Japan*, Penguin, 1960, p. 65.
4 See Hugh Cortazzi and George Webb (eds.), *Kipling's Japan*, Athlone, 1988, p. 54.
5 T. W. H. Crosland, *The Truth about Japan*, Grant Richards, 1904, p. 72.
6 Ruth Benedict, *The Chrysanthemum and the Sword* (1946), Routledge, 1967, p. 2.
7 Peter Tasker, *Inside Japan* (1987), Penguin, 1989, pp. 4–5.
8 Joe Joseph, *The Japanese*, Viking, 1993, p. 8.
9 *Fodor's 93 Japan*, Fodor's Travel Publications, 1993, pp. 78, 80, 330.
10 The book's mode of presentation continually brings us back to this central contrast: 'Americans gear all their living to a constantly challenging world . . . Japanese reassurances are based rather on . . .' (pp. 19–20); 'Their reliance upon order and hierarchy and our faith in freedom and equality are poles apart . . .'

(p. 30); 'In the United States nouveaux riches are . . . But in Japan a narikin . . .' (p. 66); 'The contrast with folkways in the United States could hardly be more marked . . .' (p. 91); 'The Japanese, however, do not follow this course . . . In the United States we stand this curve upside down . . .' (p. 177) etc.

11   Sir Rutherford Alcock, *Capital of the Tycoon,* Longman, 1863, Vol. I, p. 414.
12   Douglas Sladen, *The Japs at Home,* Hutchinson, 1892, p. 10.
13   Lafcadio Hearn, *Japan: an attempt at interpretation,* Macmillan, 1904, p. 11.
14   Percival Lowell, *The Soul of the Far East* (1888), Macmillan, 1911, p. 1.
15   A. B. F. Mitford (Lord Redesdale), *Memories* (1915), 2nd edition, Hutchinson, 1915, Vol. II, p. 514.
16   See John W. Dower, *War Without Mercy, Race and Power in the Pacific War,* Pantheon, 1986, p. 97.
17   See Sheila K. Johnson, *American Attitudes Toward Japan, 1941–1975,* American Enterprise Institute for Public Policy Research, 1975, p. 84.
18   Ian Fleming, *You Only Live Twice* (1964), Coronet, 1988, p. 38.
19   Edward W. Said, *Orientalism* (1978), Penguin, 1991, p. 300.

2. A Marked Resemblance to Monkeys

1   D. J. Enright, *The World of Dew,* Secker & Warburg, 1955, p. 14.
2   See I. L. Szyliowicz, *Pierre Loti and the oriental woman,* St Martin's Press, 1988, p. 22.
3   Pierre Loti, *Madame Chrysanthème* (1887), Calmann-Lévy, 1927, p. 82 and pp. 84–87.
4   Henry Adams, letter to John Hay, 22 August 1886.
5   Loti, *Madame Chrysanthème,* p. 299.
6   Crosland, *The Truth about Japan,* p. 72.
7   G. K. Chesterton, 'The Japanese' in *The Uses of Diversity,* Methuen, 1920, p. 47.
8   See Dower, *War Without Mercy,* p. 71.
9   George MacDonald Fraser, *Quartered Safe Out Here,* Harvill Press, 1993, p. 45.
10   Ernie Pyle, *Last Chapter,* Henry Holt, 1945, p. 5. Quoted in Dower, *War Without Mercy,* p. 78. The whole of Chapter 4 (pp. 77–93) in Dower's book is full of interesting material on this subject.
11   John Hersey, *Into the Valley,* Hodder & Stoughton, 1943, pp. 39–40 and p. 34.

12 George H. Johnston, *Pacific Partner,* Duell, Sloan and Pearce, 1944, p. 205. Quoted in Dower, *War Without Mercy*, p. 84.
13 Russell Braddon, *The Naked Island* (1951), Laurie, 1952, p. 263.
14 Ibid. pp. 245–246.
15 Laurence Oliphant, *Narrative of the Earl of Elgin's Mission to China and Japan in the years 1857, '58, '59,* Blackwood, 1859, Vol. II, pp. 18–19.
16 See Yokoyama Toshio, *Japan in the Victorian Mind,* Macmillan, 1987, p. 107, and Endymion Wilkinson, *Japan Versus Europe* (1980), Penguin, 1983, p. 55.
17 Fleming, *You Only Live Twice,* p. 32.
18 Pierre Loti, *Japoneries d'automne* (1889), Calmann-Lévy, 1926, p. 74.

3. Strange Forms of Knowledge

1 Eric Van Lustbader,*The Ninja* (1980), Grafton, 1981, p. 13.
2 Ibid., pp. 14 and 64.
3 Ibid., pp. 302 and 303.
4 Eric Van Lustbader, *White Ninja,* Grafton, 1990, p. 233.
5 Somerset Maugham, *The Razor's Edge,* Heinemann, 1944, p. 249.
6 *Time,* 21 July 1958, p. 49. (Both Suzuki and Watts were in fact rather critical of traditional Zen as practised in Japan, but such discriminations tended to get lost in the general enthusiasm.)
7 James Clavell, *Shogun* (1975), Coronet, 1976, p. 615.
8 Ezra Vogel, *Japan as Number One,* Harvard University Press, 1979, pp. 11–12.

4. Glorious Death

1 Lustbader, *The Ninja,* p. 30.
2 Cooper, *They Came to Japan,* pp. 157–158. See also pp. 57–59, 60, 78, 158, 162.
3 Engelbert Kaempfer, *The History of Japan, together with a description of the kingdom of Siam 1690–92,* James MacLehose, 1906, Vol. II, p. 311. John Tremenheere, 'Japan', *Quarterly Review,* Vol. CXIV (1863), p. 478.
4 Cooper, *They Came to Japan,* p. 162.
5 A. B. F. Mitford, 'The Execution by Hara-Kiri', *Cornhill,* Vol. XX (1869), pp. 549–554. Satow describes the same episode in Ernest Satow, *A Diplomat in Japan,* Seeley, Service, 1921, pp. 344–347.
6 Crosland, *The Truth About Japan,* p. 43. The ease with which

stereotypes can be adapted to either a positive or a negative point of view is suggested by the Punch cartoon, published in the same year as Crosland's book, which shows John Bull being instructed in patriotism by a geisha. See illustrations.

7   William F. Halsey and J. Bryan III, *Admiral Halsey's Story*, McGraw-Hill, 1947, p. 229.
8   Mass Observation Archive, *Politics 1938–56*, Box 4.
9   John P. Marquand, *Stopover Tokyo*, Collins, 1957, p. 117.
10 Alfred Tennyson, 'A Ballad of the Fleet' and 'The Charge of the Light Brigade'. Thomas Campbell, 'Hohenlinden'.
11 Alan Seeger, 'Rendezvous'.
12 See Johnson, *American Attitudes Toward Japan*, p. 91.
13 Fleming, *You Only Live Twice*, p. 70.
14 *Newsweek*, 7 December 1970, p. 31. For Glazer's comment, see Iriye Akira, *Mutual Images*, Harvard, 1975, p. 143.
15 George Orwell, *Homage to Catalonia* (1938), Penguin, 1966, p. 231.
16 See Dower, *War Without Mercy*, p. 39.
17 John Hersey, *Hiroshima*, Penguin, 1946, p. 13.
18 Ishihara Shintaro, *The Japan That Can Say No* (1989), trans. Frank Baldwin, Simon & Schuster, 1991, p. 28.

5. An Unfathomable Planet

1   Isabella Bird, *Unbeaten Tracks in Japan* (1880), Virago, 1984, p. 8.
2   Loti, *Japoneries d'automne*, p. 36.
3   See *Independent on Sunday*, 21 July 1991.
4   Peregrine Hodson, *A Circle Round the Sun, a foreigner in Japan* (1992), Mandarin, 1993, p. 159.
5   Michael Crichton, *Rising Sun*, Century, 1992, p. 57.
6   Sax Rohmer, *The Bride of Fu Manchu* (1933), Cassell, 1957, p. 245.
7   Loti, *Japoneries d'automne*, p. 179.
8   Hearn, *Japan: an attempt at interpretation*, p. 12.
9   Hodson, *A Circle Round the Sun*, p. 170.
10 Pico Iyer, *The Lady and the Monk*, The Bodley Head, 1991, pp. 198 and 158–159.
11 See Dower, *War Without Mercy*, p. 86.
12 Adams, letter to John White Field, 4 August 1886. Sir Edwin Arnold, *Seas and Lands*, Longmans, 1891, p. 176. Loti, *Japoneries d'automne*, p. 79.
13 See *Insight Japan*, Vol. I, No. 2, November 1992, p. 28.
14 Fred Hiatt, *The Secret Sun*, Simon & Schuster, 1992, p. 45.

15 *Daily Telegraph,* 27 October 1990.
16 Joseph, *The Japanese,* pp. 11, 13, 27, 29, 70, 20, 19.

6. A Realised Fairyland

1 Satow, *A Diplomat in Japan,* p. 17.
2 Oliphant, *Narrative,* pp. 164–165.
3 Cortazzi, *Kipling's Japan,* pp. 196–197.
4 John Lafarge, *An Artist's Letters from Japan,* T. Fisher Unwin, 1897, First Letter, Yokohama, 3 July 1886.
5 Henry Adams, letter to Elizabeth Cameron, 13 August 1886.
6 Loti, *Japoneries d'automne,* p. 5. Bird, *Unbeaten Tracks in Japan,* p. 16. Baron J. A. de Hübner, *A Ramble Round the World* (1873), trans. Lady Herbert, London, 1874, Vol. I, p. 406.
7 Cortazzi, *Kipling's Japan,* p. 248.
8 Iyer, *The Lady and the Monk,* p. 3.
9 Nikos Kazantzakis, *Travels in China and Japan* (1938), trans. George C. Pappageotes, Cassirer, 1964, p. 18.
10 Lowell, *The Soul of the Far East,* p. 121.
11 C. W. Dilke, 'English influence in Japan', *Fortnightly Review,* Vol. XX new series, 1876, p. 441.
12 Cortazzi, *Kipling's Japan,* p. 38.
13 De Hübner, *A Ramble Round the World,* Vol. I, p. 384.
14 Marie Stopes, *A Journal from Japan,* Blackie & Son, 1910, p. 266.
15 *Fodor's 93 Japan,* p. 77.
16 Lafcadio Hearn, 'My First Day in the Orient' Pt. IV, *Glimpses of Unfamiliar Japan,* Houghton Mifflin, 1894.
17 Oscar Wilde, 'The Decay of Lying' (1889) in *De Profundis and Other Writings,* Penguin, 1986, p. 82.
18 *Evening Standard,* 4 May 1993, p. 23.
19 Oliphant, *Narrative,* Vol. II, p. 2.

7. Force of Circumstance

1 Following references are to James A. Michener, 'Japan', *Holiday,* August 1952, pp. 27–39.
2 Vernon Sneider, *The Tea-House of the August Moon,* Macmillan, 1952, p. 74.
3 Oliphant, *Narrative,* p. 183.
4 Sherard Osborn, *A Cruise in Japanese Waters,* Edinburgh and London, 1859, p. 208.

5   C. A. G. Bridge, 'The Mediterranean of Japan', *Fortnightly Review,* Vol. XVIII new series, 1875, p. 207.
6   See Johnson, *American Attitudes Toward Japan,* p. 9.
7   Cooper, *They Came to Japan,* p. 133.

8. A Place to Meditate

1   John Stalker and George Parker, Preface to *A Treatise of Japaning and Varnishing,* Oxford, 1688.
2   G. H. Preble (ed. B. Szczesniak), *The Opening of Japan: a diary of discovery in the Far East, 1853–1856,* University of Oklahoma Press, 1962, p. 213.
3   Osborn, *A Cruise in Japanese Waters,* p. 41.
4   Henry Adams, letter to John White Field, 4 August 1886.
5   Osman Edwards, *Residential Rhymes,* T. Hasegawa, Tokyo, 1900.
6   Sir Henry Norman, *The Real Japan* (1892), T. Fisher Unwin, 1893, p. 135.
7   Cortazzi, *Kipling's Japan,* p. 40.
8   Ibid., p. 102.
9   Ibid., p. 105.
10   C. A. G. Bridge, 'The City of Kiyoto', *Fraser's Magazine,* Vol. XVII new series, January 1878, p. 70.
11   Iyer, *The Lady and the Monk,* pp. 148–150.
12   *The Sunday Times,* 2 January 1994.
13   See Benedict, *The Chrysanthemum and the Sword,* p. 165.
14   *Daily Telegraph,* 10 July 1993.
15   *Independent,* 25 May 1994.

9. A Natural Infirmity

1   Fleming, *You Only Live Twice,* p. 35.
2   W. S. Gilbert, *Patience,* Act II.
3   Fleming, *You Only Live Twice,* p. 11.
4   Cortazzi, *Kipling's Japan,* pp. 74, 86 and 92.
5   *Guardian,* 4 March 1986.
6   Henry Adams, letter to Theodore F. Dwight, 17 July 1886.
7   Loti, *Japoneries d'automne,* pp. 3 and 9.
8   Arnold, *Seas and Lands,* p. 168.
9   Loti, *Madame Chrysanthème,* p. 220.
10   Quoted in Johnson, *American Attitudes Toward Japan,* p. 52.
11   Francis L. Hawks, *Narrative of the Expedition of an American*

Squadron to the China Seas and Japan (1856), ed. Sidney Wallach, Coward-McCann, 1952, pp. 170 and 230.

12 De Hübner, *A Ramble Round the World*, Vol. I, p. 320. Dilke, 'English influence in Japan', p. 443. Sladen, *The Japs at Home*, p. 78.

13 Cortazzi, *Kipling's Japan*, p. 92.

14 Ibid., p. 213.

15 Stopes, *A Journal from Japan*, pp. 29, 137, 133.

16 Christopher Fryke and Christopher Schweitzer, *Voyages to the East Indies*, Cassell, 1929, p. 99.

17 Crosland, *The Truth About Japan*, p. 46.

18 Townsend Harris, *The Complete Journal of Townsend Harris*, ed. M. E. Cosenza, 2nd edition, Tuttle, 1959, p. 310.

10. The Inhuman Aesthetic

1 *The Economist*, 5 June 1993, p. 73.

2 Arthur Koestler, *The Lotus and the Robot* (1960), Hutchinson, 1966, pp. 191 and 193.

3 Clavell, *Shogun*, p. 93.

4 Norman Mailer, *The Naked and the Dead*, Rinehart, 1948, p. 248.

5 Studs Terkel, *The Good War*, Pantheon, 1984, p. 64.

6 Kazantzakis, *Travels in China and Japan*, pp. 114 and 115. Fifty years earlier, Percival Lowell had responded to Japanese gardening in a similarly positive way: 'Wherever the Japanese has come in contact with the country he has made her unmistakably his own. He has touched her to caress, not injure, and it seems as if Nature accepted his fondness as a matter of course, and yielded him a wifely submission in return.' (*The Soul of the Far East*, pp. 127–128.)

7 Benedict, *The Chrysanthemum and the Sword*, p. 207.

8 Koestler, *The Lotus and the Robot*, p. 200.

9 Fleming, *You Only Live Twice*, p. 75.

10 Clavell, *Shogun*, pp. 480 and 531.

11 Koestler, *The Lotus and the Robot*, p. 196.

11. A Bevy of Damsels

1 Following references are to Ashley Heath, 'The New People', *The Face*, April 1993, pp. 62–68.

2 Oliphant, *Narrative*, p. 197.

3   *The Times*, 2 November 1858.
4   Cortazzi, *Kipling's Japan*, p. 44.
5   Ian McQueen, *Japan, a travel survival kit*, Lonely Planet Publications, 1986, p. 25.
6   Clavell, *Shogun*, p. 332.
7   Fleming, *You Only Live Twice*, p. 83.
8   Norman, *The Real Japan*, p. 174.
9   W. E. Griffis, *The Mikado's Empire* (1876), Harper & Bros., 1883, p. 559.
10   George Smith, *Ten Weeks in Japan*, London, 1861, pp. 276–277.
11   Arnold, *Seas and Lands*, p. 280.
12   Basil Hall Chamberlain, *Things Japanese*, Kegan Paul, 1890, p. 365.
13   *Independent*, 25 May 1994.
14   James A. Michener, *Sayonara* (1953–1954) in *The Source, The Bridges at Toko-Ri, Caravans, Sayonara*, Secker & Warburg, 1976, p. 1053.
15   Pearl S. Buck, *The Hidden Flower* (1952), Pocket Books, 1954, pp. 144–145.
16   Ibid., p. 168.
17   Clive Holland, *My Japanese Wife* (1895), R. A. Everett, 1903, p. 40.
18   Mitford, *Memories*, Vol. II, p. 442.
19   Arnold, *Seas and Lands*, p. 163.
20   Loti, *Madame Chrysanthème*, pp. 59 and 51. Henry Adams, letter to John White Field, 4 August 1886.
21   Loti, *Madame Chrysanthème*, p. 213.
22   Joseph, *The Japanese*, p. 242.
23   Kazantzakis, *Travels in China and Japan*, p. 164.

12. Butterflies with Hearts

1   Holland, *My Japanese Wife*, pp. 92 and 11–12.
2   Griffis, *The Mikado's Empire*, pp. 559–560.
3   Hearn, *Japan: an attempt at interpretation*, pp. 397–398.
4   *Daily Telegraph*, 5 June 1993.
5   Michener, *Sayonara*, pp. 1002 and 1075.
6   Hearn, *Japan: an attempt at interpretation*, p. 393.
7   Richard Mason, *The Wind Cannot Read*, Hodder & Stoughton, 1947, p. 84.
8   Michener, *Sayonara*, pp. 1066 and 1102.

13. A Lewd People

1   Robert J. Collins, *Japan-Think, Ameri-Think*, Penguin, 1992, p. 98.
2   Alfred Tennyson, 'Locksley Hall', ll. 167–168.
3   Holland, *My Japanese Wife*, p. 49.
4   Quoted in Rana Kabbani, *Europe's Myths of Orient*, Macmillan, 1986, p. 30.
5   See P. G. Rogers, *The First Englishman in Japan: the story of Will Adams*, Harvill Press, 1956, p. 124.
6   Cooper, *They Came to Japan*, pp. 46, 64, 65.
7   Smith, *Ten Weeks in Japan*, p. 251.
8   Preble, *The Opening of Japan*, p. 123.
9   Ibid., p. 181.
10 L. de Beauvoir, *Voyage autour du monde* (1869), Paris, 1873, p. 525.
11 Preble, *The Opening of Japan*, p. 183.
12 Edward Yorke McCauley (ed. Allan B. Cole), *With Perry in Japan, the diary of Edward Yorke McCauley*, Princeton University Press, 1942, p. 108.
13 Smith, *Ten Weeks in Japan*, p. 104.
14 Tremenheere, 'Japan', p. 478. Robert Fortune, *Yedo and Peking*, London, 1863, p. 94. E. B. de Fonblanque, *Niphon and Pe-che-li*, Saunders, Otley & Co., 1862, p. 132. Frank Harris, *My Life and Loves*, ed. J. F. Gallagher, W. H. Allen, 1964, pp .913–914.
15 Fonblanque, *Niphon*, p. 132.
16 A. B. F. Mitford (Lord Redesdale), *Tales of Old Japan* (1871), Macmillan, 1910, p. 37. Hugh Cortazzi, *Victorians in Japan, in and around the Treaty Ports*, Athlone, 1987, pp. 286 and 282.
17 Griffis, *The Mikado's Empire*, p. 555.
18 Holland, *My Japanese Wife*, p. 165.
19 Charles Dickens, *The Old Curiosity Shop* (1841), Chap. IX.
20 Norman, *The Real Japan*, p. 174.
21 Mason, *The Wind Cannot Read*, p. 99.
22 Iyer, *The Lady and the Monk*, p. 364.
23 Ibid., p. 365.
24 Mason, *The Wind Cannot Read*, p. 86.
25 J. D. Bisignani, *Japan Handbook*, Moon Publications, 1983, p. 35.
26 Harris, *My Life and Loves*, p. 192.
27 Ibid., p. 916.
28 Ibid., p. 916.
29 Ibid., pp. 937–938.
30 Kazantzakis, *Travels in China and Japan*, p. 25.
31 Collins, *Japan-Think, Ameri-Think*, p. 88.
32 Fleming, *You Only Live Twice*, p. 80.

14. Cultural Penetration

1   Kazantzakis, *Travels in China and Japan*, p. 15. Loti, *Madame Chrysanthème*, p. 3.
2   See Earl Miner, *The Japanese Tradition in British and American Literature,* Princeton University Press, 1958, p. 57.
3   Crosland, *The Truth About Japan*, p. 15.
4   See Jean-Pierre Lehmann, *The Image of Japan: From Feudal Isolation to World Power, 1850–1905,* George Allen & Unwin, 1978, p. 175.
5   William Plomer, *Paper Houses* (1929), Penguin, 1943, p. 10.
6   Kazantzakis, *Travels in China and Japan*, p. 162.
7   Michener, *Sayonara*, pp. 995 and 997.
8   Ibid., pp. 1027–1028.
9   Ibid., pp. 1050, 1040, 1077.
10   Ibid., pp. 1050–1051.
11   Ronald Kirkbride, *Tamiko* (1959), Pan Books, 1960, p. 9.
12   Ibid., p. 143.
13   Michener, *Sayonara*, p. 1095.
14   Ibid., p. 1113.
15   Rohmer, *The Bride of Fu Manchu*, pp. 52–53.
16   Ironically, it later emerged that Tokyo Rose had been working for the Allies.
17   Lustbader, *The Ninja*, p. 38.
18   Eric Van Lustbader, *The Miko*, Granada, 1984, pp. 303–304 and 129.
19   Ibid., p. 332.
20   *Travelog*, Channel 4, 8 December 1993.
21   Fleming, *You Only Live Twice*, pp. 122 and 124.
22   Hiatt, *The Secret Sun*, pp. 11 and 145.
23   As quoted on the cover of the Black Swan edition of *The Lady and the Monk*.

15. A Streak of Violence

1   Kazantzakis, *Travels in China and Japan*, pp. 159–160.
2   Mason, *The Wind Cannot Read*, pp. 82–83.
3   Ibid., p. 83.
4   Cooper, *They Came to Japan*, pp. 141–142.
5   Ibid., p. 159.
6   Clavell, *Shogun*, p. 36.
7   Alexander Knox, 'Japan', *Edinburgh Review,* Vol. XCVI, 1852, p. 382.
8   Satow, *A Diplomat in Japan*, p. 47.

9   Mitford, *Memories,* Vol. I, p. 389.
10   Fonblanque, *Niphon,* p. 15. De Hübner, *A Ramble Round the World,* Vol. I, p. 462. Alcock, *The Capital of the Tycoon,* Vol. I, p. 125.
11   Loti, *Madame Chrysanthème,* p. 142.
12   Cortazzi, *Kipling's Japan,* p. 181.
13   Kabbani, *Europe's Myths of Orient,* p. 8.
14   Simon Harcourt-Smith, *Japanese Frenzy,* Hamish Hamilton, 1942, p. 6. Fleming, *You Only Live Twice,* p. 71.
15   See Dower, *War Without Mercy,* p. 142.
16   Hodson, *A Circle Round the Sun,* p. 259.
17   Homer Lea, *The Valor of Ignorance,* Harper & Bros., 1909, p. 228. Lothrop Stoddard, *The Rising Tide of Color* (1920), Chapman & Hall, 1922, p. 49.
18   Mason, *The Wind Cannot Read,* p. 43.
19   Benedict, *The Chrysanthemum and the Sword,* p. 203.
20   Cortazzi, *Kipling's Japan,* p. 181.
21   Fleming, *You Only Live Twice,* pp. 38 and 42.
22   *The Times,* 10 February 1904.
23   Harcourt-Smith, *Japanese Frenzy,* p. 191.
24   Dower, *War Without Mercy,* p. 36.
25   *The Times,* 4 December 1991.
26   Hiatt, *The Secret Sun,* p. 156.
27   Quoted in George Elison, *Deus Destroyed: The Image of Christianity in Early Modern Europe* (1973), Harvard University Press, 1988, p. 16.
28   Kurt Singer, *Mirror, Sword and Jewel, The Geometry of Japanese Life* (1973), Kodansha, 1989, p. 24.
29   Fleming, *You Only Live Twice,* p. 12.

16. The Sadist

1   De Hübner, *A Ramble Round the World,* Vol. II, p. 61. Cortazzi, *The Victorians in Japan,* p. 258.
2   Mass Observation Archive, File 1034, 7 January 1942.
3   Ken Worpole, *Dockers and Detectives: popular reading – popular writing,* Verso, 1984, pp. 50–51.
4   Quotations are from the screenplay of *The Camp on Blood Island* by Val Guest and J. M. White, July 1957, and from the novel based on it, published by Panther in 1958.
5   Lord Russell of Liverpool, *The Knights of Bushido, A Short History of Japanese War Crimes,* Cassell, 1958, pp. vii, 105, 93.

6   This works both ways. At the end of the sixteenth century local
     Japanese residents thwarted Franciscan efforts to set up a
     church in Osaka on the grounds that the meat-eating friars
     were cannibals.
7   Braddon, *The Naked Island*, p. 249.
8   Lord Russell of Liverpool, *The Knights of Bushido*, p. 240.
9   Ibid., p. 238.
10   Crichton, *Rising Sun*, p. 123.
11   Joseph, *The Japanese*, pp. 221, 222, 223.
12   Ibid., pp. 106–107 and 127.
13   *Sun*, 23 September 1988.
14   Following quotations are from Catherine Eade, 'Manga Mania',
     The Big Issue, no. 66, 15–21 February 1994, pp. 10–11.
15   *Passengers*, Channel 4, 12 August 1994.
16   Hodson, *A Circle Round the Sun*, p. 136.
17   Crichton, *Rising Sun*, p. 64.
18   Quoted in R. Daniels, *The Politics of Prejudice* (1962), Smith,
     1966, pp. 20 and 47.
19   Guest and White, *The Camp on Blood Island*, p. 145.
20   Ibid., p. 41.
21   Ibid., p. 89.
22   Ibid., p. 133.
23   Ibid., p. 103.

17. Bushido

1   Mitford, 'The Execution by Hara-Kiri'.
2   Enright, *The World of Dew*, p. 19.
3   Singer, *Mirror, Sword and Jewel*, p. 41.
4   Cooper, *They Came to Japan*, p. 41.
5   Lustbader, *The Ninja*, p. 117.
6   Jean-Pierre Melville's 1967 film takes as its epigraph a sentence
     purporting to be from *The Book of the Samurai*: 'There is no
     greater solitude than the samurai's, unless perhaps it be that of
     the tiger in the jungle.'
7   Robert Stone, *Dog Soldiers* (1973), Star (W. H. Allen), 1976, p. 75.
8   Singer, *Mirror, Sword and Jewel*, pp. 166–167.
9   Marie Conte-Helm, 'Appearance and Reality', *Proceedings of the
     British Association for Japanese Studies*, Vol. 9, 1984, pp. 19–20.
10   Hiatt, *The Secret Sun*, pp. 6–7 and 13.

18. Samurai in Suits

1   Lafcadio Hearn, *Kokoro* (1896), Gay, 1900, p. 52.
2   Cortazzi, *Kipling's Japan*, p. 76.
3   *Annals of the American Academy of Political and Social Science*, Vol. 34, July–December 1909, pp. 223, 228, 47.
4   See Daniels, *The Politics of Prejudice*, p. 9.
5   Fleming, *You Only Live Twice*, p. 77.
6   *Time*, 2 March 1970, p. 25.
7   Lustbader, *The Miko*, p. 43.
8   Ibid., p. 41.
9   Lustbader, *White Ninja*, p. 60.
10   Hiatt, *The Secret Sun*, p. 250.
11   *Time*, 10 May 1971, p. 85.
12   See James Fallows, 'Containing Japan', *The Atlantic*, May 1989, pp. 40–54, and 'Getting Along with Japan', *The Atlantic*, December 1989, pp. 53–64.
13   Crichton, *Rising Sun*, pp. 230 and 122.
14   Ibid., pp. 225, 20, 242.
15   *Annals of the American Academy of Political and Social Science*, Vol. 34, July–December 1909, p. 43.
16   In 1987 Toshiba was found to have breached the rules governing trade with communist countries by supplying to the Russians equipment which reduced the propeller noise of their submarines, thus making it easier for them to escape detection by NATO trackers.
17   Crichton, *Rising Sun*, p. 230.
18   See William Horsley and Roger Buckley, *Nippon, New Superpower*, BBC Books, 1990, p. 240.
19   Hiatt, *The Secret Sun*, p. 8.
20   Crichton, *Rising Sun*, p. 324.
21   Hodson, *A Circle Round the Sun*, pp. 98 and 165.
22   Joseph, *The Japanese*, pp. 262–263, 261, 265.
23   See Marie Conte-Helm, *Japan and the North-East of England: from 1862 to the present day*, Athlone, 1989, pp. 141–142.
24   Joseph, *The Japanese*, p. 241.
25   Martin Cruz Smith, *Red Square*, Harvill Press, 1992, p. 77.
26   The survey was carried out at the University of Wales during the first six months of 1991 by D. W. Anthony, Director of the Japanese Studies Centre, and D. M. Ungersma of the School of Journalism Studies.
27   Joseph, *The Japanese*, pp. 235 and 236.
28   *Independent*, 25 May 1994.
29   Hodson, *A Circle Round the Sun*, p. 117.

19. Back to the Yellow Peril?

1   Harcourt-Smith, *Japanese Frenzy*, p. 218.
2   Dower, *War Without Mercy*, pp. 54 and 55.
3   Reported in *The Sunday Times*, 23 June 1991.
4   *The Sunday Times*, 16 June 1991.
5   *Time*, 15 December 1941, p. 17. Quoted in Dower, *War Without Mercy*, p. 37.
6   See M. Weglyn, *Years of Infamy: the untold story of America's concentration camps*, Morrow, 1976, p. 271.
7   See P. Jacobs, S. Landau and E. Pell, *To Serve the Devil*, Vintage Books, 1971, Vol. II, pp. 189–190.
8   Crichton, *Rising Sun*, p. 230.
9   Terkel, *The Good War*, p. 543.

Select Bibliography

A full bibliography of material relevant to the study of western images of Japan would have to include practically everything published or broadcast about the country and its people. The following is a list of written works referred to in this book. Where quotations have been made from an edition other than the first, the original publication date is given in brackets.

Adams, Henry, *The Letters of Henry Adams*, ed. Levenson, J. C. et al., Belknap Press (Harvard University), 1982–1988.

Alcock, Rutherford, *Capital of the Tycoon*, Longman, 1863.

Annals of the American Academy of Political and Social Science, vol. 34, July–December 1909.

Anthony, D.W. and Ungersma, A.M., 'Reporting Japan', University of Wales, 1991.

Arnold, Edwin, *Seas and Lands*, Longman, 1891.

Beauvoir, L. de, *Voyage autour du monde* (1869), Paris, 1873.

Benedict, Ruth, *The Chrysanthemum and the Sword* (1946), Routledge, 1967.

Bird, Isabella, *Unbeaten Tracks in Japan* (1880), Virago, 1984.

Bisignani, J.D., *Japan Handbook*, Moon Publications, 1983.

Bowring, Richard and Kornicki, Peter *The Cambridge Encyclopedia of Japan*, Cambridge University Press, 1993.

Boxer, C.R., *The Christian Century in Japan, 1549–1650*, University of California Press, 1951.

Braddon, Russell, *The Naked Island* (1951), Laurie, 1952.

Bridge, C.A.G., 'The Mediterranean of Japan', *Fortnightly Review*, vol. 18, new series, 1875.

———'The City of Kiyoto', *Fraser's Magazine*, vol. 17, new series, January 1878.

Buck, Pearl S., *The Hidden Flower* (1952), Pocket Books, 1954.

Chamberlain, Basil Hall, *Things Japanese*, Kegan Paul, 1890.

Chesterton, G.K., 'The Japanese' in *The Uses of Diversity*, Methuen, 1920.

Clavell, James, *Shogun* (1975), Coronet, 1976.

Collins, Robert J., *Japan-Think, Ameri-Think*, Penguin, 1992.

Conte-Helm, Marie, 'Appearance and Reality', *Proceedings of the British Association for Japanese Studies*, vol. 9, 1984.

——*Japan and the North-East of England: from 1862 to the present day*, Athlone, 1989.

Cooper, Michael, *They Came to Japan, An Anthology of European Reports on Japan, 1543–1640*, Thames & Hudson, 1965.

Cortazzi, Hugh, *Victorians in Japan, in and around the Treaty Ports*, Athlone, 1987.

– and Webb, George (eds.), *Kipling's Japan*, Athlone 1988.

Crichton, Michael, *Rising Sun*, Century, 1992.

Crosland, T.W.H., *The Truth about Japan*, Grant Richards, 1904.

Daniels, R., *The Politics of Prejudice* (1962), Smith, 1966.

Dickens, Charles, *The Old Curiosity Shop*, Chapman & Hall, 1841.

Dilke, C.W., 'English influence in Japan', *Fortnightly Review*, vol. 10, new series, 1876.

Dower, John W., *War Without Mercy, Race and Power in the Pacific War*, Pantheon, 1986.

Edwards, Osman, *Residential Rhymes*, T. Hasegawa (Tokyo), 1900.

Elison, George, *Deus Destroyed: The Image of Christianity in Early Modern Europe* (1973), Harvard University Press, 1988.

Enright, D.J., *The World of Dew*, Secker & Warburg, 1955.

Fallows, James, 'Containing Japan', *Atlantic*, May 1989.

——'Getting Along with Japan', *Atlantic*, December 1989.

Fleming, Ian, *You Only Live Twice* (1964), Coronet, 1988.

Fonblanque, E.B. de, *Niphon and Pe-che-li*, Saunders, Otley & Co., 1862.

Fortune, Robert, *Yedo and Peking*, London, 1863.

Fraser, George MacDonald, *Quartered Safe Out Here*, Collins-Harvill, 1993.

Friedman, G. and Lebard, M., *The Coming War with Japan*, St. Martin's Press, 1991.

Fryke, Christopher and Schweitzer, Christopher, *Voyages to the East Indies*, Cassell, 1929

Gibson, William, *Neuromancer*, Ace, 1984.

Griffis, W.E., *The Mikado's Empire* (1876), Harper & Bros., 1883.

Guest, Val and White, J.M., *The Camp on Blood Island*, Panther, 1958.

Halsey, William F. and Bryan, J., *Admiral Halsey's Story*, McGraw-Hill, 1947.

Harcourt-Smith, Simon, *Japanese Frenzy*, Hamilton, 1942.

Harris, Frank, *My Life and Loves*, ed. J.F. Gallagher, W.H. Allen, 1964.

Harris, Townsend, *The Complete Journal of Townsend Harris*, ed. M.E. Cosenza, 2nd edition, Tuttle, 1959.

Hawks, Francis L., *Narrative of the Expedition of an American Squadron to the China Seas and Japan* (1856), ed. Sidney Wallach, Coward-McCann, 1952.

Hearn, Lafcadio, *Japan: an attempt at interpretation*, Macmillan, 1904. *Kokoro* (1896), Gay, 1900

——'My First Day in the Orient' from *Glimpses of Unfamiliar Japan*, Houghton Mifflin, 1894.

Herrigel, E., *Zen in the Art of Archery*, Routledge & Kegan Paul, 1953.

Hersey, John, *Hiroshima*, Penguin, 1946.

——*Into the Valley*, Hodder & Stoughton, 1943.

Hiatt, Fred, *The Secret Sun*, Simon & Schuster, 1992.

Hilton, James, *Lost Horizon*, Macmillan, 1933.

Hodson, Peregrine, *A Circle Round the Sun* (1992), Mandarin, 1993.

Holland, Clive, *My Japanese Wife* (1895), R.A. Everett, 1903.

Horsley, William and Buckley, Roger, *Nippon, New Superpower*, BBC Books, 1990.

Hübner, J.A. de, *A Ramble Round the World* (1873), trans. Lady Herbert, London, 1874, vol. 1.

Insight Japan, vol. 1, no. 2, November 1992.

Iriye Akira, *Mutual Images: essays in American-Japanese relations*, Harvard University Press, 1975.

Ishihara Shintaro, *The Japan That Can Say No* (1989), trans. Frank Baldwin, Simon & Schuster, 1991.

Iyer, Pico, *The Lady and the Monk*, The Bodley Head, 1991.

Jacobs, P., Landau, S. and Pell, E., *To Serve the Devil*, Vintage Books, 1971, vol. 2.

James, Clive, *Brrm! Brrm!*, Jonathan Cape, 1991.

Johnson, Sheila K., *American Attitudes Toward Japan, 1941–1975*, American Enterprise Institute for Public Policy Research, 1975.

Johnston, George H., *Pacific Partner*, Duell, Sloan and Pearce, 1944.

Joseph, Joe, *The Japanese*, Viking, 1993.

Kabbani, Rana, *Europe's Myths of Orient*, Macmillan, 1986.

Kaempfer, Engelbert, *The History of Japan, together with a description of the kingdom of Siam 1690–92*, James MacLehose, 1906, vol. 2.

Kazantzakis, Nikos, *Travels in China and Japan* (1938), trans. George C. Pappageotes, Cassirer, 1964.

Kerouac, Jack, *The Dharma Bums* (1958), André Deutsch, 1959.

Kipling, Rudyard, *Kipling's Japan*, ed. Hugh Cortazzi and George Webb, Athlone, 1988.

Kirkbride, Ronald, *Tamiko* (1959), Pan Books, 1960.

Knox, Alexander, 'Japan', *Edinburgh Review*, vol. 96, 1852.

Koestler, Arthur, *The Lotus and the Robot* (1960), Hutchinson, 1966.

La Farge, John, *An Artist's Letters from Japan*, T. Fisher Unwin, 1897.

Lea, Homer, *The Valor of Ignorance*, Harper & Bros., 1909.

Lehmann, Jean-Pierre, *The Image of Japan: From Feudal Isolation to World Power, 1850–1905*, George Allen & Unwin, 1978.

Loti, Pierre, *Japoneries d'automne* (1889), Calmann-Lévy, 1926.
———*Madame Chrysanthème* (1887), Calmann-Levy, 1927.
Lowell, Percival, *The Soul of the Far East* (1888), Macmillan, 1911.
Lustbader, Eric Van, *The Miko*, Granada, 1984.
———*The Ninja* (1980), Grafton, 1981.
———*White Ninja*, Grafton, 1990.
McCauley, Edward Yorke, *With Perry in Japan, the diary of Edward Yorke McCauley*, ed. Allan B. Cole, Princeton University Press, 1942.
McQueen, Ian, *Japan, a travel survival kit*, Lonely Planet Publications, 1986.
Mailer, Norman, *The Naked and the Dead*, Rinehart, 1948.
Marquand, John P., *Stopover Tokyo*, Collins, 1957.
Mason, Richard, *The Wind Cannot Read*, Hodder & Stoughton, 1947.
Mass Observation Archive, File 1034, 7 January 1942.
———*Politics 1938–56*, Box 4.
Maugham, Somerset, *The Razor's Edge*, Heinemann, 1944.
Michener, James A., 'Japan', *Holiday*, August 1952.
———*Sayonara* (1953–1954) in *The Source, The Bridges at Toki-Ri, Caravans*.
———*Sayonara*, Secker & Warburg, 1976.
Miner, Earl, *The Japanese Tradition in British and American Literature*, Princeton University Press, 1958.
Mitford, A.B.F. (Lord Redesdale), 'The Execution by Hara-Kiri', *Cornhill*, vol. 20 (1869).
———*Memories* (1915), 2nd edition, Hutchinson, 1915, vol. 2.
———*Tales of Old Japan* (1871), Macmillan, 1910.
Murasaki Shikibu, *The Tale of Genji*, trans. Arthur Waley, Allen & Unwin, 1925–1933.
Norman, Henry, *The Real Japan* (1892), T. Fisher Unwin, 1893.
Oliphant, Laurence, *Narrative of the Earl of Elgin's Mission to China and Japan in the years 1857, '58, '59*, Blackwood, 1859, vol. 2.
Orwell, George, *Homage to Catalonia* (1938), Penguin, 1966.
Osborn, Sherard, *A Cruise in Japanese Waters*, London, 1859.
Plomer, William, *Paper Houses* (1929), Penguin, 1943.
Preble, G.H., *The Opening of Japan: a diary of discovery in the Far East, 1853–1856*, ed. B. Szczesniak, University of Oklahoma Press, 1962.
Pyle, Ernie, *Last Chapter*, Henry Holt, 1945.
Rogers, P.G., *The First Englishman in Japan: the story of Will Adams*, Harvill Press, 1956.
Rohmer, Sax, *The Bride of Fu Manchu* (1933), Cassell, 1957.
Russell of Liverpool, Lord, *The Knights of Bushido, A Short History of Japanese War Crimes*, Cassell, 1958.
Said, Edward W., *Orientalism* (1978), Penguin, 1991.
Satow, Ernest, *A Diplomat in Japan*, Seeley, Service, 1921.
Shukert, E.B., and Scibetta, B.S., *War Brides of World War II*, Presidio, 1988.

Select Bibliography

Singer, Kurt, *Mirror, Sword and Jewel, The Geometry of Japanese Life* (1973), Kodansha, 1989.

Sladen, Douglas, *The Japs at Home*, Hutchinson, 1892.

Sledge, E.B., *With the Old Breed at Peleliu and Okinawa*, Presidio, 1981.

Smith, George, *Ten Weeks in Japan*, London, 1861.

Smith, Martin Cruz, *Red Square*, Harvill, 1992.

Sneider, Vernon, *The Tea-House of the August Moon*, Macmillan, 1952.

Stalker, John and Parker, George, *A Treatise of Japaning and Varnishing*, Oxford, 1688.

Stoddard, Lothrop, *The Rising Tide of Color* (1920), Chapman & Hall, 1922.

Stone, Robert, *Dog Soldiers* (1973), Star, 1976.

Stopes, Marie, *A Journal from Japan*, Blackie & Son, 1910.

Storry, Richard, *A History of Modern Japan*, Penguin, 1960.

Szyliowicz, I.L., *Pierre Loti and the oriental woman*, St. Martin's Press, 1988.

Tasker, Peter, *Inside Japan* (1987), Penguin, 1989.

Terkel, Studs, *The Good War*, Pantheon, 1984.

Tremenheere, John, 'Japan', *Quarterly Review*, vol. 114 (1863).

Vogel, Ezra, *Japan as Number One*, Harvard University Press, 1979.

Weglyn, M., *Years of Infamy: the untold story of America's concentration camps*, Morrow, 1976.

Wilde, Oscar, 'The Decay of Lying' (1889) in *De Profundis and Other Writings*, Penguin, 1986.

Wilkinson, Endymion, *Japan versus Europe* (1980), Penguin, 1983.

Worpole, Ken, *Dockers and Detectives: popular reading – popular writing*, Verso, 1984.

Wyndham, John, *The Midwich Cuckoos*, Michael Joseph, 1957.

Yokoyama Toshio, *Japan in the Victorian Mind*, Macmillan, 1987.

Index

Index

194–207; comparisons between
China and, 5–6, 27, 52, 74–5, 195;
comparisons between Germany
and, 13–4, 19, 44, 198, 208, 210;
feminine aspects of, 89–91, 94–5, 97,
142–56; history of relations between
the west and, xii, 3–5, 76–7; images
of antithesis between the west and,
xiii, 8–11, 13, 24–5, 35, 39, 52–8,
149–50, 160–61, 198; smallness of
scale of, 45, 92–5, 97, 116
Japan Festival (London), 'Visions of
Japan', 33–4, 86
Japan Handbook, see Bisignani, J.D.
Japanese,
    attitude to death of, 35–44, 103–4;
    attitude to sex of, 125–41, 178–83;
    chivalrous ideals of, 184–93;
    inherent violence of, 162–9, 196–7;
    represented as: artistic, 66–85,
    190–1, childlike, 73, 92, 94–5, 97,
    116–7, 121, 134–7, comic, 22–4, 54,
    204–6; conformist, 46–7, 49, 52–3;
    cruel, xii, 99–103, 137, 159–61,
    170–83; dishonest, 95–7, 200, 225;
    doll-like, 45, 50, 99, 118, 121, 123;
    fanatical, 37, 39, 53, 73, 163, 165,
    168, 171, 193, 202, 204–5; imitative,
    6, 17, 96–7; ingenious xi, 79, 85, 96,
    196; inscrutable, 53, 165, 168–9,
    188; paradoxical, 3–4, 5–8, 110, 152,
    155; picturesque, 62–6, 83, 85–7, 92,
    98–9, 104–5, 147, 162; robotic, 12,
    20, 46, 49–54, 99, 206; subhuman,
    13–21, 30, 46–7, 50, 54, 117;
    superhuman, 28–34, treacherous,
    166–9, 196–7, 200, 225
Japanese-American Citizens League
    210
Japanese-Americans, 42–3, 210–1
Japanese Constitution, 166, 192
Japanese gardens, 64, 72, 85, 86–8,
    99–102, 115, 152
Japanese woman, 109–56, 160; as
    cultural emblem, 142–56; as
    handmaiden, 110–9; as ideal wife,
    120–4; as sexual partner, 125–41,
    150–2
japonisme, 80–1, 84
Jesuits, 4–5, 54, 76, 79, 169, 184
Jewison, Norman, *Other People's
    Money*, 201
Johnson, Grove, 181

Johnson, Sheila K., *American Attitudes
    Toward Japan, 1941–1975*, 214, 216,
    218
Johnston, George H., 21, 215
Joseph, Joe, *The Japanese*, 8, 11, 13, 18,
    19, 26, 28, 56–7, 118, 175–7, 202–4,
    206, 213, 217, 220, 224, 226

Kabbani, Rana, *Europe's Myths of
    Orient*, 163, 221, 223
kabuki, 72
Kaempfer, E., *History of Japan*, 36, 215
kamikaze, 35, 37, 39, 197, 206
karate, 55, 190
Karate Kid films, 190–2, 193
katana, 160, 186–8, 190
Katsura Rikyu Garden, 61
Kazantzakis, N., *Travels in China and
    Japan*, 66, 101–3, 118, 139, 142, 145,
    159, 217, 219, 220, 222, 223
Keats, John, 66, 84
Kerouac, Jack, *The Dharma Bums*, 32
Ketchell, Robert, 87
Kipling, Rudyard, 5–6, 11, 64, 65, 66–7,
    69, 81–3, 86, 90–1, 92, 95, 101, 111,
    113, 123, 137, 143, 162–3, 166, 167,
    213, 217, 218, 219, 220, 223, 224, 225
Kirin beer, 151
Kirkbride, Ronald, *Tamiko*, 147–9, 222
Knox, Alexander, 'Japan', 161, 223
Kobe, 6, 36, 65, 93, 133, 184
Koestler, Arthur, *The Lotus and the
    Robot* 6–7, 11, 49–50, 99–100, 101–4,
    219
Korea, 27, 74, 146
Korean War, The, 74, 125, 145–6
Kurosawa Akira, *The Seven Samurai,
    Yojimbo*, 187–8
Kyoto, 8, 61, 72, 76, 79, 81–2, 88, 90,
    93, 114, 162, 171, 192, 194, 196
Kyoto Garden (Holland Park), 69
Kyushu, 5, 82

L.A. Law, 201
La Farge, John, *An Artist's Letters
    from Japan*, 64–5, 217
Lea, Homer, *The Valor of Ignorance*,
    164, 223
Legend of the Overfiend, 179–80
Lehmann, Jean-Pierre, *The Image of
    Japan*, 144, 222
Leone, Sergio, *A Fistful of Dollars*, 188
Liberty, Arthur L., 23

235

Index

A NOTE ON THE AUTHOR

Ian Littlewood was born in York in the United Kingdom and studied at Oxford University and the University of Sussex, where he now teaches English. He has also taught at universities in Tokyo, France, and Colorado. His other writings include literary companions to Paris and Venice, a study of Paris's architecture and art, and *The Writings of Evelyn Waugh*.